Princess Michael
of Kent

Princess Michael of Kent

Peter Lane

C. 1

Salem House
Manchester, New Hampshire

B

MICHAEL

First published in the United States
by Salem House Publishers, 1986
a member of the Merrimack Publishers' Circle,
Manchester, New Hampshire 03101

ISBN 0-88162-166-8

Library of Congress Catalog Card
Number 85-72576

Printed and bound in Great Britain

Contents

For my grandchildren
Kathryn, Helen and Benjamin

Illustrations

Between pages 128 and 129

PICTURE CREDITS

BBC Hulton Picture Library: 1, 2; family sources: 3, 4, 5, 6; The Photo Source: 7, 8; Camera Press: 9, 10, 11, 12, 13, 14, 15, 16, 21, 24, 25; private sources: 17, 18, 19, 23; The Press Association: 20; IPC Magazines: 22; Syndication International: 26, 27, 28, 29, 30, 31, 32, 33, 34.

Acknowledgements

In November 1984 I wrote to Princess Michael asking for her co-operation on this, the first full-length book devoted to her life. In her reply she explained that she was sending 'not the office standard letter of refusal to your request but a regretful note from me personally instead.' Although she signed the 'note' 'Yours sincerely, Marie-Christine', she had earlier warned me that 'all my family, my friends, my schools, educational institutions, etc., have been requested to co-operate with no one with regard to articles or a book about me. I am simply not yet ready to become a book.'

I am grateful to the many people in 'my family, my friends' who chose to ignore the Princess's request and gave me their active help. I regret that most of these invaluable sources have asked that no acknowledgement be made of the contributions which they made. I owe a deep debt of gratitude to the authors of the family histories of the following princely or noble families: Schwarzenberg, Szapáry, von Reibnitz and Windisch-Graetz. I am equally grateful to the members of those families who, having read my original manuscript, provided valuable information which helped to improve, in particular, Chapters 1–3. I acknowledge my gratitude to many workers in the field of royal genealogy and in particular to the Society of Genealogists and to P.W. Montague-Smith and M.L. Berbier who drew up the tables showing the common ancestries of Prince and Princess Michael.

I am grateful to many of Princess Michael's friends – in Australia, Britain and Europe, who either provided me with information or suggested sources from which information could be obtained. Without their help I could not have written in particular Chapters 3, 4 and 14.

As a Catholic and a historian, I consider that the most important chapters in this book are 5-9. I am deeply indebted to many people for help in writing these 'Catholic' chapters. Monsignor Ralph Brown, JCD, the Vicar-General of the Archdiocese of Westminster and long-serving *officialis* of the

Marriage Tribunal of the Archdiocese of Westminster, is a world authority on the many-sided question of Catholic marriage and annulment. His definitive study *Marriage Annulment* (Kevin Mayhew, 1977), from which he generously gave me permission to quote, was an invaluable aid while I was working on Chapters 4 and 5. Monsignor Brown was, personally, a guide and mentor as I wove my way through the political, religious and human problems which form the basis for Chapters 6–9. He was kind enough to read Chapters 5–9 and to make constructive comments.

Two of Monsignor Brown's colleagues also read these 'Catholic' chapters. Monsignor David Norris, Vicar-General, brought to his reading his own special interest in constitutional history; Monsignor George Leonard provided the perceptions of the Private Secretary to Cardinal Hume. I am grateful to both of them for their careful reading of the script and for their gentle advice which helped me avoid a number of pitfalls.

I am equally indebted to Father Jean Charles-Roux, a priest of the Institute of Charity and a former diplomat. Father Jean provided the essential link with the Vatican and was my adviser on the complex world of church politics. He was also, through his close friendship with the aristocratic families involved and because of his innate kindness, the 'gentle persuader' who gained for me that invaluable access to the Princess's relations and friends. He was also kind enough to read and to have read by others, the completed manuscript, and I am grateful for the courteous way in which he helped improve it.

I appreciate the hospitality which I received at the Apostolic Nunciature, where Archbishop Bruno Heim helped put a human face on some aspects of Church politics and kindly explained the role which he had played in the questions examined in Chapters 5–9.

I acknowledge the considerable help which I received from the staffs of several libraries. In particular I wish to thank the staffs at the Wiener Library, London, of the London Library and of the Catholic Central Library.

I received considerable help from the staffs of several Embassies and High Commissions. In particular I am grateful for the help provided by the staffs of the Czechoslovak Embassy, London, and by the Ministerstvo Kultury CSR, Prague; the Embassy of the Hungarian People's Republic, London, and the National Archives (Magyar Orszagos Levelter), Budapest; the Austrian Embassy and, through the staff there, the contact with and help from the Anglo-Austrian Society, the Austrian Institute and the Heraldisch-Genealogische Gesellschaft in Vienna. The

Librarian at the Australian High Commission, London, put me in touch with many Australian newspapers, and I am grateful to the editors of the *Sydney Morning Herald*, *The Australian* and the Sydney-based *Daily Telegraph* and *Sun* for the cuttings which they sent and for the contacts they provided.

Leo Simmonds, a personal friend and Assistant Personnel Manager at the *Daily Express*, was kind enough to help me gain access to the cuttings files of many national newspapers. In spite of my strictures on journalists in general, I am indebted to many who have written about Princess Michael, if only because their work helped provide some of the framework for my book.

As ever, I owe a special debt to my wife, Teresa, and my two youngest children, Damien and Gerard, for their patience and good humour during the long period I spent researching and writing this book. The travelling, visiting and reading brought me into contact with many kind people; for my wife and two boys there was no such relief. My thanks to the three of you for allowing me so much self-indulgence.

Finally, back to Princess Michael, the subject of the exercise. One or two of those who read parts of the manuscript sent copies of Chapters 5–9 to Prince and Princess Michael. I gratefully acknowledge a letter which states 'that Her Royal Highness appreciates the sincerity of your scholarship, and in particular your interest in the "Catholic" question ... the most important issue ...' It only remains for me to acknowledge that, in spite of the considerable help I have received, the responsibility for what appears – with its possible errors and omissions – remains mine.

P.L.

Introduction

'She's an instant person. You either love her or dislike her the moment you meet her.' This was the verdict of John Barratt, formerly private secretary to Lord Mountbatten and, for two years, private secretary to Prince and Princess Michael of Kent. 'She's not one of the wishy-washy mediocre sort who grow on you. Perhaps that's one of the reasons she's always been controversial.'

One of her close friends wrote to tell me that, 'The key to Marie-Christine's character is that there is much more of the hot-blooded Hungarian [inherited from her mother] in her than the cool, sensible German [which she may have inherited from her father]. Impulsive, reckless, passionate, generous, quick to find fault and just as quick to forgive, a perfectionist, romantic, intensely loyal to her friends yet with an almost biblical attitude to her enemies, artistic, easily hurt and unaware when she hurts others, optimistic and possessing an overwhelming *joie de vivre*.'

In fine, she is an unusual princess. Not because she is 'foreign-born' nor because she is 'glamorous'. Many other foreign and glamorous princesses have become much-loved members of the Royal Family. One thinks of Princess Alexandra of Denmark (who was to be Edward VII's Queen) and Princess May of Teck (George V's Queen). There was, too, Princess Marina of Greece, who became the popular Duchess of Kent in 1934 – and the mother of Prince Michael. But no other Princess has been a wartime refugee fleeing as an infant in a cot from the advancing Russians, a Sydney-educated schoolgirl, a worker, dependent on her earnings to pay the rent, a Catholic yet a divorcée – the list of unprincessy features is a long one. They help to explain the suspicion, not to say hostility, with which she was once regarded.

John Barrat may have exaggerated when he spoke of Princess Michael's being 'always controversial'. It is, however, undeniable that she was the subject (and/or object) of major and public controversies in 1978, 1983 and 1985.

In 1978 the issues were, in quick succession, the annulment of her first marriage (which angered some Catholics and puzzled more, while it baffled most Anglicans), her engagement to Prince Michael (which led to a well-publicized row over the position of Catholics in the constitutional life of the country) and, finally, Pope Paul VI's refusal to give the dispensation which was needed to allow her to have her marriage recognized by the Catholic Church. The set of issues involved a variety of people who walked down different 'corridors of power'. The Queen, Lord Mountbatten, palace officials, civil servants, Pope Paul VI, his Secretary of State, the Cardinal Archbishop of Vienna, our own Cardinal Hume and the Hierarchies of England, Wales and Scotland – all were involved to a greater or lesser degree. Many of these people were involved, once again, in July 1983, when Pope John Paul II agreed to allow Prince and Princess Michael to have their marriage convalidated in a service held at Westminster Cathedral. What had happened to the 'grave considerations' which, said the Vatican, forbade a dispensation in 1978? Why had Church authorities in Great Britain changed their minds?

I have examined the issues and personalities involved in this religious-constitutional controversy with the help of many of those who played active roles in the drama during which Princess Michael showed some of her tough tenacity – as well as the 'romantic ... artistic ... reckless' facets of her personality.

These were complex issues involving constitutional lawyers, Catholic canonists, Vatican officials and such unpublic figures as the Private Secretary to the Queen. There was, on the other hand, nothing remote or shadowy about the controversy which was aroused in April 1985. The *Daily Mirror* sparked it off when it headlined the fact that Princess Michael's father had been a member of the Nazi Party and of the SS. For some ten days or so ('the most difficult of my life') the media were dominated by allegations, half-truths and innuendoes: Princess Michael added to the controversy when, against the advice of the Palace, she gave a TV interview in her Kensington Palace home ('the most important $7\frac{1}{2}$ minutes of my life'). Her courage, honesty and determination were as obvious as the horror she had felt when her mother told her that the stories were, in part only, true. Fortunately the documentary evidence was available to support her mother's contention that the father had never been an active member of the SS and that he had become an anti-Nazi long before he was sent to fight in Russia in 1944. I have examined all aspects of this affair with the aid of the documents and with the help of many members of Princess Michael's family. It was obvious at the time that this publicity served to reveal many of the traits of her character – 'easily hurt ... optimistic' – to which her friend referred in his letter.

Much of the controversy which has surrounded Princess Michael has been due to the activities of gossip columnists and headline-seeking journalists. Once they vented their spleen on Princess Anne; her work for the Save the Children Fund as well as her obvious ability to cope with the media caused journalists to seek fresh prey. Once, too, they had been accustomed to savaging Princess Margaret; her illness has led to a fall-off in the campaign. The 'reckless, passionate ... romantic' Princess Michael who was 'easily hurt' came as a gift to deprived royalty-watchers. They have invented stories, provided the wrong reasons for some of her actions, made false allegations based on half-baked investigations and put as many words into the Princess's mouth as they have into the mouths of other members of the Royal Family. In July 1985 some sections of the popular press publicized the alleged 'friendship' between Princess Michael and a Texas businessman. The Queen's Press Secretary dismissed these stories as products of the 'sewer Press', but this did not prevent that same Press from claiming that the Queen had said this or that and had ordered this or that punishment for the Princess.

In 'The Uncelestial City', the poet Humbert Wolfe (1886-1940) wrote:

You cannot hope
   to bribe or twist,
thank God! the
   British journalist.

But seeing what
   the man will do
unbribed, there's
   no occasion to.

In the following pages I have tried to provide evidence which, her friends hope, will put an end to some of the journalistic inventions. It is to be hoped that Princess Michael will be allowed to make the contribution which she would wish to make to British life. 'I have the ambition. I want to be put to work.' May it be so.

1

A Background of Families

'My roots are deep in most of the royal houses of Europe going back many centuries' – HRH Princess Michael quoted in the *Daily Express*, 15 March 1984

In 1962 hundreds, perhaps thousands, of Australians came back to Europe for shorter or longer periods. Some came to study before returning to contribute to their continent's economic development. Some came, as 'culture vultures' with a year-long itinerary mapped out to enable them to get a taste of their cultural heritage. Some, coming on briefer holidays, were anxious to track down this or that place where one or other of their ancestors had been born and lived.

If in 1962 there was any VIP treatment for incoming Australians, it was for the already famous; cricketers, rugby players, opera stars, balletomanes and politicians such as Robert Menzies, returned to power in the election of December 1961. There was no such preferential treatment for the tall, blonde, athletic-looking Marie-Christine von Reibnitz, born in Czecho-slovakia, but a resident in Australia since 1950, when she returned to Europe in August 1962. No bevy of reporters rushed to meet her; no radio or television interviews for this Australian-looking but middle-European born returning to her birthplace. In years to come she would win automatic headlines – some favourable, others critical. Her doings and sayings would occupy many column inches; interviewers would vie with one another for the privilege of a word or two. Indeed, in April 1985, the BBC would be taken to court by TV-am programme makers for using part of a TV-am interview in BBC News programmes about Marie-Christine. But in August 1962 the British were concerned with many other things than a young (if glamorous) returning emigrant. The politically-minded were still discussing and analysing the amazing events of 13 July when a desperate

Prime Minister, Harold Macmillan, had sacked half his Cabinet in an attempt to retrieve his party's (and his own) declining fortunes. On the wider European front, there was a great deal of interest in the preparations being made for the October opening of the Second Vatican Council called by the roly-poly Pope John XXIII who seemed determined to drag the Catholic Church into the modern world. The arrival of the young Baroness Marie-Christine Agnes Hedwig Ida von Reibnitz passed unheralded and unsung, unnoticed by a world busily concerned about many other things. No one, it seemed, noticed the arrival of the young Baroness Marie-Christine von Reibnitz.

Yet it is doubtful if many of the returning emigrants came with such eagerness as did Marie-Christine, with her deep-felt interest in her family background. For if others were to find their roots in Welsh townships, Irish villages or Italian cities, Marie-Christine knew that hers lay in a multitude of palaces, castles and mansions occupied, in the past at least, by ancestors who had ruled over most of Europe. In the 1980s the satirical magazine *Private Eye* was to cast doubts on her background, describing it as 'shady' and calling her an 'impostor'. The best independent proof of her claims was provided by a report prepared by the Society of Genealogists, which displayed her family tree and totally disproved the accusations made by *Private Eye* (see Appendix).

The earliest documented references to the Reibnitz family are in 1271, when a Hans Rybicz is mentioned, and 1288, when a Heinrich Rybnicz is named. From *circa* 1300 descendants spelt their names in a variety of forms – Rybnicz, Rybicz, Ribenicz, Reibnitz and, the most usual form, Reybnicz. The family history (published in 1901) suggests that the name is probably derived from two villages, which were still in existence in 1901. One (Reibnitz) village was near Breslau (now Wroclaw, Poland); but it was the Reibnitz village by Hirschberg (now Jelania Gora, Poland) which is described in the family history as 'the cradle of the clan'.

The present spelling, Reibnitz, dates from the end of the sixteenth century, when the family also adopted the 'von', as did most other noble families of that time.

The oldest seal with a family crest (which is still used by the family) dates from a document dated 1352 which is in the Breslau Archives. This document mentioned Konrad von Ribeniz who was born in 1307 and died in 1377. Given two earlier references (of 1271 and 1288), Konrad is said to be 'in the third generation'. Some histories name him as 'the founder of the family'; while this is patently untrue, it has to be said that the family does trace its descent in unbroken line only from this 'third generation'.

Of the seven brothers in that generation, Marie-Christine descends from Nicol, who founded what genealogists call 'the Wederau line'. While there is no evidence of his date of birth, we know that in 1351 he joined the estates of Pulkau and Wederau which were inherited by his son in 1374.

British reference books disagree as to when and by whom the head of the family was granted the title of baron. *Royalty, Peerages and Nobility of the World* claims that the first baron was created by Frederick William III of Prussia 'before 1829'.[1] *Debrett*, on the other hand, claims that the barony was created in 1724 by the Holy Roman Emperor Charles VI.[2] I am grateful to the family's own historian who provided me with the evidence that the barony was conferred simultaneously on two brothers – Christoph Friedrich and Johan Leopold von Reibnitz. The family history contains on pp.62-5, the letter written by Emperor Charles VI on 16 July 1724. In this, the Holy Roman Emperor praised the reputation, good manners, generosity etc., of the family and refers to them as the 'ancient knightly family' which has been 'held in high regard for centuries in our Duchy of Silesia'. Having mentioned several of the family's ancestors who had held high office, the Emperor granted the barony to both brothers 'and all their legitimate descendants, male or female'.

The family historian points out that the barony was both an Austrian and a Holy Roman title, since Silesia was part of the Austrian Empire at the time. However, as Princess Michael points out, 'boundaries in that area change very frequently'. During the expansion of Brandenburg-Prussia in the eighteenth century, Silesia was among the regions which came under Prussian control, which may help to explain the claim that the baron was created by Frederick William III of Prussia. In fact, it was Frederick II ('the Great') who played a role in the family's history. The first two barons, Johann Leopold and Christoph Friedrich had no heirs: Johann's only son died leaving no issue and Christoph was also childless – despite four marriages. Shortly before his death, Christoph adopted his cousin Gottfried Diprand von Reibnitz (b. 1729), a step which had to receive the King's approval. This was given in a letter dated 20 January, 1757. The King wrote:

Our dear and loyal servant,
I have received your letter of 27 December from which I gather that your cousin Christoph Friedrich, Baron von Reibnitz in Stohnsdorf, has taken your son Gottfried Diprand as his own, out of his social

attachment to the same, which [adoption] I am happy to agree to. I am
your most affectionate King
(signed) Friedrich.

Table showing ancestry of Baron Günther von Reibnitz
adapted from a history of the von Reibnitz family, 1901

Generation
1 Hans Rybicz (mentioned 1271) and Heinrich Rubnicz (mentioned
   1288)
2 Conrad Ribenicz (–1364)
3 Konrad von Ribeniz (1307–1377) and Nicol (–1374), the
   founder of the Wederau branch of the family
4 Guizel (died 1420)
5 Conrad (died 1469)
6 Georg (died 1535), who was granted the barony of Wederau in 1489
7 Hans (1532–1575)
8 Georg (1550–1611)
9 Hans (1593–1678)
10 Hans (1637–1690)
11 Johann (1672–1735), who was created Baron by edict issued 16 July
    1724
12 Johann Maximilian (1701–1758) who had no children
    Christoph (1686–1757) who was also created a Baron on 16 July
    1724 and who adopted a son-successor on 27 December 1756
13 Gottfried (1729–1793), the adopted heir
14 Grust (1765–1829)
15 Carl (1803–1856)
16 Ernst (1830–1867)
17 Hans (1856–1918)
18 Günther (1894–1983)

(In Chapter 2 we shall see something of the effects of the First
World War on the various families from whom Marie-Christine
descends. Here we have to note that in 1919, Silesia, including
the von Reibnitz estates, was taken from Germany to become part
of the newly created Poland.)

Although the von Reibnitz ancestry was ancient ('*uhr adel*' –
'noble since anyone can recall'), in family-conscious Europe they
were regarded as being relatively minor nobility – as was made
plain when, in 1941, Countess Marianne Szapáry married Baron
Gunther von Reibnitz.

The Queen is alleged to have remarked, when Marie-Christine
married into Britain's royal family, that she would be 'too grand
for us'. If this remark was ever made, it may have been a reference
to Marie-Christine's maternal ancestry, which reads like a roll call
of the outstanding families of the Austro-Hungarian Empire and

before that of the Holy Roman Empire.

The American historian Jerome Blum has written:

> In the last decades of the eighteenth century an estimated one-third of all the land in the Austrian Monarchy, after Russia the largest state in Europe, belonged to a few hundred families. Their special strongholds were Bohemia and Hungary. In Bohemia in 1778 there were 174 noble families, 15 of them princes, 79 counts and 96 barons and knights. The princes owned land valued at 465 million florins. The property of the counts added up to 119 million florins and that of the barons and knights was worth only 17.6 million florins. The manors of the Schwarzenbergs alone, *richest of the princes* [italics added] were valued at 14.4 million florins ... the Schwarzenbergs owned 1.6 million acres in Bohemia with 230,000 peasants ... Prince Paul Anton Esterházy, *greatest of all Hungarian magnates* [italics added], had around 700,000 peasants, about 6.5 per cent of Hungary's entire population ... Esterházy's annual income ran from 800,000 florins to 1.7 million florins.[3]

Auersperg, Lobkowitz, Schwarzenberg and Windisch-Graetz are names which appear time and again in the family tree of Marie-Christine's mother, the former Countess Marianne Szapáry, and behind the names are family histories which link with the history of Europe itself.

In 1877, Princess Gabrielle of Auersperg married Prince Alfred Windisch-Graetz, who was to be Prime Minister of Austria-Hungary in the 1880s. Their daughter was to become Marie-Christine's grandmother. The Auerspergs are one of Austria's oldest families, tracing their origins back to 1060, their entrance to the nobility to 1530. Having supported Emperor Ferdinand 'the Catholic' during the Thirty Years War, the Auerspergs were titled counts in 1630 and, the final accolade, raised to the princely status in 1653, having a share in offices in Church and State. Their sense of their importance was illustrated by an earlier Princess Gabrielle, who in 1815 rejected the courting of Alexander I, Tsar of all the Russias. Only the supremely confident could afford to reject overtures from such a source.

The princely Auerspergs were related many times over to the Esterházys. That family's history took off with the Peace of Nikolsburg in 1621 which ended the struggle between the Hungarian nobility and the Emperor. This treaty was largely the work of a Transylvanian landowner, Nikolaus Esterházy. As a reward he was given the castles and estates at Forchenstein and Eisenstadt. The family remained loyal to the Emperor during the great siege of Vienna and during the troubles of the early eighteenth century when most other Hungarian magnates rose against the Emperor. He used his influence with the successful Emperor to get permission to buy up, cheaply, the lands of other less perceptive landowners.

The Esterházy base was at Eisenstadt in Austria, still dominated by Schloss Esterházy, built between 1663 and 1672 around an inner courtyard in Italian baroque forms, its four corner towers once crowned with cupolas. In 1687 Paul Esterházy was named Palatine of Hungary and Prince Regent: he set about providing the family with a background worthy of its rise to princely rank, a huge complex in the high-lying western part of the town; it was never completed, but the Bergkirche and Kalvarienberg churches give some indication of what he conceived. Better known, however, was the great Esterházy Palace in Bratislava, which the family made the cultural and social centre of Hungary, remembered as the scene of many Haydn triumphs – the composer for many years enjoyed the Esterházys' patronage.

The Esterházy family owned, at one time, nearly seven million Hungarian acres. No one could compete with their wealth. Prince Metternich, the arbiter of Europe from 1815 to 1848, was pleased to have his daughter, Marie, marry into the family. Other nexus-making marriages included those of Count Francis Esterházy and Princess Anna Lobkowitz, in 1893, and Count Nicholas Esterházy and Princess Frances Schwarzenberg in 1895.

The Lobkowitz family was another which had benefited from their loyalty to the Catholic Emperor during the religious struggles of the Thirty Years War. In 1624 Emperor Ferdinand 'the Catholic' raised the family to the princely status.

Like the Esterházys, the Lobkowitzes were great patrons of the arts. Beethoven's third symphony, the *Eroica*, had its first public performance in the heavy baroque palace of Prince Lobkowitz in Vienna. The Prince bought the score, his private orchestra gave the performance, and music-lovers of all classes were admitted to the concert.

Among the audience was Prince Karl Schwarzenberg, then the head of the family described by Blum as 'the richest' of the princely families. The Schwarzenberg fortune, like that of their imperial masters, had depended in the first instance on a fortunate marriage. Although the family had been ennobled as far back as 1405, it had lacked means. This was put right in 1617, when the twenty-eight-year-old Count Georg Schwarzenberg married the eighty-two-year-old Anna Neumann, heir to a considerable fortune which she made over to her young husband, making him the owner of lands in Carinthia and Styria, mines at Bleiberg, a good deal of invested capital and letters of credit worth a fortune in themselves. Thus was launched 'the most powerful family in the Austro-Hungarian Empire'.[4]

The builder of the great Schwarzenberg Palace in Vienna was Prince Johann, who died after being accidentally shot by the Emperor Charles VI during a hunt: 'My life was ever at the disposal of Your Supreme Majesty,' he remarked ironically.[5]

Prince Karl Schwarzenberg was Austrian Ambassador to France during the Napoleonic empire and in 1812 commanded the Austrian army which fought alongside the French – he retained the post when, in 1813, Austria changed sides and declared war on France. Prince Felix Schwarzenberg became Austrian Prime Minister in 1848 and engineered the abdication of Emperor Ferdinand and the succession of the eighteen-year-old Francis Joseph to the imperial throne. While his brother-in-law Field Marshal Prince Windisch-Graetz put an end to the Czech national rebellion of 1848, Schwarzenberg dealt with the rebels at home and re-imposed imperial control. Two years later the brothers-in-law contrived the 'Humiliation of Olmutz', in which Prussia agreed to subordinate itself to Austria. Between them they had saved the Empire, ensured continued Austrian domination of German affairs and saved the aristocracy whose wealth had been threatened by the rebels' attempt to free the peasants in the Empire. The Prince did not, of course, go unrewarded.

In 1851 was born Prince Alfred Schwarzenberg, to become President of the Austrian Upper Chamber and of the Council of Ministers. More importantly for our story, he was also to become the father of that Princess Hedwig who married a Count Szapáry, whose daughter Marianne became the mother of Marie-Christine.

The Szapárys were one of Hungary's truly ancient families, having arrived in the country with Arpad, its first king, in 986, when they were already *uhr adel* – noble. The present family traces its descent from George Szapáry, who lived about 1543. The head of the family was created a baron in 1640, and a descendant was made a count in 1722. Count Frederick Szapáry, Marie-Christine's grandfather, held a series of high political offices. He was for a time a member of the Imperial Council of Foreign Affairs, and in 1913 he was appointed Ambassador to the Court of the Tsar at St Petersburg. It was Count Szapáry who, in 1914, had to announce to the Tsar that their two countries were at war.

It is usual, when a member of the royal family informs the monarch of his or her proposed marriage, that various authorities are asked to check (to 'vet') the background of the potential newcomer. In most cases it is a mere formality, but when Marie-

Christine contemplated entering the Royal Family in 1977-8 there was more interest than usual, since she was both divorced and a Roman Catholic. Amid the plethora of family history that was unearthed were the scandals of her parents' marriage and of her father's war-time activities, which we shall examine later; less seriously, genealogists discovered that Marie-Christine and Michael of Kent were distant – very distant – cousins.

First, they are both descendants of Prince Ferdinand August of Lobkowitz (1655–1715), she from his first marriage, he from the second. This makes them cousins, nine generations removed. Secondly they share another common ancestor in Moritz, Landgrave of Hesse-Cassel (1572-1632). Thirdly they also share descent from Ludwig II, Count of Lowenstein (1530-1611), who was the progenitor of all the European sovereigns of Europe still reigning in the 1980s.

It is clear from this brief examination of her family background that Marie-Christine's pride in her ancestry is well justified. As she herself says, her roots are indeed deep 'in most of the royal houses of Europe'.

2

The Family and the War, 1939–45

'It was the best of times, it was the worst of times ...'
The Tale of Two Cities, Book 1, Chapter 1

Baroness Marie-Christine von Reibnitz was born on 15 January 1945 on her mother's estate at Tachau (now Tachov), one of the estates which her mother had inherited from her own mother, Princess Hedwig. One romantically inspired journalist mistakenly wrote of the birth taking place in 'a shooting-box amid the rolling woodland stag country near Kladruby in Czechoslovakia'. (A 'shooting-box' is a country mansion on that part of an estate where stags are hunted.) The 'shooting-box' at Schloss Kladrau (now Kladruby) is a large and beautiful mansion in front of a lake in the forest. Marie-Christine and her mother were forced to move there when the German army made the castle into their headquarters. Today the 'shooting-box' is a holiday camp for Russian soldiers stationed in Czechoslovakia.

It is possible to imagine the celebrations which, in more favourable times, might have accompanied the birth and christening of a new member of the extended family of the Austrian-Hungarian and German nobility. But January 1945 was not 'the best of times'; indeed, as Dickens had written of 1789, 'it was the worst of times' for middle Europeans. There was little opportunity for the reunions and festivities which, in more normal times, would have surrounded the christening of Marie-Christine Anne Agnes Hedwig Ida von Reibnitz. Her birth was registered at Carlsbad – which has given rise to journalistic claims that this is where she was born.

In fact, Marie-Christine was fortunate not to have been born in prison; her mother had been released from a Nazi camp in time to give birth to her child. Her father was not present at her birth, registration or christening, for he was in a Russian prisoner-of-war camp. Fears of a Russian take-over of the heartland of

Europe had once led him and many other aristocrats to support Hitler and the Nazi Party. In January 1945 those fears were about to be realized.

The peace treaties which followed the end of the First World War marked a major stage in the decline of the power of the imperial nobility. Austria, the prime mover in the events which had started that war, was the greatest sufferer. Emperor Franz Josef had died in November 1916; his grand-nephew, Emperor Karl I, abdicated in November 1918; the ancient Habsburg dynasty ceased to exist. Once the centre of a multi-racial empire, Austria was left as a small and landlocked republic of some six million people. Vienna became a shadow of its former imperial self, too large for the contracted needs of the small republic.

Hungary had been an almost equal partner with Austria in the great Empire, and its Magyar nobility had provided many of the leading statesmen and officials who ran that extended state. By the Treaty of Trianon (1920), Hungary was stripped of Slovakia, which was transferred to the Czechs, of Transylvania, which was conquered by the Romanians, and of Croatia, which became part of the new kingdom of Yugoslavia. The Esterházys, Szapárys and others of the proud Magyar aristocracy had to watch as the ancient kingdom was despoiled by peasant democracies. When their relatives, including the Schwarzenbergs, Windisch-Graetzs and Metternichs, had helped draw the map of Europe at the Congress of Vienna, the imperial nobility had acted as the arbiters of the Continent; in 1919-20 the imperial nobility played no active part in the drawing up of the various treaties. It was, in Churchill's phrase, 'the age of the common man'.

In the new republic of Hungary the nobility held on to most of their great estates; major land reforms had to wait until the Russian occupation of Eastern Europe after 1945. The Szapáry and Esterházy families were given the opportunity of adopting to a new political situation with, at least, their economic and social bases almost intact. The Austrian nobility, including the Schwarzenbergs, were less fortunate. The new republic abolished the old laws of entail which had secured the permanence of large estates; thousands of acres changed hands as big estates were broken up to become the property of small owner farmers. The town houses and palaces of Vienna were affected by ambitious Socialist programmes financed by heavy taxes on city property which almost eliminated incomes from house rents and forced all but the richest of large house-owners to sell up.

Some of the imperial nobility had had the foresight to invest in industrial and commercial developments in the nineteenth century. Many of them became directors of railroads, steel firms and banks. The patent to establish the famed Austrian Credit-Anstalt in 1855 was granted to four princes and three bankers. Two of the princes were Auersperg and Schwarzenberg, who were also among the founders of the Austrian Syndicate for Chemical and Metallurgical Production. They and their fellow-magnates owned most of the beet-sugar refineries, breweries and distilleries. Some of Marie-Christine's ancestors frowned on such interest in business activity as being contrary to the status and traditions of their caste. Prince Alfred Windisch-Graetz, for example, remarked that *'Geschafte macht kein Windisch-Graetz'*. ('No Windisch-Graetz goes into business.') However, the haughty Prince Alfred had in fact invested heavily in industry.

After 1920 and the drop in their incomes from land and house rents, many members of the old nobility tried to make up the shortfall by speculation on the stock exchanges. They were encouraged in this by the post-war boom of 1920-22, when gains were easily made. However, the rashness of most of their dealings was revealed by the onset of the depression in 1922 – a depression which, in more or less savage degree, was to last until 1939. For many of Marie-Christine's family, the great inflation of 1923 proved to be the disaster which wiped out inheritance and savings and forced them to sell jewellery and silver plate. The Schwarzenbergs converted their Viennese mansions into luxury hotels, while others even opened their castles and country houses to take in paying guests.

The Wall Street Crash of 1929 provided another landmark in the decline of the former imperial nobility. Many of them lost money as stock exchanges in Europe plummeted in the wake of the American disaster, for much of the apparent recovery of Austria and Germany had depended on a flow of loans from the prosperous USA, and, following the Crash of 1929, US banks called in their loans. In May 1931 the Schwarzenberg-led Credit Anstalt collapsed. German banks, which tried to rescue it, were pulled down in their turn. In Austria and Germany, bank after bank declared a moratorium which froze the hundreds of millions which London bankers had invested in the middle-European banking system. In London, the Labour government resigned, to be replaced by a National Government. In Germany, the Nazi Party and the Communist Party both made great gains at the elections which took place during the days following the collapse, days in which the number of bankruptcies and of the unemployed shot up.

In the aftermath of the economic crisis of 1931, Hitler came to power in Germany. It is worth noting that he won power by using the democratic system. Unlike Mussolini in Italy, he did not seize power as he might have done and as some of his closest advisers wanted him to do. Nearly fourteen million Germans voted for him in 1931 and 1932; millions more welcomed his advent to power, even if they had not voted for the Nazi Party.

This is not the book in which to examine why so many and varied social groups joined or supported Hitler and the Nazi Party. It is, however, relevant to our story to ask why many Catholic aristocrats did so and why, in particular, Baron Günther von Reibnitz joined the Nazi Party in 1930 – when Hitler's rise to power was far from assured. The answer to both questions lies in events and developments in both Germany and Austria after the First World War.

When, in the aftermath of the Russian Revolution of 1917, the Tsar and his family were murdered, along with thousands of members of the Russian aristocracy, it was, for Europe's surviving aristocrats, a matter of family concern (von Reibnitz's mother, for example, was a Russian aristocrat). And there was, in 1919-20, a real threat of a Bolshevik take-over in Germany, so that in the years that followed, when Hitler posed a challenge to Communist elements in Germany, aristocrats, especially Catholics who viewed with horror the Russian state's atheism, embraced his doctrines.

Von Reibnitz was a Catholic aristocrat. He was, in addition, a Silesian, appalled at the way in which his homeland had been used as a pawn by the victorious Allies during the treaty-making at Versailles after the war. In 1930 von Reibnitz saw Germany's Social Democratic government as incapable of coping with the Bolshevik threat and as having failed to persuade the Allies to undo the injustices of Versailles. These considerations help to explain why he joined the Nazi Party. His membership card shows that he was member no. 472,855.

In March 1938 Hitler ordered his troops into Austria, which was then forcibly incorporated into the Greater Reich. In September 1938 Britain and France forced the Czech leaders to allow Germany to take over part of Czechoslovakia (the Sudetenland), hoping this would appease Hitler, but while this move diminished and weakened the small republic, it failed to satisfy him. On 15 March 1939 the democratically governed state which had been created by treaties of 1919 and 1920 fell to pieces: Slovakia became an independent state; part of Carpathia was seized by the Hungarians; Bohemia, including the vast estates of the Windisch-Graetz family, became a German 'protectorate'. Marie-Christine's mother's family had to accept the presence of German administrators in their homeland.

Countess Marianne Szapáry, in her castle at Tachau or at the 'shooting-box' at Schloss Kladrau, had not yet met her future husband, von Reibnitz, though her brother, Count Ladislaus, had become friendly with the Baron through meeting him at various shooting competitions. Countess Marianne, unlike von Reibnitz, resented the success of the Nazis, whom she saw not as the 'saviours of Christian Europe' but as illegal occupiers of her homeland.

In the mid 1930s the young Countess and her brother Ladislaus had devoted themselves to sport. She was among the competitors in the Hungarian ski team at the Winter Olympics of 1936; he – now and in later years – represented Hungary (before 1939) and Austria (after 1945) in no fewer than three Olympics, for shooting; he was also six times European shooting champion, he skied, ski-jumped, boxed and drove racing cars. (The reason for their prowess in sport was that, their mother having died from tuberculosis, their father was determined that his children should have healthy lungs. Every winter they moved to the mountains, where Marianne gained her Olympic-class skiing skill.) However, at the same time – and, more dangerously, later – Marianne Szapáry was taking part in anti-German and anti-Nazi demonstrations and marches, activities for which she was to suffer during the war.

The outbreak of the Second World War in September 1939 marked another stage in the decline in the fortunes of the European aristocracy and, more especially, in those of the landed magnates of eastern Europe. Many fled. Countess Marianne, remaining on her Carlsbad estate in Nazi-occupied Bohemia, read of the successes of German troops in western Europe in 1940 and 1941. Hitler, it seemed, was to achieve what imperial forces had not been able to achieve in 1914-18, namely the defeat of France and the supremacy of 'Deutschland über alles'. In 1941 and the early part of 1942 German and Austrian troops surged to victory against the retreating Russians.

In the First World War Baron Günther von Reibnitz had been a cavalry officer and had sustained a bad sabre injury to his leg. This did not, however, prevent his being called up in 1939, as a captain (*Hauptmann*) in the reserve list. He was in the 31st Panzer Regiment which took part in the invasion of Poland and fought at Pless Nikolai and at Pozesna Ruska in September 1939.

In April 1985 Britain's tabloid newspapers made a series of allegations against Baron von Reibnitz, connected with his

membership of the Nazi Party, his membership of the SS and his
wartime activities. *The Mirror* and the rest of the tabloids made
their allegations sound like newly discovered secrets. As the
editor of *Burke's Peerage* commented: 'Serious researchers had
known about these things since 1978' when Marie-Christine's
background was investigated by the Palace before the Royal
Assent was given to her proposed marriage to Prince Michael. In
London and in Berlin documents exist (and had existed long
before April 1985) which show that von Reibnitz was merely an
honorary member of the SS-Gestapo. Goering, founder
commander of both organizations, used his position to give such
honorary membership to a variety of people whose friendship he
wanted to win. In hindsight and in the light of the knowledge we
have of the horrific work of the SS and the Gestapo, it may seem a
grisly way to honour one's friends. The fact is that many people
accepted such honorary membership. There was the politician
Ribbentrop – who was not even a soldier; there were industrialists
– enrolled as a sign of Nazi approval for their work; there were
aristocrats who were nominated in the hope that they would give
some 'class' to the organizations. Von Reibnitz was one such
honorary member; there is no evidence that he ever wore the
hated black uniform with its SS slashes and death's head insignia.
There is no evidence that he played any part in the running of
concentration camps. The noted Nazi-hunter Dr Simon
Wiesenthal, no friend to anything to do with Nazis or, in
particular, the Gestapo, laughingly dismissed the notion that von
Reibnitz might, somehow or other, have been involved. 'If this
man had been in a concentration camp, he would be known by
name to me. He is not.'

In June 1941 von Reibnitz was sent to Karlsbad to take a cure
so that he could be fit to go to the Russian front. The
forty-seven-year-old veteran of the First World War was too
much of a student of military history to expect that he would
return unscathed from the fighting. The French had found
'General Winter' too much of an opponent for even Napoleon-led
troops; there was no reason to expect that Hitler-controlled troops
would be any luckier.

In Karlsbad von Reibnitz met his old shooting rival Count
Ladislaus Szapáry and was invited to lunch with Countess
Marianne, whose castle was not too far away. She admits that she
fell in love immediately with the much older man (she was thirty
years old), though 'I wouldn't even have gone on talking to him if
he had still thought Hitler's régime was a good thing.'[1] In part,
she was attracted by his looks – tall, dashing and handsome; in

part, she was influenced by the fact that he was, apparently, a close friend of the brother whom she loved and on whom she relied and still relies. But, she says, perhaps the most important influence was a sympathetic regret for this Catholic aristocrat who, they both agreed, had no great expectations of returning from the Russian front. She wanted him to leave for Russia with some sort of happiness. They fell in love, enjoyed a whirlwind courtship of a few days and were married in the chapel at the Countess's castle. Communications between Hungary, Bohemia and Austria were almost non-existent at the time. That is why, I was told, it was not possible to consult or even inform relatives, let alone seek their approach. In view of subsequent developments, that may now seem to have been one unfortunate result of wartime restrictions.

Von Reibnitz had to apply to the Race Purity main office in Berlin for permission to marry the once-Hungarian, now Czech Countess. This was required so that he could prove that neither of them had any Jewish blood. He signed his letter of application with his honorary rank of SS *Sturmbannführer* (equivalent to the rank of Major) even though he was actually serving as a Captain in the Wehrmacht. Perhaps he hoped that his SS rank would get his application dealt with more efficiently. Perhaps he was mindful of the fact that, while a serving Captain, he was officially attached to the SS south-east district headquarters at Breslau in Silesia (now part of Poland). Here he was a provincial gamekeeper, looking after fishing, shooting and falconry – a judicious use, one might think, of the man's proven abilities and interests, but far removed from the infamous work of other sections of the SS – the running of concentration camps.

In spite of his SS posting at Breslau, von Reibnitz left his wife to return to his Panzer division in Russia. She was pregnant with a child who was to be born while he was on duty in Russia; he was first to see his infant son, Baron Frederick, when he returned on leave early in 1944. By that time he had become totally disenchanted with the Nazi Party. Friends claim that he had become a 'born-again' Catholic and that his new-found convictions drove him to become an opponent of the régime. Others claim that he had found out about the work of Himmler, Eichmann, Mengele and others and wanted to distance himself from them.

As for the Countess, years later she told her son of her own open opposition to the régime: how she had refused to give the 'Heil Hitler' sign and greeting when she went to Tachau to run the timber business; how she had been caught listening to the BBC; how the Germans who had conquered Czechoslovakia saw her as an anti-Nazi. When she was summoned to Berlin to appear before the Gestapo to answer for her behaviour, the Baron, who might have stayed quiet, chose to appear alongside his accused wife. 'He showed enormous courage ... What really happened to him then was that he came under the cloud which still hung over me. A year later ... the SS in Breslau ... accused him of giving hunting permits to Jews ... other petty things such as he refused a prominent Nazi a hunting permit.'[2] It was, said the Countess, the beginning of the end for von Reibnitz. Early in 1944 he was expelled from the SS. After a trial, *in absentia*, he was thrown out of the Nazi Party later that year and sent to fight in Russia. Not long after, the Russians took him prisoner.

Countess Marianne had become outraged at Nazi behaviour in the wake of the Stauffenberg bomb-plot. The mother of an infant son and pregnant with Marie-Christine, she took part in anti-Party demonstrations and was arrested and sent to a concentration camp. The smearing journalists who attack Princess Michael with their misconstrued accounts of her father's past ignore the courage of the mother who bore her. Perhaps 'SS Links' makes a better headline than 'Heroine Mother'. Marie-Christine was saved from being born in camp by a quirk of the peculiarly Germanic code of civil law. While this did nothing to prevent Himmler and the SS from doing their worst, it did say that no woman was to be allowed to give birth to a child in prison. This, it was felt, would give the child an unfair start in life. That is why Countess Marianne was freed and why she was allowed to return home in time for her baby to be born in January 1945. By then the German authorities had more to do than concern themselves with a mother and her child. From east and from west the country was occupied by invading forces – Russian, American, British and French.

The tide had turned against Germany in 1942. The Red Army smashed through countries which had been occupied – Poland, Romania, Hungary, Czechoslovakia and Yugoslavia. The von Reibnitz estate in Silesia came under Russian control; so did the great estates of the Esterházys and Szapárys in Hungary. In Bohemia, Countess Marianne and her two infant children waited for the end. In their mansion they were surrounded by mementos of an age which was about to vanish completely, but in the tumult of 1944 and early 1945 they merely eked out an existence, waiting for the arrival of the Red Army.

First came the tank divisions ... composed of picked soldiers, the columns of guns and lorries, the parachute divisions, motor cyclists, technical units ... But this ... is only its vanguard. More than anything else the Red Army is a mass ... columns of marching soldiers, dirty, tired, clad in ragged uniforms. Tens and hundreds of thousands of columns moving on the dusty roads of central and eastern Europe. They march slowly in close rank with a long even step. Sometimes a song burst from the marching column, usually something slow and poignantly sad. So they march, men young and old, men from Russian towns and villages, from the Ukraine and the Tartar Republics, the Ural Mountains and the Caucasus, the Baltic countries, Siberia and Mongolia. ... And columns of women and girls in military grey-green uniforms, high boots and tight blouses, with long hair greased with goose fat ... And children, mainly small boys; the *bezprizorni* from burnt-out villages and towns. Soldiers found them in the woods, exhausted and half mad with hunger and fright, without parents, without a home or a name ... Behind the spearheads drive the staff ... In German luxury cars ... and lorries laden with furniture, beds ... radios, frigidaires, wardrobes, couches ... cases of china, kilometres of textiles, fur coats, carpets, silver ... and lorries with tons of Russian delicacies, caviar, sturgeon, salami, hectolitres of vodka and Crimean wine ... Behind the staffs more marching columns, without a beginning and without an end. And finally the rearguard; miles and miles of small light carts drawn by low Cossack horses. A grey old man sits in front of the cart ... in the back, under the canvas hood, there is a heap of straw and fodder, packages, tins of food and on top lies a sick soldier, a drunken woman, a pen containing a goose, a leg of smoked pork ... They drive today ... as the Tartars used to drive centuries ago; in crowds and hosts, uncounted and uncountable, infinitely foreign and lost in all these western countries of which they have never heard and which they are utterly unable to understand; a flood from the steppes, spreading across Europe.[3]

With their family memories of persecution of the aristocracy after the Russian revolution, the aristocrats in Communist-occupied Europe dreaded their fate. More than most people, the descendants of the imperial nobility were dismayed by the Yalta agreement of February 1945, in which Britain and the USA gave the Soviet Union *carte blanche* in eastern Europe.

Hundreds of thousands of refugees were already fleeing in the face of the Russian advance. Many of these had owned little, if anything; many had lost whatever they may have owned in the devastation of war; some had 'few jewels or money which they hid in their clothing', as Marie-Christine's mother recalled later on, 'but we were luckier than most'. She was lucky in the location of the estate which she had inherited from her mother 'right on the border with Bavaria'. Part of the estate was a series of forests. To help her run it more efficiently, Countess Marianne had taken a course in forest management. As a result, she knew her forest better than any invading Russian soldiers and so was able to elude them and pass into Bavaria. She says little of her own skill: this I learnt from a relative. She does, however, admit that she was fortunate. What would have been her fate if her estate had been further inside Czechoslovakia? 'Another fifty kilometres inside the border ... and we could not have made the journey,' hampered as they were with a young boy and an infant of a few months. As it was, ' ... we walked through the forest, across the border and into Bavaria where the Americans were.'

It is possible now, in the calm of peace and with the benefit of hindsight, to over-romanticize the escape, with its overtones of *The Sound of Music*. Indeed, journalists have over-romanticized it – and made a series of mistakes. The *Daily Express* gave the lead which, slavishly, others followed: 'As the advancing Russian army smashed its way into Czechoslovakia ... a Silesian nobleman ... piled what necessities he could into a small handcart and pulled it through the forest ... his toddler son plodded along ... a baby called Marie-Christine ... golden curls on top of this pathetic pile of a family's dreams in her cradle as the handcart creaked and pumped its way to freedom.'[4]

It seems a pity to spoil such a good 'yarn', but the truth was very different. In the first place, the 'Silesian nobleman' was in a Russian camp, wondering if he would ever get back home. The Countess was helped by her brother, Count Ladislaus. He was not married and so had no family of his own to rescue. He adored his sister, who reciprocated the affection. It is not surprising that he was to become her children's guardian and their lifelong friend. They were joined in their flight by the children's governess and her sister, who was the Countess's maid. There were two horses pulling a cart, and the baby Marie-Christine was tucked away in the hay on top. It was hardly a 'pathetic pile of a family's dream', for Countess Marianne and her brother made several journeys back to the castle to salvage more possessions. Among these was the fortune in diamonds which her father had given her. Count Frederick Szapáry, realizing that the harsh Treaty of Versailles would lead, inevitably, to another war, had purchased a large quantity of not too big, Amsterdam-cut, perfect blue diamonds. Some he had given to his three children; the bulk had been deposited for them in numbered accounts in a Swiss bank. Countess Marianne could face the uncertain future with more hope than could the majority of refugees.

To say that is not, however, to suggest that the flight was some sort of rich lady's picnic. As Countess Marianne now admits, there were many worrying questions to be faced in the troubled world of February 1945. Would she ever return to her estate in Bohemia? Would she again enjoy the splendour of Vienna? How far would Russian occupation of eastern Europe extend? And would it be further extended once the fighting ceased? True, she admits, she and Count Ladislaus had inherited vast estates from their parents and grandparents. Somewhere, surely, in Hungary, Bohemia and Austria, something would remain? And from wartime wreckage, she and, if he returned, her much-loved husband would be able to carve out some sort of future for Frederick and Marie-Christine.

Among her vast inheritance, Countess Marianne had a house in the Austrian lake district at Altmunster in the Salzkammergut, and another in Kitzbuhel. Here they learned that Baron von Reibnitz was, according to the German military authorities, 'missing, presumed dead' in Russia. In fact, he was in a Russian prisoner-of-war camp. On May Day 1945, while the Russian guards were drunkenly celebrating, he escaped and travelled back through Poland to join his family. He was merely one of the many refugees who made their uneasy way across war-ravaged Europe. The family collectively was merely one unit among the large numbers who had been uprooted.

Marie-Christine was to carry lively memories of her early years in Kitzbuhel, which was in the US-occupied zone of divided Germany. She remembers that it appeared always to be full of American troops who, with typical generosity, organized parties for the children of the enemy whom they had so recently helped to defeat. When she broadcast on the World Service programme *Outlook*, Princess Michael recalled the gifts that she took away from some of these parties – baby dolls and stuffed animals, the outward sign of an American wish to come to terms with the conquered people.

The Countess also shared, with her brother and sister, a palace or town house in Vienna, an apartment building also in Vienna and the huge estate of Dobersberg (where Count Ladislau lives in 1985) to the north-west of Vienna.

Between 1945 and 1950 the Austrian nobility were joined in Vienna by many of the Czech, Polish and Hungarian nobility, refugees from Communist rule. Post-war Vienna suffered the food shortages commonplace in devastated Europe; in the severe winter of 1946-7 people queued for whatever fuel the occupying powers allowed into the small, shattered country. The presence of foreign troops was a reminder of the defeat in which Austria had shared, the Russians a grim reminder of the danger of a Communist take-over of Austria. In February 1948 a Communist *coup* in Czechoslovakia brought to an end the uneasy coalition in which the Communists had shared power with representatives of democratically based parties. That *coup* was one of the many incidents in the so-called Cold War which threatened to develop into a Third World War.

Against the global background of widespread uncertainty, the affairs of the von Reibnitz family pale into relative insignificance. At least they were ensured of shelter in the Countess's houses in Altmunster and Kitzbuhel or they could stay in the Vienna apartment building. They suffered less than most from the general shortage of food and fuel, for the family estates were a source for both, while there was always enough money available to buy whatever might be going. For millions of other refugees, life in post-war Europe was much harder; thousands were homeless, many finding inadequate shelter in bombed-out ruins. Thousands of families were separated one member from another; they sought each other out in one or other of the myriad of advisory offices which sprang up to try to aid the refugees. The Americans, who had spent so lavishly to bring about the defeat of Germany and her allies, now spent on an equally massive scale to provide aid for the refugees who thronged post-war Europe. The USA contributed $2.7 billion in aid to the United Nations Relief and Rehabilitation Administration (UNRRA). By 1948, when UNRRA ceased operation, 25 million tons of goods had been shipped, the chief European recipients being Austria, the Ukraine, Czechoslovakia and Poland. By 1948 11 million 'displaced persons' had been helped to find their way home, but some half million remained in refugee camps in Germany.

Older readers will remember the harsh realities of Britain in the immediate post-war years. In some way, life was harder than it had been even during the war itself. Only in 1946-7 did the British have to endure bread rationing, as the government diverted grain to help overcome the shortage of food in occupied Europe. In hindsight it seems as if there were shortages of everything: clothes, furniture, food of all kinds, sweets, tobacco, petrol, coal, newsprint – most things were strictly rationed. In this respect, the problems facing the von Reibnitz family were certainly no greater, and in general much smaller, than the problems facing the majority of people in Britain – which had, after all, been victorious during the war.

However, in another respect the von Reibnitzes were faced with unusual problems – problems shared with the 'war-criminals' of the Nazi years and with those Germans who had been openly associated with them.

In 1947-8 Baron von Reibnitz was tried by a Bavarian 'de-Nazification' court.

Under the terms of Allied Occupation Law, there were five categories of Nazi involvement:

1. *Hauptschuldige*, major offenders, were all the top-ranking Nazis.
2. *Belastete* were activists, militarists and profiteers, including industrialists.
3. *Mindebelastete* were lesser offenders, active Nazis who had joined the Nazi Party in their youth but who were not known to have committed any major crimes.
4. *Mitlaufer* were described as 'small fry' who had been forced to maintain some form of allegiance in order to keep their jobs.
5. *Entlastete* were those who could be exonerated because they could provide proof of anti-Nazi opposition to the régime.

In April 1947 a de-Nazification court decided that von Reibnitz was a 'lesser offender'. However, he appealed against this finding. In May 1948 a court in Upper Bavaria reclassified him as a mere follower rather than a supporter of the régime. The court found that although von Reibnitz had had the right to wear the SS uniform, he had never done so. It recognized that he had been one of those outspoken Catholics who had expressed opposition to the régime, so that he had aroused the disapproval of top SS officials – who had arranged for him to be dismissed from the Party and from the SS. In particular, the court recognized the Baron's work on behalf of foreign forced labour, declaring that he had gone 'well beyond normal limits' to help these and other victims of racial abuse.

We have seen that in July 1941 von Reibnitz and the Countess had feared that he would not return alive from the Russian front and that they had rushed into marriage so that he could have, as it were, 'a last hurrah' of happiness. However, against the odds, he was now back with his wife and family. The Countess was delighted to have back the man she loved, the father of her two young children. Together, she hoped, they would re-build a life in war-ravaged Europe. It is impossible to imagine how she felt when he came to tell her that, when he 'married' her in 1941, he was already a married man and the father of a teenage daughter. He claimed that the first marriage had been a failure from the start, that he had chosen to 'forget' about it when snatching a few weeks happiness before what he had seen as certain death on the Russian front.

Now the Countess was faced not only with the everyday

problems of life in war-torn Europe. As a devout Catholic she had also to consider what she was to do about her 'marriage'. She went to consult a Cardinal. His decision was sympathetic but firm. Since she had married von Reibnitz in good faith, the children were legitimate – in the eyes of the Church. However, because of the existing first marriage, the Countess could no longer live with her 'husband'. The Church recognized that von Reibnitz had a responsibility to maintain his children but, said the Cardinal, he could not exercise a husband's role as regards the Countess.

Von Reibnitz could not accept this way of life. He left the Countess and the children to travel in Africa, where he had many friends and connections for going on safari. He arranged to give a series of lectures on the way of life he knew best – hunting, fishing and shooting. While in Mozambique he met the widowed Baroness Rosemarie von Buddenbrock, who had a large estate in Mozambique which had at that time, not been cultivated as she and her late husband used it only for big-game hunting. Von Reibnitz proposed marriage; she accepted, and, not following his 1941 duplicity, he told his new fiancée of his previous marriages and divorces.

The former playboy and cavalry officer worked hard to set himself up as a citrus farmer and a game-hunter. It had been commonplace for 'failed' members of the British nobility to be sent to the colonies by their unhappy families. Kenya, further north along the African coast, had been developed by some such. Von Reibnitz may have hoped to imitate the men who had carved out vast estates in the so-called White Highlands there. He may have been encouraged by the welcome given to aristocratic refugees by Salazar, Portugal's dictator, who ran the colonies of Angola and Mozambique in the interests of the mother country and of the Europeans (largely Portuguese) who made their homes there. Perhaps von Reibnitz hoped to become one of the favoured few, able to enjoy a high standard of living in a country where land was cheap, labour plentiful, wages low and the white man held in high regard.

Working a twelve-hour day, von Reibnitz organized the building of a ranch-style house, a beautiful park and a large farm on which he grew citrus fruit, bananas, maize, peanuts, sunflowers (for their oil), avocados, cotton and coffee. His farm became so widely recognized as a show-piece that people came from all over Africa to see it. Indeed, when the revolution took place in Mozambique, the new government set a special guard around the farm so that it would be kept intact and neither looted nor broken up into small plots. Von Reibnitz's favoured form of recreation was to go with friends on safari – an experience which, in their turn, his children were to enjoy. He stayed in Mozambique until 1981, when, aged eighty-seven, he returned to Europe, suffering from angina which, in 1983, was the cause of his death.

Once von Reibnitz had deserted his family, Countess Marianne had to make important decisions concerning her, and her children's, future. She had several options. She might stay in Europe, where she had a variety of estates and the comforting web of inter-family relationships on which she could rely for whatever help she might need, and where, after all, she had made her own life to this date. However, in 1950 Europe was not the place it had been in the days of imperial glory before 1914 or even in the period between the wars. Her own country was in ruins, Europe as a whole struggling to recover from the ravages of war; the crisis over Allied rights to travel to West Berlin had shown that the danger from Russian expansionism was still very real, that the Cold War might, at any time, explode into a shooting war. Also, though she might have lived in comfort in any of her homes, she would have found in them daily reminders of von Reibnitz, the husband whom she had given up because of her religious convictions.

Many of her friends suggested that Countess Marianne ought to build a new life for herself and her children in the United States. Here, more than anywhere else outside Europe, she would have found the kind of elegant and aristocratic society to which she was accustomed. She would have had the help of her rich Vanderbilt-Szapáry cousin, her lifelong friend. Marie-Christine might have grown up among the cream of American society.

If Countess Marianne had been driven merely by considerations of the worldly well-being of her children, she might well have decided to have lived in the USA. But worldly ambition has never been a driving force in the Countess's life. She long ago made it clear that she did not care whom her children married so long as they were in Church and remained loyal Catholics. That is not to say that she was not ambitious for her children. Herself a hardworking student and graduate, estate manager and family organizer, sportswoman and Olympic competitor, she could hardly be described as unambitious. As she admits, she wanted her children to have academic ambitions: 'No child of mine shall ever fail an exam' was more than a cliché. A close friend says that, ideally, the Countess would have liked her son to be a priest and her daughter an academic. Little here of materialistic considerations: so there was no settling in the USA.

Some of her friends suggested that she should settle in Britain. Here too she would have found family links which would have been helpful. There was another of her cousins, Princess Weikersheim, the sister of Prince Fritzi Windisch-Graetz who had married a niece of Lord Mountbatten. Her daughter, Mrs Alexander McEwan, would have been of help to Marie-Christine, whom she might have chaperoned into society as she grew up. There were also a number of the Countess's friends from skiing days, including the Duchess of Portland, distantly related to the Queen Mother, and the Countess of Selkirk, sister-in-law of the late Duke of Hamilton. There would have been no shortage of the well placed, ready and willing to make it easy for the Countess and her children to settle in Britain.

Strangely enough, it was some of these British friends who suggested that she should think of going to Australia – at least for some time, during which she might have a chance to gather herself after the collapse of her marriage. Many of the British aristocracy owned land in Australia. Post-war tax changes had led to the situation in which such expatriate landowners had to pay tax on their estate-income to both the Australian and British governments – unless they spent six months in Australia, when they avoided the British tax levied on their Australian holdings. Many British aristocrats spent half the year in Australia. They had discovered for themselves – and they told Countess Marianne – that Australia was, indeed, a land of great opportunities, particularly for the rich and the young. As a clincher, the Countess learnt of the opportunities for 'great skiing' which existed in Australia.

Thus, along with thousands of other middle Europeans, Countess Marianne emigrated to Australia. Even Australian friends are surprised when they hear of this decision. At least, they say, von Reibnitz may have hoped to replicate some form of 'superior' life in colonial Mozambique: he would have servants to command (and obey him); he would enjoy a life-style far superior to that of the surrounding majority. But Countess Marianne can have had no such illusions about life in Australia, where the concept of 'equality' was far greater than that of 'service' and where democracy flourished in a way unknown in middle Europe. Perhaps the choice of the far-away island continent was an indication of a wish to bring to an end a life of unhappiness; Nazi occupation, broken marriage, wartime and post-war deprivation, Cold War, Russian threat – perhaps it had been too much.

3

Growing Up in Australia, 1951–68

'I am a baroness.' 'So what?' — an exchange alleged to have taken place in a school playground, Sydney, Australia

We have seen that the Countess's father had taken care to ensure that his children would never be poor. When she left for Australia, she took with her her diamonds and, unlike the majority of hopeful emigrants, she and her children travelled first class. In addition to the paternal diamonds, she also took her share of the fabulous emeralds in the shape of partridge eggs that Tsar Nicholas II had given to her beautiful mother, Princess Hedwig. In post-war Europe the market was being flooded with the jewellery of refugee aristocrats. This would not be the case in Australia.

Sydney, where the family settled, was founded in January 1788; its oldest surviving building dates from 1815 and its cathedral from 1868. In the collective memory of the Szapáry-Esterházy-Schwarzenberg-Lobkowitz family, these dates are but as yesteryear. The relatively 'new' country had not acquired even the superficiality of cultural life, let alone the depth evident almost everywhere in Austria and Hungary. There was, when the von Reibnitz family arrived, no opera house — a sad comparison with the castles and mansions they were leaving behind, in which Haydn and Beethoven had had their works performed. Nor had the brash young city of Sydney used the opportunities open to its developers to become a place of beauty. Nowhere was there the mansions, palaces, great parks and squares that Countess Marianne had known in Europe's great cities, and in Vienna in particular.

Before long she met and married a Polish nobleman, Count Tadeusz Rogala-Koczorowski. Before the war, he had been a

Polish diplomat. At the outbreak of war in September 1939 he was stationed in Paris and, with the fall of his country, became one of the many exiled Poles. After the war, he emigrated to Australia and, when he married Countess Marianne, he was employed in the surveyor's office at Sydney town hall. They lived in a 'normal' house in the exclusive Double Bay suburb of Sydney. It held certain mementos of a more glorious past – original oil-paintings, hundreds of years old, but these could only stir the memory; the reality of life was that Countess Marianne became an ordinary housewife – cooking, cleaning, shopping and bringing up her children.

Students of children's educational progress know the importance of the mother's influence over the child's development. There is no doubt that Countess Marianne exemplifies this dominant importance of the mother over the child's success. Her family and friends point out that, whatever her circumstances, she would have demanded very high academic standards from her children. She had, after all, achieved such standards for herself; it was reasonable for her to want the same for her children. She was, one friend says, 'a total blue-stocking, uninterested in glamour or social standing. Her standards are moral and academic and her deep religious beliefs have always ensured her optimistic nature. Overall, her sense of humour and lack of bitterness are what strike one most about this fascinating and intelligent lady.'

Among the journalistic inventions about the Sydney-based Countess was one that she worked as a hairdresser and cosmetician to pay the fees at the smart girls' school to which her daughter went as a weekly boarder.[1] One sees why an inventive journalist might want to write such a line: a romantic picture of a hard-working mother, an aristocrat lowering herself to scrape together the school fees. The truth is very different.

As a young woman, Countess Marianne had wanted to go to Paris with one of her Apponyi cousins – who later married Prince Esterházy. However, both young women had very strict parents who would not have taken kindly to the suggestion that their daughters should be let loose in Paris. So the enterprising youngsters asked that they be allowed to go there to study. But to study what? At that time Countess Marianne suffered from a skin disorder; she used this as the basis for her petition to her parents. The famous dermatologist Dr N.G. Payot had been treating her whenever he visited Hungary. He taught in Paris. Why not, she asked her parents, let her go there to take a course with the doctor? This would enable her to provide for her own treatment when she came home – and would be yet another academic string to her well-strung bow.

When the Countess settled in Australia, she noticed how dry were the skins of Australian ladies. She decided to invest in the franchise of Dr Payot's products for Australia – the sort of entrepreneurial decision which had once driven her Schwarzenberg and Auersperg ancestors. Having obtained the franchise, she sold the products through a number of beauty salons – 'very successfully', I was told. It may be that she shares her friend's regret that 'when Countess Marianne met and married her second husband, he made her give up her little business enterprise, which had lasted only a year and a half. The products still exist – but someone else now makes the profits.' When I discussed this 'hairdresser and cosmetician' story with members of the Countess's family, they were both annoyed and amused. Their amusement stemmed from the fact that, as one of them told me, 'The Countess has never learnt to put a curler in her own hair, let alone in anyone else's.' 'I hope,' said another, 'that you finally put an end to this silly story.' I doubt whether one can hope for such success.

We have seen that that story was linked with the notion that the Countess needed to earn money to pay her daughter's school fees. (This, incidentally, ignores or begs the question; 'Who paid the fees for Baron Frederick's education?' Maybe, in journalistic eyes, there is more mother-care in finding fees for a daughter's than for a son's schooling.) Once again, the truth is very different. Countess Marianne did not, in fact, have to pay very much for her children's schooling. Her son won scholarships to his school and to university. As for Marie-Christine's school, when the famous Hungarian Cardinal Mindszenty wrote that various branches of her family had done so much for the Church over the centuries it was time that the Church did something for the family, the teaching nuns who read this letter 'drastically reduced' the level of her fees. (In passing, I fear that some journalist will now make a story out of 'Corruption in high places; Szapárys use their influence ...' or some such. It is, in fact, very difficult for the aristocrat to win.)

Marie-Christine's first school was the junior, or prep, school called Baratburn, a small building in the grounds of the Rose Bay Convent complex where she was taught by the nuns of the Sacred Heart Order. However, since she did not want to be a full-time boarder, when she was aged eight she moved to the sister-convent at Elizabeth Bay, Kincoppal, where she could be a weekly boarder. This school was situated on a promontory of land projecting into the harbour – rather as does the spit of land on which stands the

Sydney Opera House. Many years later it was sold by the nuns –
'for a fortune', I was told. The city's most exclusive apartment
buildings now stand on the site. It commands a view which,
according to Marie-Christine, is the most beautiful she has ever
seen.

When they closed their school at Kincoppal, the nuns
transferred their pupils to Rose Bay Convent, which, to the
delight of Countess Marianne, consciously aimed to produce
high-achievers. The girls were made aware of the hopes which the
school and their parents had for them. In Marie-Christine they
had, in almost every respect, an ideal pupil with whom to work.
She had some advantages over the Australian-born majority in
that, as the Countess explained, 'We always spoke French at
home.'[2] With a Polish stepfather, a Hungarian mother and the
English-speaking children, French was 'the only language that the
Countess had in common with her husband'. His English was
minimal when he arrived in Australia and he never really became
fluent. In an interview for the BBC World Service, Princess
Michael explained that when she was living in Kitzbuhel she had
a British governess and that in Australia she and her mother used
to listen to the BBC World Service 'to help us learn English'. In
particular she recalled the many times they had listened to Max
Robinson's commentaries from Wimbledon, and to Dylan
Thomas's *Under Milk Wood*. At that time, she says, she had no
idea where Wales was, but she did learn to appreciate Thomas's
use of the language. Indeed, she and Prince Michael still listen to a
recording of the poet reading his own work; she claimed, on
Desert Island Discs, that when Prince Michael gets slightly
annoyed by her insistence on having the house tidy, he mocks her
as 'the tidy Mrs Pritchard' who features in Thomas's work.

Since her mother and her aunts had been very good tennis-
players, it is not surprising that Marie-Christine also did well at
the game.' She also enjoyed swimming, learned to ride and was a
welcome addition to the parties given by her schoolfriends. One
of them remembered: 'She was a knockout socially. When she
walked into a party, everything would stop. Even at seventeen she
had a fantastic way with men. She had that certain knack of
meeting somebody and being able to talk to him as if he was the
only chap in the world.'

Her social success was due, in part, to the centuries of breeding
which had gone to the 'production' of the Szapáry-Windisch-
Graetz-Auersperg-von Reibnitz families, but she owed a great
deal to her mother, who was determined that her daughter would
succeed. She sent Marie-Christine to evening classes to learn to

sew – as she herself always regretted that she had never learnt. Marie-Christine could not afford to buy the expensive clothes that her rich friends could buy, so she had to learn to make her own. The Countess brought to the process her own cultivated taste. Other girls relied either on the products of the Sydney shops – hardly trend-setters in the world of fashion – or on the 'inspirations' of their mothers, with none of the flair of the descendant of centuries of imperial nobility. It is not surprising that Marie-Christine's friends remember that; 'She always had poise, charm and style far beyond her years ... It was really amazing the way she did it, because at that stage she was a very big girl. To be honest, I should say fat. She was nicknamed "the Amazon" by the boys.' (Shades here of the 'Val', for 'Valkyrie', nickname which, according to some journalists, is used in the Royal Family. It is likely that 'Amazon' and 'Our Val' are more the product of imagination than of reality. All the photographs of her 'Sydney period' show her as a tall, slim girl; indeed, one friend goes so far as to write that she 'was rather on the thin side'. As for the 'Our Val' story, the truth is that the Princess is known as 'MC' inside the Royal Family.)

The mother watched, with pleasure, the growth of her daughter and her successes – academic, athletic and social. She also made her aware of her ancestry. This was easily done: in the modest suburban house there were paintings and jewellery which provided, as it were, 'visual aids' for a lesson on family history. There were, too, letters from European relatives, many of which included photographs of members of the extended family and of their homes. Here, again, ample opportunities for tracing out the family tree, for explaining who this one was, what that one had done. And, as we saw in Chapter 1, they had done so much – in the Empire, in Europe and in the cultural field.

Marie-Christine may have had dim recollections of European estates and mansions, but while these may have helped her appreciation of where she stood in 'history', at another level, they may have inhibited her. She never invited her schoolfriends back to the family home. Some of them think that this was because she was sensitive about the simplicity of that home which was less 'grand' than their rich, middle-class homes. Others think that she feared that her home would not provide the fitting background for the 'Baroness', for, as one remembered, 'She did try to play up the Baroness bit. But perhaps she was just trying to make up for the disadvantage of being foreign.'

Once again, as one of her friends noted, 'the right fact but the wrong reason.' Only a few of Marie-Christine's close friends knew, or know, that she did not enjoy the best of relationships with her stepfather, who had been a Polish diplomat before 1939 and who had found it difficult to settle to a new life in Australia. It is likely that Marie-Christine was unwilling to have her schoolfriends become aware of this domestic unhappiness.

As to the journalistic claim that 'she played up the Baroness bit', there are good grounds for doubting this often-told story. Her mother kept a low profile, never boasting about her background, largely because she felt that she could not entertain in the style which her rank called for. Certainly she brought her children up to face the reality of their new situation. The Countess is a very realistic person and not one to risk causing irritation or scorn by boasting, especially in Australia, a country where the majority are unfamiliar with European aristocracy. As a highly intelligent woman, she knew only too well how many Australians in the 1950s viewed the rush of immigrants from Europe with suspicion. To many of them, there seemed to be little, if any, difference between a semi-literate Greek and a Hungarian countess: they all had accents which the locals could barely understand. The last thing Countess Marianne wanted for her children was for them to cause aggravation through snobbery. Indeed, Princess Michael says that they deliberately kept a low profile almost out of a form of inverted snobbery, because it seemed to the family that almost every other European who arrived, sometimes the servants of former aristocrats, actually claimed to be their former masters or mistresses. Her mother, she says, laughed about these impostors privately – but kept the mockery inside the family. She was so secure in herself, knowing who and what she was, that she did not need to assert herself or 'show off' – and, says Princess Michael, she taught her children to do the same.

Marie-Christine matriculated in December 1960 – a reminder that the Australians enjoy their summer (and children suffer examinations) at the end of the year. She was then not yet sixteen – the youngest girl ever to matriculate in New South Wales, a credit to her mother's academic inspiration and her own innate ability. But she was still too young to go on to university. Perhaps as a reward for her hard work, her mother decided to send her to Mozambique to stay with her father. In fact she was to spend almost two years in Africa because he sent her to stay with a number of her friends throughout Africa so that she could see more countries.

An Australian schoolfriend remembered: 'She had an enormous regard for her father', although she had not met him since she had left Europe. 'Her brother, Frederick, had gone to visit him in Africa, and as a schoolgirl she just seemed to live for the day when she could leave school and follow him.'

When she took part in Roy Plomley's *Desert Island Discs* programme, Princess Michael recalled the shock she had when she met her father, now almost sixty-seven years of age. 'He seemed old enough to have been my grandfather,' she said. She has told many people of the mixture of pleasure and sadness which she experienced during the nine months which she spent at the luxury ranch-house on her stepmother's estate. Her father left her very much to her own devices; they seem to have had all too little in common. (In passing we might ask, as some 'investigative journalists' did in 1985, 'Why did the Baron not tell his daughter about his Nazi past while she was with him?' To which, in fairness, one might ask, 'Why should he? Would any other similarly placed father?')

Princess Michael has happy memories of her years in Africa. There was the chance to enjoy the continent's beauty and the company of her stepmother, who was very kind to her. In May 1984, when Marie-Christine appeared on a BBC talk show, *Private Lives*, she talked about that visit. Her father, she said, took her on a safari to hunt big game. But, she claimed, even in the middle of the jungle, he lived 'the high life': in the evening the table was laid out complete with silver, the white-gloved servants poured the champagne and wines and helped the guests, including the wide-eyed Australian schoolgirl, to a variety of dishes. It is not surprising that her friends remember that she returned to Sydney 'exhilarated and excited by what she had seen and desperate to see more of the world, particularly the country of her birth'.

TV viewers in Britain heard about this exciting adventure. They did not hear the full story because the programme had been recorded, and only an edited version went out. I have been fortunate in having watched a video recording of the unedited programme. BBC viewers did not hear what the *Daily Mirror* was to call 'tales concerning her deprived and bare-foot past'. The main reason for the cuts was that Princess Michael used words ('coloureds' and 'natives') which the BBC feared might cause racial upset by those who chose to misunderstand her. One of the 'tales' which the Princess told – and which the *Mirror* half-reported – concerning her having travelled on a bus 'used by the natives' because she could not afford to pay for the 'transport favoured by the whites'. She had, it was reported, dyed her hair, blacked her face to a gleaming ebony and became 'indistinguishable from the Nubians'. The *Mirror* cast its doubts on whether this actually happened.

Because of the cuts in the programme, BBC viewers did not hear the full story. After Marie-Christine had spent some time with her father in Mozambique, he sent her travelling to friends in South Africa and Namibia. When it was nearing Christmas, he sent her an air ticket to come home to Mozambique for the holiday. As she was having such a wonderful time, Marie-Christine cashed in her ticket and spent the money. When it was almost Christmas and she realized she had to leave for Mozambique, she was in a dilemma. Her hosts knew her father had sent her the ticket and she was too ashamed to ask them to buy another. She found she had just enough money left to take the bus. But the bus was intended not for white passengers but for black and coloured travellers. As she had been to Cape Town and seen the famous 'Cape Coloured' (people of mixed white and black descent), she thought she could pass as one, even with her light eyes, particularly if she dyed her hair (and in South Africa no one would want to pretend to be Coloured!). There is no doubt the adventure of it all also appealed to her as well as the circumstances.

During the recounting of this story, Princess Michael did not use any of the phrases which I have quoted from various newspapers' comments on the programme. It seems a pity that they did not use her own words and not implied that she used others.

At the end of her African holiday it was back to the Sydney suburb to pick up the threads of her Australian life. Among the journalistic myths of this short period of her life are the stories that she went to work in a Sydney boutique and that her ambition was 'to be a secretary'.[3] As to the first: far from working in someone else's shop, Marie-Christine set up her own dress-design business, making a small 'collection' from which her friends placed orders. There was no shop, no 'boutique'. Her business was very successful and fulfilled its main purpose of providing enough money for her to travel back to Europe as soon as possible. As to the secretarial ambitions: such limited aims would have been totally out of character then as now.

It had always been intended that the von Reibnitzes would return to Europe one day. Indeed, Countess Marianne's original intention had been to stay in Australia for only four or five years. Once she had saved enough money (from her dress-design business), Marie-Christine set off for what proved to be a process of education that was vital to her future life. Her first stop was in Trieste, where she stayed with her Windisch-Graetz cousin, the brother of Prince Fritzi, and his family. They have remained her very close friends. It was with them that she discovered Venice, 'across the water', which she described as 'my favourite bolt-hole'. If she were on a desert island, Princess Michael would like to have a Mahler record to remind her of this period and that favourite city.

After this break she went back to Vienna and her favourite uncle and guardian, Count Ladislaus. He had married in later life. His wife was the daughter of the Dutch Ambassador to Vienna, Charlotte Star-Bussmann. She had been educated at Heathfield in Britain and was to prove a great friend and ally. 'Aunt Charlotte' was to be a particularly valuable adviser and guide when Marie-Christine first moved to Britain.

Marie-Christine recalls that year in Vienna. Here, she says, she met an endless list of people of her own generation and extended family. 'In England one doesn't even know one's first cousins; we have an intimate knowledge of our first, second, third and even fourth cousins.' The family 'swopped stories' about various comings and goings: some had gone to live in Spain, others to Canada, many had gone to South America, more to the USA, while Marie-Christine had her own Australian stories to tell. In her interview on the *Outlook* programme for the BBC World Service, she remembered how they all appeared to be, compared with their parents and grandparents, 'a restless generation' who seemed to live with 'their cases packed in foreign countries ... waiting to go back'. In spite of its many links with her extended family, or perhaps because of those links, Vienna is not one of Princess Michael's favourite cities. Indeed, if she were on Roy Plomley's desert island, she would have with her a recording of the operatic tragedy *Tosca* to help her recall visits to the Vienna Opera House when she first went to Vienna. Why such a sad work? 'Because I am a Central European ... I like a good tragedy.'

With an eye to her own future Marie-Christine took a course in art history studies at Florence, Vienna and Paris. Such a hard-headed attitude to life may have disappointed some of the older relatives who, she says, hoped that from the coming together in Vienna, an inter-family marriage might emerge. For her part, Marie-Christine found that her studies served to increase her fascination with design in general. She had thought, when considering her return to Europe, that she would make a career in dress design, but her art studies convinced her that interior design was the career which she wanted.

However, there was no opportunity for studying interior design in Austria. 'It was considered that what had been good enough for your grandmother should be good enough for you.

Only the *nouveau riche* would consider changing the long-established.' This helps to explain why the Australian-educated Marie-Christine came to Britain in 1965; it was one place where she could be at home and, at the same time, study interior design.

She was helped to settle in Britain by her mother's many friends and relatives who lived in and around London. One of her mother's skiing friends was Miss Evelyn Pinching, who owned a large apartment in Eaton Square. She provided Marie-Christine with a small flat — the residence of the servants in more prosperous days. Miss Pinching ran her own interior design business and accepted Marie-Christine as an apprentice, paying her a small salary to supplement the allowance which she received from her uncle Ladislaus. For £3 a week, Marie-Christine 'mixed the paints, laid the carpets, stripped the paper, did the carpentry ...' so that, as she explained, she would be the better able to supervise others when she came to run her own business.

As soon as she felt that she had learned enough to be able to set herself up as an interior decorator, the practical Marie-Christine realized that she would also have to learn to run an office. While she was a guest on the programme *Desert Island Discs*, she explained that she knew that office-organization would be essential to her future but that, while a competent designer, she had no idea of what happened in an office, so she went to work for an advertising agency. Her 'boss' remembered: 'She was poised, self-confident and charming. She was very good at meeting people, organizing and talking to clients over the telephone. But she was inclined to talk to clients as though she was an executive. She was miscast as a secretary.'

There was another reason why her employer found it impossible to retain the services of the 'striking and self-assured' Marie-Christine: she developed a very active social life in London. Many of her relatives lived there, working for international firms or in their countries' diplomatic services. She was a welcome addition to their circle and through them was introduced into London society. Her employers became increasingly disenchanted with the 'attractive and competent' secretary who had to refuse to work late at night because of one or other social engagement. He also acknowledged that because of her many late nights she was only 'fairly' punctual the morning after.

Marie-Christine was, indeed, 'miscast as a secretary'; she was, as it were, merely playing at the part, with higher things in mind. As soon as she felt that she could run an office, she left to set up her own business, Szapáry Designs. Very intelligent, tall, glamorous, well-dressed and well-connected, it is not surprising that she was a success. She admitted to Roy Plomley that she had been 'very successful' and become 'very rich' within a short space of time. Her success allowed her to enjoy visits to friends on the Continent – the Windsich-Graetzes in Trieste and Uncle Ladislaus in Vienna.

In August 1968 Countess Marianne came to Europe. This was, for the people of Czechoslovakia, 'the glorious Dubček summer' when an attempt was made to create a new form of politics – 'Socialism with a human face'. Countess Marianne thought that, in the light of the liberated atmosphere that seemed to prevail, she could risk taking Marie-Christine to western Bohemia to show her their former home and her birthplace. They were driven by the retired chauffeur who had been Princess Windisch-Graetz's coachman. He could speak Czech – which the Countess did not. After a nostalgic tour of western Bohemia, they returned to stay at the French Embassy in Prague. The Ambassador, Roger Lallouette, was an old friend. After dinner one evening, while they were sitting on the terrace overlooking the garden, the Ambassador was called to the telephone. He returned and, even at that late hour, asked his guests to pack and leave for Austria immediately. He did not try to explain the need for the haste, but as the Countess and Marie-Christine reached the border, they heard on the radio that Russian troops had invaded. It is not surprising, perhaps, that in her broadcast on the BBC World Service Princess Michael admitted that she had long had a deep respect for and love of Britain, where there is a 'special quality of life ... respect for the individual ... unlike so many foreign countries'.

Within a year of that tour with her mother, Marie-Christine met the Etonian banker Tom Troubridge, who seemed in many ways to be the personification of that peculiarly British way of life which she so admired.

4

Mrs Thomas Troubridge,
1971–7

'Tom's a very private man with a lot of self-esteem' –
private conversation

Marie-Christine first met Tom Troubridge at a boar-hunt on the German estate of a relative. He was a leading member of the British branch of the Kleinwort merchant banking business, and he knew some of her relatives as banking colleagues and competitors.

In 1969 Troubridge was thirty years of age, a successful banker who was extremely popular with a wide range of people. He had spent some time studying banking – and learning German – in Munich. He had many friends in Germany and mixed easily in aristocratic circles. His friends were never in any doubt that he would like to marry a European, preferably one who would make him even more a part of those aristocratic circles he enjoyed frequenting.

That he and Marie-Christine met at a boar-hunt may sound strange to British readers who would not find it odd if the couple had met at, say, a hunt ball. In Germany and Austria the boar-hunt has often been the occasion for significant meetings. In 1937, for example, Lord Halifax accepted an invitation to a boar-hunt at Berlin, organized by Goering.

The outcome of the meeting between Tom Troubridge and Marie-Christine was, for a time at least, a happy one. They found that they had a good deal in common: her 'international' friends were, in many cases, his business associates; they were both accomplished linguists; they shared many cultural interests. Today some of their friends claim, but only in hindsight, to have known that their relationship was doomed from the start. No one showed any such perspicacity in 1969.

No one knows the nature of the 'chemistry' which drew them

to one another. Their friends are prepared, however, to venture to suggest some of the practical reasons for the development of the relationship over the next two years. Troubridge's friends admit that he was a carefree bachelor who led an active social life at home and abroad, his London base being a Georgian house, 1b Gertrude Street, a quietish backwater on the borders of Fulham and Chelsea. He appreciated that the tall, strikingly good-looking, intelligent and lively Marie-Christine would be an admirable hostess and partner. This is not to ascribe cynical motives to Troubridge. It is, rather, to accept what the bachelor Prince Charles once said – when asked what he would look for in a potential bride, he remarked: 'She would have to be up to the job.' Troubridge considered that Marie-Christine would be 'up to the job' of being wife and companion and would be able to provide him with that entrée into European society which he loved – especially to the shooting parties to which, via the Szapáry connections, she had access.

Some of Marie-Christine's friends, who remained loyal to her during her later struggles with Church and State, suggest that she had 'practical' reasons for responding to Troubridge's advances. One of them, perhaps more honest than others, said that, in the Troubridge marriage, 'Marie-Christine looked for the security provided by his money.' Other friends, however, claim that this is to misunderstand the situation. Troubridge never misled Marie-Christine into thinking that he had money beyond his salary and a small private income. Certainly he had none of that inherited wealth which allowed her European relatives to enjoy a high standard of living. Unlike the castle- and estate-owning Europeans, Troubridge had a charming house but little else. As to the security which he seemed to offer: Marie-Christine could have got such security – and more – from a number of eligible men to be found among the serried ranks of family relatives. It is worth noting that some of the rank-conscious Europeans said that, 'He was not much of a catch.' This is a little unfair, for Troubridge was, like Marie-Christine, 'well born' and a friend of minor royalty, the descendant of a family with a long and proud history.

The Troubridge family first appeared in the history books in the person of Thomas Troubridge (1758-1807), who had a distinguished naval career. Between 1783 and 1793 he was an officer in the Naval forces which helped win India for Britain. During the French Revolutionary Wars he fought at Cape St Vincent (1797) under the command of Jervis, and at Aboukir Bay (1798) under Nelson. In Nelson's opinion he was 'the most meritorious officer of his rank in the services'. He helped in the attack on southern Italy and the capture of Malta (1799), following which he was created the first Baron Troubridge, the 321st in the order of precedence. He became a Rear-Admiral and a Lord of the Admiralty. He died when his ship was wrecked while on his way to take command at the Cape of Good Hope.

His son, Sir Edward, had a similarly distinguished naval career, taking part in the important Battle of Copenhagen (1801) and serving with Nelson on the *Victory* until 1803. Like his father, he became a Rear-Admiral, Lord of the Admiralty and an MP representing Sandwich from 1831 to 1847.

His eldest son, Thomas, broke with tradition by becoming a distinguished army officer, taking a leading role at the Battle of Inkerman (1854) where he was field officer of the day with the Light Division. Although badly injured, losing his right leg and left foot, he remained at his station, for which he was mentioned in despatches, received a medal, was made a CB and became aide-de-camp to the Queen. From the family's point of view his major importance lies in his marriage, in November 1855, to Louise Gurney, niece of Elizabeth Gurney, better known as Elizabeth Fry, the noted campaigner for prison reform.

Ernest Charles Thomas, Baron Troubridge (1862-1926), was yet another of the family's distinguished naval officers. Between 1901 and 1913 he served in a number of naval-diplomatic posts, first at Vienna (1901-4) at a time when Marie-Christine's relatives were helping to run the Austro-Hungarian Empire, later in Madrid and Tokyo before returning to become Private Secretary to successive First Lords of the Admiralty, McKenna and Winston Churchill. During the First World War he saw action in the Mediterranean before re-entering the diplomatic world as aide to the Crown Prince of Serbia and in 1920 as British representative to the Danube Commission. He was knighted for his service to the nation.

His son, Thomas Hope Troubridge, followed his father into the Navy. He played an outstanding part in the Second World War, winning the DSO, the DSM, a bar to his DSO and a CB; he also became a KCB. His wife, the mother of Sir Peter and of Tom Troubridge, was Lily Kleinwort, of the once-German banking family whose ancestors first settled in London early in the nineteenth century.

The summary of the history of the family may serve to indicate that Tom Troubridge was 'well born' as well as wealthy enough to provide Marie-Christine with a comfortable home. When they returned from Germany to London, they continued to meet. He enjoyed meeting some of the aristocratic friends who had introduced her into London society and he approved of her development of her business. She was charmed with his Georgian house in Gertrude Street which had much of the comfort which she remembered at her mother's home in Double Bay.

Their friendship blossomed in a series of concerts and parties, the 'good-time' Troubridge not disguising (and why should he?) his zest for the carefree existence which he had led before (and after) he met her. She, for her part, welcomed the attention she received from Troubridge's friends who, although not of 'the highest birth', represented the class where money meets minor royals as well as entertainers of the jet set. Marie-Christine fitted well into this milieu: attractive, intelligent, with a wide range of interests and an innate, inherited ability to fit in.

In 1970 Troubridge introduced Marie-Christine to his family, including his elder brother, Sir Peter. This was a sign that, for him at least, this was a more serious than usual relationship, for he had not been given to 'bringing home' for inspection, as it were, other of his many female acquaintances. Marie-Christine proved to be as much 'at home' in the family atmosphere as she had been in the more relaxed climate of London's social life. The family approved of her. For her part, she was impressed by the solidity of life as lived by the Troubridges; they might not have had the wealth, land or power of her ancestors, but, after all, neither had her relations in modern Europe; that was a thing of the past. The Troubridges represented for her much of what was best about British life – a sufficiency of wealth, a good deal of comfort and a sense of permanency.

On 25 May 1971 the engagement of Tom Troubridge to Baroness Marie-Christine von Reibnitz was formally announced. For the first time, as far as this story is concerned, Marie-Christine's religion posed a problem. She was, and is, a practising Catholic, although as one of her clerical friends pointed out, 'of the European kind; *sympatico, non fanatico*'. She appreciated that she was bound by the laws of her Church as regards marriage. We shall be forced to examine some of those laws in more detail in subsequent chapters. Here we are concerned only with the Church's laws on 'the form' of a Catholic marriage. The Catholic Church rules that, normally, a Catholic is required to marry in a Catholic Church (before a priest and two witnesses). However, in the more liberal days since the conclusion of the Second Vatican Council, the Church has been prepared to allow dispensations from these laws on 'the form' of marriage. In 1971 such dispensations were dealt with under the provisions of a document labelled *Matrimonia Mixta*; at the time of writing, such dispensations would fall under Canon 1127 of the current Canon Law. The power to dispense with the Church's requirements as to 'form' lies with the bishop of the diocese in which the applicant for the dispensation lives.

Troubridge, for his own, no doubt, good reasons, refused to have his marriage celebrated in a Catholic church. He did agree to the compromise of a joint Catholic-Anglican service in his local Anglican church. So in 1971 Marie-Christine, using the good offices of some of her clerical friends, approached Archbishop's House, Westminster, to ask that her marriage to Troubridge might take place in the Anglican Chelsea Old Church. It was Troubridge's local church – although he was not a regular church-goer.

The dispensation was readily granted. In case the reader might suspect that this was a concession made by 'an Establishment-minded Church' to 'one of the privileged', it should be noted that such dispensations are regularly given by bishops up and down Britain; many Catholics will have seen one of their children married in an Anglican church after having received a dispensation from the local bishop. In such cases, as with Marie-Christine's application, the bishop will insist that a Catholic priest be present at the ceremony, playing the part of 'the essential Catholic witness' to the marriage.

Why do some Catholics want to have their marriage celebrated in an Anglican and not in a Catholic church? By the very fact of bothering to ask for a bishop's dispensation, these Catholics have provided evidence of their adherence to their faith; they have not walked away from the need to obey the laws of their Church. There may well be as many answers to the question as there are marriages celebrated in this way. For some Catholics, this will be their way of acknowledging that their Anglican partner and his/her parents have accepted the introduction of a Catholic into the family. It is unfortunately true that, while overt bigotry may have decreased in most parts of the country, there is still in many parts the remnants of, at the least, suspicion of Catholics. The Catholic who finds a ready welcome into an Anglican family may well feel that it is incumbent to say, in action, 'Thank you'. Then there will be Catholics who wish to make an ecumenical gesture by having their wedding take place in an Anglican church. This, they say, will please the Anglican relatives, who have every right to their beliefs. Since it is a dispensable matter of 'form' only, why not offer the ecumenical olive branch? Then there will be the cases where the major consideration is more social. Will the guests of the Anglican partner feel so uncomfortable in the hitherto unknown surroundings of a Catholic church that the atmosphere may become somewhat strained? When and why people have to stand, kneel, bow, answer a response and so on, may be minor and 'dispensable' hindrances. And, of course, there will be even more worldly considerations which will affect the choice of the Anglican, rather than the Catholic, church. Will the wedding 'look better' if it takes place in that fifteenth-century church with its approaches, entrance, screens, woodwork and the like, than in that early twentieth-century Catholic church squashed in between Sainsbury's and Curry's on a busy main road? For some social aspirers this may be a major consideration.

Why does the Catholic Church, often accused of being 'rigid', grant dispensations from part of her canon law? Perhaps it is worth noting that the law is of human, not divine origin and, being man-made, is man-dispensable. Catholics have become accustomed to their Church making changes in existing laws – on fasting before receiving Communion, on Saturday evening Masses fulfilling the obligations as regards attendance at weekly Mass. It is not, so to say, radically revolutionary for the Church to agree to dispensation as regards the form of marriage. Indeed, in an increasingly post-Christian and pagan society, the Church authorities may well feel that by the fact of applying for a dispensation, the Catholic partner has shown a degree of commitment and thoughtfulness which may well be absent from some so-called Catholic marriages which have taken place in Catholic churches 'to please Gran'. And, like some Catholic partners, the Church may well wish to give a sign of goodwill towards fellow-Christians – one small step along the road to a desirable Church unity. This, if it is to happen, will have to take place at the very human level: bishops and commissions may legislate for unity, but it will come about only if ordinary men and women will it to happen. The perceptive Church may well see a marriage dispensation as a slight nudge in that direction.

Marie-Christine and Tom Troubridge were married, then, at Chelsea Old Church on 15 September 1971, with one of her clerical friends, Father Jean Charles-Roux, being present as the 'essential Catholic witness'.

Journalists have surrounded this wedding-day with a number of untruths and one serious allegation, which, in view of the evidence of the untruths, may be seen to be equally false. From various reporters we learn that 'Marie-Christine's mother flew in from Australia along with her son, who gave his sister away.' The truth is that her brother was not at the wedding, and Marie-Christine was 'given away' by her uncle and guardian,

Count Ladislaus Szapáry. Baron Frederick, Marie-Christine's brother, was married in Australia the day before she married Troubridge in Chelsea. Frederick knew and liked Troubridge, and Marie-Christine knew and liked her sister-in-law. The reporters go on to comment on the fact that 'her rank-conscious father' was not at this wedding to 'a commoner'. It is true that he was not at the wedding: he had recently had a heart attack, but both couples had accepted the Baron's invitation to spend their honeymoons with him in Africa and go on a safari.

It was always open to journalists to have found out the truth about these issues for themselves. Some papers also reported that 'The newly married couple had a blazing row in the vestry of the church while they were signing the marriage register.' True, the reporters admit that the handful who witnessed the signing – and the supposed row – are reluctant to talk about it. I am grateful to the close friend who has written to tell me, 'I was there, and there was no row. This is typical "gossip column research".'

To the casual observer, the post-honeymoon life of the Troubridges may appear to have been somewhat idyllic. They made their home at Tom's once-bachelor residence in Gertrude Street and are reported by one 'friend' to have enjoyed 'the incessant whirl of their social life'. One is entitled to doubt this 'whirl' description, because a few months after they were married Marie-Christine began an intensive history of art course at the Victoria and Albert Museum which entailed, she remembers, 'homework every night'. She could hardly have led such a giddy social life if she was studying every evening – and, as a friend writes, 'I know that she took the course very seriously.'

Among their widening circle were bankers and industrialists such as Charles Villiers, former head of British Steel, whose daughter Diana was to become a close friend and comfort for Marie-Christine. There were diplomats whose friendship had to be cultivated as part of Troubridge's work at Kleinwort's. There were also members of the 'Chelsea set', among whom Tom had enjoyed his bachelor life and with whom he was determined to continue to enjoy himself.

Once she had completed her two-year-long studies at the Victoria and Albert Museum, Marie-Christine continued to work as an interior decorator. Nor was this a 'front' or pin-money-earning hobby. 'She was very good at it,' says a friend, and it became increasingly important for her to have a private income – as we shall see.

Most weekends were spent either at the country house of Tom's mother, Lady Troubridge or, during the winter, at various shooting parties. Troubridge had, and still has, a passion for shooting. He had never cared for horses and did not share Marie-Christine's love of horse-riding which she could indulge at various country homes. There were inter-house parties such as the one at Barnwell Manor, home of Prince William of Gloucester, Tom's Eton schoolfriend and Cambridge contemporary, at which Marie-Christine was introduced to Prince Michael of Kent (who then, in 1972, was infatuated with another young lady). Neither Prince Michael nor Marie-Christine could have any idea then that their paths were to become even more crossed.

Marie-Christine remembers that first meeting: 'I thought he was the funniest man I had ever met. We just kept laughing and talking together. But I didn't think he had really "noticed" me at all. He was with such a pretty girl.'[1] The Prince was quick to counteract that impression: 'I was very struck by this tall Austrian lady. I was very impressed. I remember we had a long talk about the history of art sitting in a hut eating sausages.' She once said: 'He was a charming spare man I used to invite to dinner parties or when I had extremely eligible European relatives over. I thought, this young man is all alone, I'll produce the right girl friend for him. I saw myself as a sort of fairy godmother, waving my magic wand.'[2]

The casual observer might have envied the Troubridges their life-style: comfort at home, frequent dinner parties for the well-connected and 'eligible', country house week-ends with aristocracy and royalty, but close friends knew, even by Christmas 1971, that the marriage was flawed – perhaps fatally. One friend caught Marie-Christine off guard at a small reception at Christmas, noticing that her face showed all the signs of strain and sadness. There were, it transpired, two reasons why, during this festive season, Marie-Christine was depressed, even having attended Midnight Mass. Tom, she claimed, never gave her enough money to run the home and provide for herself. If it had not been for the money she earned by her interior decorating, she would not be able to dress and entertain as he wished her to. We shall see that shortage of money is a recurrent, indeed almost continual, complaint made by the now Princess Michael of Kent. It may be, therefore, that in 1971 this problem was more apparent than real. She insisted that Tom had not realized that 'two cannot live as cheaply as one', that he assumed, somewhat naïvely, that he and Marie-Christine could continue to live as he had lived without increasing his expenditure. For the girl who had hoped that her marriage would provide her with some of that solidity she had found in the Troubridge family life-style, this meanness, as she saw it, came as a shock.

But, and much more seriously, there was Tom's attitude to her hopes for a family. 'I am nearly twenty-seven,' she told a friend at Christmas 1971, 'I am getting on and I want to have children. And he won't.' His unwillingness to have children is explained by one of his friends: 'Tom loved his life-style, and one of the possible reasons for not wanting children could have been the likelihood of his having to cut down on his most extravagant hobby, namely shooting. He would fly anywhere in the world for a shooting invitation.' This attitude towards children was to be the single major cause of the final break-up of the marriage. We shall examine that break-up in later chapters. Here we should note that even as early as Christmas 1971 and long before that first meeting with Prince Michael, the marriage was fatally flawed, the two partners differing over one of the fundamentals of marriage.

It may well be impossible to provide dates as markers along the road to the breakdown of a marriage. What can be said in the case of the Troubridge marriage was that Tom's posting, in 1972, to represent Kleinwort's in Bahrain may be seen as such a marker.

Marie-Christine won a contract which took her to Bahrain too, where she restored an old house and also redecorated her husband's offices. She loved the Middle East as much as he did. Troubridge, an Arabic-speaker, was merely one of a string of bankers anxious to help the rich rulers of the oil states cope with the flood of petro-dollars flowing into the Middle East. The rulers of some of the smaller states, such as Bahrain, welcomed advice as to investments, purchases of property and companies in Britain and elsewhere, guidance as to the complexities of exchange rates, international banking and the like.

Life in any of the Muslim states of the Middle East is difficult for most Europeans and, in the opinion of men who have to work there, 'impossible for the women' because of the religious-based and custom-established attitudes towards women. In the case of the lively Marie-Christine, the 'impossible' was made worse, if that can be said, by Tom's behaviour. Although she loved the exotic Gulf and their beautiful house, she was saddened by his behaviour towards her. Busily engaged in his banking work, happy among the male company of fellow bankers, diplomats and Arab politicians, 'He had no need for me.' This had been the case in London, but there she had the compensation of her own work. There was little call for female interior decorators in the desert Bahrain so that her loneliness and sadness were deepened.

It was no surprise then that, as a friend says, 'They agreed it was very difficult for her to live out there. So she came back to

London and he stayed out there.' There are many men who work in the Middle East while their wives live in Britain; not all such marriages end in divorce, but in the case of the Troubridges, Marie-Christine's return to Britain was the outward sign of the failure of the marriage. It may be, as friends claim, that it had failed before she went out to Bahrain, that her stay out there was a futile attempt to hold on to what, they say, was already a dead relationship. If so, then Marie-Christine has to be credited with a brave try, a perhaps natural reaction of an inherently good woman unwilling to accept the inevitable.

When she came back to London, Marie-Christine returned to live in the Troubridge home – her home, after all – in Gertrude Street, from where she ran her interior decorating business, Szapáry Designs Ltd. She obtained Tom's agreement to her suggestion that, for various understandable reasons, she should ask her friend Diana Villiers to move in with her. Diana was willing to do so because, she said, 'Marie-Christine was friendly and outgoing and fun to be with.'

Among her 'fun' activities was horse-riding. She used to ride most days in Richmond Park, where Prince Michael's sister, Princess Alexandra (married since 1963 to the Hon. Angus Ogilvy) lives in Thatched House Lodge. It was in Richmond Park that she met Prince Michael again.

In January 1985 Princess Michael gave an interview timed to appear on her fortieth birthday. In this she gave an account of the Richmond Park meetings, an account which fits in with the memories of many of her friends. For they recall that Prince Michael had often been a guest at dinner parties given by Tom and Mrs Troubridge before the Bahrain interlude. They also remember how Prince Michael and Marie-Christine were placed next to one another at a Red Cross charity luncheon at Patricia Rawlings' house, shortly after she had returned from Bahrain. One of her friends said that, 'Prince Michael was very struck with her.' Another friend describes how he surprised them commiserating with each other – he because of the end of a close relationship which he had enjoyed with Patricia Rawlings, she because of the failure of her marriage to Troubridge. They were, says this friend, a comfort for each other. In the interview given in January 1985, Princess Michael remembered that star-struck luncheon date. During their conversation, both realized that 'For the first time since they had known each other, they were emotionally free.' She recalled: 'For a long time we cried on each other's shoulders. I saw him for about a year simply as a friend. Now, I'm very glad that we had that time because friendship is something you never lose – and when you're in the rocking chair, friendship is what counts.'

She then went on to give an account of the early morning rides in Richmond Park. She explained that the police horses stabled at Thatched Lodge had been sent there for retraining and that they were liable to be rather tricky rides. 'The one he usually rode was a grey with a – shall we say *difficult* temperament, on which he used to have to try to find me in the vastness of Richmond Park. As luck and Cupid would have it, my horse – my beautiful, dancing Anglo-Arab steed – fell madly in love with this other rather churlish animal and from miles away would whinny and gallop up to him. Then it was "Oh, hello – what a surprise! How nice to see you!" Everything was very tentative at that stage but I do remember thinking, "He doesn't seem to enjoy riding very much – how strange that he perseveres!" '

Princess Michael explained that their friendship 'slowly developed' throughout 1974 and in subsequent years. There were, as we have seen, the early morning meetings in Richmond Park. There were, too, evening meetings when, she recalled, 'We'd go on his motorbike, because you can't recognize anyone under a crash helmet which covers the mouth and chin.' This life went on for three years. One of her friends, with whom, she was living during this period, remembered: 'We would talk about him the way bachelor girls do. You know – "Has he telephoned? Do you think he'll take me out to dinner tonight? I've just had a wonderful week-end with him" – those kind of remarks.'

One of her friends claimed that during this first year Marie-Christine 'fell in love with Prince Michael'. Princess Michael remembers that she was 'immediately and forcefully attracted' by his physical courage, typified perhaps by his winning the British Bobsleigh Championship in 1972. That, as one friend noted, 'takes great courage'. Princess Michael says, 'I love bravery. He will take on the most terrifying things, not in a daredevil way but simply refusing to be afraid.' She also loved and loves his 'humour and integrity. I know that here is someone who will always do what is right. If I am in any doubt on an issue, I know his instincts will be right.'

As their friendship deepened, Marie-Christine moved out of the Troubridge home in Gertrude Street, where she had been living with Diana Villiers, into her decorating studio in Cadogan Gardens, where she lived alone until her marriage in 1978.

The friendship between Mrs Tom Troubridge and Prince Michael became known to the circle of their friends and relatives. Troubridge, in Bahrain, learned about it but maintained a 'discreet and gentlemanly silence and did not view the Prince as having broken his marriage'.[3] Nearer home, the perceptive Lord Mountbatten watched the burgeoning relationship. To some outside observers, such as Beaverbrook and his *Express* newspapers, Mountbatten's was an influence on the Royal Family to be fought and regretted; to others, who had the pleasure of his assistance, he was a beneficent senior male 'royal'. To young royals, including Prince Philip and Prince Charles, he was an instructive aid, Philip being 'the son we never had' and Charles being 'born of a Mountbatten'.

Lord Mountbatten was a useful ally to Prince Michael and Marie-Christine. She describes him as their 'good angel'. He had, of course, known Prince Michael all his life and had felt a special concern for the youngest Kent because of the death of his father on active service during the war. At least two of Marie-Christine's cousins were related to Lord Mountbatten by marriage, and she had met him at their homes. She admits that this was an important factor in her life; 'Knowing my family was one of the things that decided him that my husband and I would "work". In many ways he *made* our marriage – without his support and help and championing of our cause, I doubt whether it would have happened.'

In 1976 Lord Mountbatten acted. He told Marie-Christine that she 'ought to marry that young man'. When asked, 'Why?', he replied, 'Because he is madly in love with you.' In 1984 Princess Michael claimed that until then she 'had never thought of it', believing that her religion, marriage and 'foreignness' would debar her from marriage into the Royal Family. She knew, for example, that her friend Prince William of Gloucester had been refused permission by the Queen to marry the divorced Mrs Nicole Sieff. As a friend writes; 'What reason had she to hope that her situation might be viewed differently, especially as she had another disadvantage – she was a Catholic?'

However, there were, after all, cases of divorce and remarriage in other families to which she was related; there were plenty of cases of 'mixed' marriages. Perhaps the problems were not as great as people imagined. In any event, it was Mountbatten who helped the couple to examine the constitutional-religious problems that faced them if, indeed, they wished to get married.

5

The Annulment of the Troubridge Marriage

'I knew nothing about it and wasn't involved in any way. It was a Roman Catholic thing and I don't know how they go about these things' – (Tom Troubridge, quoted in the *Daily Express*, 14 March 1984)

It was relatively simple for Marie-Christine to get a civil divorce from Tom Troubridge. Their marriage was dissolved in the summer of 1977, after they had lived apart for $3\frac{1}{2}$ years.

It was very much more difficult for her to get her Church to declare that her first marriage had been null and void, that, as it were, it had never taken place. Only if she obtained such an annulment would she be free, as a Catholic, to remarry. We shall see that Troubridge (who, in 1981, married Mrs Petronella Forgan and followed his banking career in the United States) is not the only one who does not 'know how they go about these things'. Indeed, few Catholics understand the annulment process; it is not surprising, therefore, that non-Catholics find it an almost mysterious business.

I hope that the following pages may help to explain the process. I have examined the attitudes of different 'wings' in the Anglican Church towards the remarriage of divorced people. I have also examined the Catholic teaching on marriage and on annulments in order to outline the annulment process. Because it is a matter of major importance in Princess Michael's life, I hope that what follows may help to a better understanding of 'this Roman Catholic thing'.

Princess Michael has read reports which suggest that the Church went out of its way to arrange an annulment for her 'just because I wanted to marry a prince'. Rightly, she protests that, 'It was all quite legitimate, absolutely within Catholic law.' She knew that some people in Britain thought it was 'some cosy

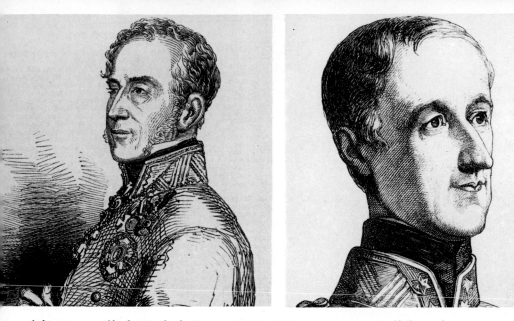

(left) Prince Alfred Windisch-Graetz (1787–1862), great-great-grandfather of Princess Michael. In 1849–50 he led the imperial armies in their victories over revolutionaries in Austria, Bohemia and Hungary, and so helped his brother-in-law, Prime Minister, Prince Felix Schwarzenberg, to preserve the power of the Austrian Emperor. (right) Prince Felix von Schwarzenberg (1800–52). He succeeded in re-asserting Austria's control of the German Federation at Olmutz in 1850.

Princess Michael's maternal grand-parents: Count Friedrich Szapáry and Princess Hedwig Windisch-Graetz. Their marriage linked two distinguished aristo-ratic families.

Schönblick, the Silesian country house of Princess Michael's father, Baron Günther von Reibnitz.

Princess Michael's father with a stag after a hunt on his estate in Silesia. He shared a passion for shooting and hunting with Count Ladislaus Szapáry, who introduced von Reibnitz to his sister, Countess Marianne.

The 'shooting box' on one of Countess Marianne's estates in Bohemia where Princess Michael was born in January 1945.

Spanning the generations. A photograph taken on 3 May 1951, when Queen Mary visited the South Bank Festival along with her grandchildren, Prince William of Gloucester and Prince Michael of Kent (far right).

Prince Michael of Kent on active duty in Cyprus with the UN peacekeeping force, of which his squadron of Royal Hussars formed part. In 1981 he was forced, reluctantly, to give up his army career.

Prince Michael's sister, Princess Alexandra of Kent with her husband, the Hon. Angus Ogilvy and their children, James and Marina, in the garden of Thatched House Lodge, Richmond Park.

Lord Louis Mountbatten who played important part in the lives of Prince and Prince Michael.

(*below left*) Most Rev. Thomas J. Winnir Catholic Archbishop of Glasgow since 197 who vigorously defended Pope Paul VI's de sion not to issue a dispensation for the marria of Prince and Princess Michael in June 1978.

(*below right*) Archbishop Bruno Heim who, Apostolic Delegate (from 1973) and as Ap tolic Pro-Nuncio (after 1982) was the Pop personal representative in London until retirement in 1985.

On the way to the registry office in Vienna on 30 June 1978, the radiant bride has her mother, Countess Marianne, on her right and, on her left, Princess Olga, sister of the late Princess Marina of Kent.

After the registry office marriage in the Vienna Town Hall: from left to right: the Duke of Kent, Princess Alexandra (partly concealed), Prince Michael and his bride, Lady Helen Windsor, niece of the Prince, Princess Anne, Lord Mountbatten and, at the back, the Hon. Angus Ogilvy.

Dressed for dinner and ball on her wedding night, Princess Michael is escorted by Sir Peter Scott, Secretary to Prince Michael.

Arriving for the celebration of the private Mass 1 July 1978, the day after the registry office wedding. The officiating priest, Fr. Hofrat Sigismund Pawlowski, welcomes Princess Michael.

Marie-Christine   Michael

One of Princess Michael's favourite photographs, taken in
the garden of the Palais Schwarzenberg on her wedding day.

On the Occasion

of the Marriage of

His Royal Highness Prince Michael of Kent

and

The Baroness Marie - Christine von Reibnitz

Friday 30th June, 1978
Palais Schwarzenberg

SERVICE OF PRAYER
AND BLESSING

AT
LAMBETH PALACE

30th October, 1978

Michael   Marie-Christine

The many civil and religious stages involved in the marriage: in Vienna, at Lambeth Palace and (left) at Westminster Cathedral. Here, on 29 July 1983, the Prince and Princess received Roman Catholic validation for their marriage, following the Pope's recognition of their civil wedding. Princess Michael wore the suit she had worn in Vienna five years earlier.

arrangement that you make with a cheque book'. She knew differently by the time her annulment came through: 'That's not so at all. You have to discuss *very* personal things ... *not* easy to do, and that is why a lot of people don't even try to get annulments, because they have to discuss things that you would barely discuss with your doctor.'[1]

There is, today, both an awareness of and a wide acceptance of divorce. The annual reports of the Registrar-General show that the number of divorces is increasing by something like a quarter of a million a year. The general public has become, as it were, innured to the tragic reality that many marriages fail. At the same time, it has become clear that the Established Church, the Church of England, is in some disarray over the question of the treatment of divorced people who wish to remarry.

The marriage of Prince and Princess Michael of Kent in 1978 provided an opportunity for the airing of diverse Anglican views. By chance, the question of the remarriage of divorced people had just been debated by the General Synod of the Church of England, which had rejected 'liberal' proposals put forward by a Commission headed by the Bishop of Lichfield. On 14 July 1978 the Bishop of London, who had voted against the Commission's proposals, wrote to *The Times* to explain 'why some of us with reluctance had to vote against them'. His statement is significant as it comes from what may be called the 'Catholic' wing of the Anglican Church and contains proposals for an Anglican adoption of the Catholic concept of annulment.

> We share the view of the Commission that there are a number of instances when it would be proper for the remarriage of someone who has been divorced to take place in church.
>
> We cannot however accept the view that it should be permissible for someone who has already taken the solemn vows of the marriage service towards a living person to take the same vows towards another person, until the Church has formally pronounced upon the marital status of the party involved.
>
> The situation could, I believe, be eased if the General Synod were to give authority to the Bishop to examine the previous marriage and the reasons for its dissolution, and then, if he felt justified, either to pronounce the marriage to be morally and spiritually dead, or to dispense the person involved from his or her life vows. An agreed Code of Practice could be drawn up to ensure that the bishops act in agreement with one another. The way would then be open for the second marriage to take place in church and the vows taken and administered with a clear conscience.[2]

The Bishop of London was, at least in 1978, in a minority. The

Religious Correspondent of *The Times*, Clifford Longley, seemed to represent the majority view when he wrote:

> ... The Church of England runs the risk of alienating a large and growing faction of the population if it does not unbend on the remarriage of divorced people in church ...
>
> ... the Church of England has such an emphatic tradition of divorce that it is not easy to see how it could change without looking guilty of a charge of accommodation to the prevailing mores. The Anglican marriage service is quite unambiguous about the permanence of marriage vows, and the Anglican understanding of marriage is quite unambiguous about who the vows apply to.
>
> ... In classical Anglican teaching on marriage, permanence and fidelity are principles by which everyone is bound, whatever their beliefs. There is not one law for Christians and one for the rest.[3]

The report then went on to pour scorn on 'the subtleties of Roman Catholic distinctions between "sacramental" and "non-sacramental" marriages, the former only being governed by the rule of indissolubility'. This refers to the Catholic refusal to accept as valid the 'marriage' of a Catholic in a register office. However, the report went on, albeit reluctantly, to approve of the Catholic teaching on annulment:

> The Roman Catholic Church, in spite of the confusion [which] its marriage discipline causes, has stumbled upon insights in the course of the development of its annulment procedure. It has built those insights into the elaborate machinery of matrimonial tribunals, which tend to ignore status [defined as the relationship between an individual and society] and concentrate only on relationship [defined as the relationship between two individuals].

The Catholic Church claims a right to establish certain laws concerning the existence and contracting of marriage. It claims that when Christ founded His Church, he committed into the hands of Peter and the Apostles the guardianship of the Sacraments within the Church, which, by extension, has the right to legislate upon the Sacraments. Certain laws on marriage are called divine laws, considered to have been established by God and to be merely re-stated by the Church. Other laws have been made by the Church and are called ecclesiastical laws. Some laws prevent a valid marriage taking place – for example, it is not possible for a man to marry his mother or his sister: these prohibitions are of Divine Law. Another law forbids two first cousins marrying: this is usually seen as an ecclesiastical law. When laws which the Church has either re-stated from the Divine

Law or formulated as ecclesiastical law prohibit marriage either absolutely or less severely, such laws are called impediments. These impediments which arise from Church law may be dispensed with. Those of divine origin cannot be dispensed. A marriage tribunal is concerned with all these impediments.

For a long time in the history of the Church there was some debate as to what exactly constituted a marriage. Teachers at the school of law at Bologna held that the element which made marriage was consummation. However, the law school at Paris maintained that it was consent which made the marriage valid. Pope Alexander III (1159-81) declared that the weight of tradition came down on the side of the Paris school. From that time onwards the Church taught that it was consent which made marriage, although some canonists insisted that consummation was also essential.

Marriage was one of the many questions examined by the Fathers of the Church at the Second Vatican Council (1962–4). They decided that a Christian marriage involved a union 'which has been established by God and qualified by His laws. It is rooted in the conjugal covenant of irrevocable personal consent. Hence, by that human act whereby the spouses mutually bestow and accept each other, a relationship arises by the Divine Will which, in the eyes of society too, is a lasting one.'[4] In this humanly pastoral language the Church draws attention to the fact that the union 'forged by the consent of the parties' is irrevocable and lasting, permanent 'until death do us part'.

The Fathers went on to say: 'By their very nature, the institution of matrimony and conjugal love are ordained for the procreation and education of children'. This is not to say that there is a compulsion to have children. It is, however, to say that having children is one of the purposes of marriage. Taken together with the statement on the free giving of consent, this reference to children implies that each of the partners, as a result of the consent freely given and accepted, is entitled to be a parent. Because of the possibility of there being children, the Church declares that this 'mutual gift of two persons, as well as the good of the children, imposes total fidelity on the spouses and argues for an unbreakable oneness between them'.

We may, then, summarize the Catholic position by reference to the three points made so clearly by the Vatican Council, namely the permanence of the bond, the right to children within the union and the total fidelity imposed on the couple as a result of the other two essentials. It is clear that a couple might enter into a state which could be loosely called 'marriage' by doing all the necessary external things required by the laws of the Church while, in fact, never truly entering into the married state.

When the Catholic novelist Evelyn Waugh proposed to Evelyn Gardner 'over dinner in the Ritz Grill, he suggested that they should get married "and see how it goes". It was a fatal phrase, for it gave Evelyn Gardner the sense that Waugh was not wholly committed to the alliance.'[5] If Waugh really meant what he said, he obviously had no intention of providing that essential element of 'permanence'.

There have also been well-publicized examples of people who were forced into marriage against their will. Perhaps the most notorious 'forced' marriages were those which involved the daughters of the socially ambitious Vanderbilt family. Consuelo Vanderbilt was the first of the foreign wives of the ninth Duke of Marlborough. This 'dollar' princess told her own story in *The Glitter and the Gold* in which she detailed the various ways in which her mother drove her into a marriage to the Duke – against her will – and how the Church annulled that marriage on the grounds that she had not given her 'free consent' to the contract. Any 'marriage' contracted without the full consent of both partners would be, of its nature, null and void. Equally, the person giving the consent must be a complete human being. Thus insanity would prevent a person giving proper consent, and a union entered into by a person who was probably insane at the time would not be a Christian marriage.

It is important to note that the documents of the Vatican Council, in common with traditional Catholic teaching, refer to 'Christian marriage'. Catholic teaching on marriage applies equally to Catholic and non-Catholic. The only additional law to which Catholics have to conform is the rule of the Church that, normally, baptized Catholics must be married in the presence of a priest and two other witnesses. This is termed the 'form' of marriage. For special reasons the Church may dispense with the 'form': thus a Catholic may receive a dispensation allowing the celebration of a valid and lawful marriage in a non-Catholic church before a minister of another denomination. This law on 'form' applies only to members of the Catholic Church. Marriage between two non-Catholics is valid, sacramental and indissoluble even if it takes place in a register office. Apart from the case of Catholics who are bound to the 'form' of marriage, a marriage can (canonically) take place anywhere.

The Catholic Church has developed its 'doctrine of nullity' over many centuries. It is not something to be glibly dismissed as 'an accommodation to the prevailing mores'. It is true, however, that the number of people applying for annulments has increased in the recent past. This is a reflection of the reality of a modern situation. 'It is not possible to state – as *was* the case – that Catholics "are not really involved" in [the] growth rate of divorce figures ... reason alone indicates that they cannot be unaffected by this social feature of our present day.'[6] To those who believe that the Catholic Church is 'priest-ridden', it may come as a surprise to learn that it was a layman who first perceived the modern need for a greater Catholic involvement in the study of marriage problems, separations and divorces. In 1945, when Mrs Graham-Green suggested that there ought to be a Catholic Marriage Advisory Council (CMAC), her husband, Major Graham-Green approached Cardinal Griffin, who gave the idea his blessing and encouragement. The CMAC was born in July 1946.

In the past, there was a widely held view among Church lawyers that persons would come to a marriage tribunal with the conviction that their marriages were invalid for some reason. It was the task of canon lawyers to examine this claim. Canon lawyers are, by training and experience, concerned with Church law; many people see them as occupying the opposite end of the clerical spectrum from 'pastoral' clergy, the men who have to deal with people not in some abstract or merely legal fashion but as they really are. Pastoral clergy, it is said, have more under-standing of people's problems than have the canonists with their concern for 'the law'.

Modern canonists deny that there is this deep division between themselves and their pastoral brethren. There has been, for example, a very radical alteration in the approach of canonists to the question of Marriage Tribunals:

> They no longer expect people to come along with claims of nullity to be examined. What in fact happens is that people whose marriages have broken down come to a Tribunal and try to find out if there is anything that can be done to permit them to enter new marriages ... Although the procedure is very similar [to what it had always been] what is different is the starting point of canonists. The starting point now is very much to see if the person in question can be helped (by whatever means) to resume, or enter into or continue his or her life within the Church on a fully sacramental basis.[7]

It has to be agreed that, in general, the Church authorities do not help their own case. There is, obviously, a great deal of Catholic ignorance about annulments. If there were not, people would not think that annulments are 'arranged' only for 'the rich'. In fact, the Westminster Diocesan Tribunal receives around eight hundred applications for annulment every year. About five hundred of these are dismissed as being defective, not providing even superficial evidence on which an annulment case might be based. That leaves three hundred or so applications to be taken through the process. About two hundred of these appeals are decided in favour of the applicant, a figure which may surprise most 'good' Catholics. They know, of course, that this or that princess has received an annulment; they do not know that two hundred or so 'ordinary' Catholics are similarly treated every year in a single diocese.

There is also the accusation that it is only the rich who can get annulments. The process *is* both time-consuming and expensive, but at Westminster only some ten per cent of those who receive annulments pay all the costs of their cases. Indeed, a canon lawyer intimately involved in the Tribunal process was quick to point out that, 'In Marriage Tribunal work, the Church had a system of legal aid long before our civil courts adopted one.'

There does not appear to be any good reason why both these facts – on numbers and costs – should not be more widely publicized. If what is being done is 'of the Lord', the Church has nothing to hide. On the contrary, a greater public awareness of the process might well be the means of enabling many others, currently unaware of the possibility, to get their 'rights' before a Tribunal. (We shall see that this was one side effect of the great publicity given to the annulment of the Troubridge marriage in April 1978, and to the convalidation of the marriage of Prince and Princess Michael of Kent in July 1983.)

The word 'tribunal' is used in two different senses. In the first sense, the tribunal is a department of the diocesan government and looks after the day-to-day administration of marriage cases (and not merely nullity cases). It is presided over by a canon lawyer called the *officialis*, who makes the arrangements for prospective clients to be interviewed, for applications to be dealt with in the office, for evidence to be taken and for personnel to be assigned to each case. He will usually have the help of a number of priests and lawyers concerned with the administration of cases. In another sense, the word 'tribunal' is used to describe the actual panel of priests, with their different functions, who deal with each specific marriage case. In this sense, the tribunal is also called a court. At Westminster, as many as thirty cases are dealt with at any one time, under the ruling of the tribunal (using the word in the first sense) although being dealt with by a number of separate 'courts'. Some of the priests involved in one court will also belong to other such courts, which helps ensure some sense of uniformity of treatment by the several courts.

Mrs Thomas Troubridge was advised that her husband's refusal to have children provided good grounds for an appeal to a marriage tribunal. (Since she lived in the archdiocese of Westminster, her case was heard there.) She had to present her case to a court composed of a minimum of six persons. Three of these were judges, priests experienced in canon law and in the work of marriage tribunals. One of the judges was the President of the Court. He managed the daily correspondence and detail connected with the case. He was also the *ponens*, the person who led the discussion of the case at the decision hearing and who eventually produced the lengthy 'sentence' giving the reasons in law and fact for the decision. The court also had a 'defender of the bond of marriage'. The task of this experienced canon lawyer was to bring forward arguments showing why the marriage under consideration should be regarded as valid.

Mrs Troubridge, like every other petitioner before a court, was represented by an advocate appointed to assist her in the presentation of her case. At the end of the proceedings, he produced the arguments showing why the marriage should be declared null and void.

The court had a notary to take down the evidence and whose signature on the documents showed that they and other papers were authentic.

At Westminster, where there is a large volume of work, it is necessary to have an organization servicing the various officials and courts. There are, in fact, some twelve lay people who work full time for the Westminster tribunal and many others who are called upon from time to time to provide, for example, the specialist knowledge which their education and experience have given them. Thus, there is a team of psychiatrists on whom the tribunal is free to call.

In the first instance, Mrs Troubridge was advised by Lord Mountbatten. Politically wise, he knew that the Apostolic Delegate, Archbishop Bruno Heim, would be able to advise both him and Mrs Troubridge. There was, too, Father Jean Charles-Roux, once a diplomat, now a priest of the Institute of Charity and a friend of many exiled aristocrats. With the advice of the Apostolic Delegate and Father Jean, Mrs Troubridge was well placed to put her case to the tribunal.

The annulment proceedings began with an interview with one of the priests who assist the tribunal. The priest drew up a *libellus* or petition which Mrs Troubridge signed and which was formally presented to the tribunal (using the word in its first sense). The president of the tribunal appointed a court consisting of three judges, a 'defender of the bond', an advocate and a notary. This court examined the petition to establish whether it could be accepted for trial. The court then issued a citation. This is the technical term for the letter sent to Tom Troubridge advising him that his former partner had petitioned for the examination of the marriage and explaining to him the grounds on which she claimed their marriage had been invalid. (To be valid, a marriage has to be 'open' to the possibility of procreation. Troubridge's absolute bar in this respect deprived his wife of one of her rights and so rendered the marriage invalid.)

Troubridge is said to have acknowledged a series of letters concerning the case; he knew the dates on which meetings of the court took place and was asked, repeatedly, whether he wished to intervene, whether he wished to give evidence or whether he wanted to leave the whole matter to the court. Indeed, it is a requirement of the tribunal's proceedings that a note be entered into the documents of the case stating that the respondent has been cited, that he has received the citation – and, if such be the case, that he has not replied.

At the first formal meeting of the court, Mrs Troubridge had to present the precise grounds of the alleged nullity. The notary prepared a document setting these down in legal terms. This document was signed by the judges, the defender of the bond, a proxy acting for Mrs Troubridge and the notary. At this first meeting she was questioned by the court and her evidence was taken down. At this and subsequent meetings she was questioned by her own advocate and by the defender of the bond. During these later hearings, of which there were many, at least one of the judges was present along with the defender of the bond and the notary.

One of the Princess's friends commented on the fact that it took over eighteen months for her case to be settled. There were several reasons for this long delay, one being that everyone involved in the case was 'too polite. No one wanted to say anything calculated to hurt anyone else.' There was, too, a natural reluctance on the part of Marie-Christine to discuss 'very personal things ... things that you would barely discuss with your doctor.' The case might have become bogged down in a sea of calm politeness and reluctance. In the end, some of her advisers worked hard not only to persuade her to 'tell all' but to get twenty-two witnesses to come forward on her behalf. That many of these were members of Troubridge's own family must have weighed heavily in her favour.

It is worth noting that Church courts do not follow the legal procedures of an English civil court. The whole process is a documentary one; it is also completely confidential; no members of the public are present other than those immediately involved in the case, including witnesses who have been invited to give evidence. The method of giving and taking evidence also differs from that followed in English courts. There is no cross-questioning, no oratory by advocates, no attempt to discredit witnesses. 'Hearsay' is accepted into the evidence, to be evaluated later for what it is worth. There is much less formality than in an English court. The judge puts questions to the witnesses and often asks that they talk about the matter for a while before trying to give a direct answer to the question asked. The judge may even help the witness to formulate an answer which contains the basic information required by the court. This may lead some people to suspect that the judge may lead the witness to give an answer which was never intended. In fact, the whole of the statement is read back to the witness at the end of the session, and the witness has the chance of changing whatever he wishes in the testimony. People, including English lawyers, who have taken part in nullity cases are certain that the depositions contain precisely what the witness means to say.

I have talked about this aspect of the work of nullity courts with two English lawyers who were plaintiff and defendant in the case involving their own marriage. Both of them agree that, as Princess Michael has also said, the questions were searching and brought out things that few people would wish to have revealed. One of the partners was a non-Catholic. It was refreshing to hear his statement that the method of questioning was much the better way of arriving at the truth of a situation. He was glad that the court had not been conducted on the adverserial or accusatorial lines normal in English courts. He did not believe that that type of questioning and of 'attacking the credibility of the other' would have got anywhere near establishing the reality of the situation in which he and his Catholic-lawyer partner found themselves.

These two had taken the oath of secrecy required of everyone taking part in nullity cases. This ensures that those 'very personal things' to which Princess Michael refers remain secret. I have admired the way in which people involved in Princess Michael's case refuse even to comment on her statement outlining the grounds on which she got her annulment; they neither deny nor confirm that it was 'children' which was at the root of the breakdown and the cause of the nullity. I approached a number of priests for advice about the nullity process in general. As soon as I let it be known that I was preparing this book on Princess Michael, two priests refused to talk, even in general terms, about annulment. They had been involved in later hearings concerning the case.

Each session of the court may last as long as three or four hours. In Princess Michael's case there were several such long and searching hearings. The court in this case, as in all others, refused to hurry witnesses, preferring to allow people time to search their memories and so help establish the truth. Once all the evidence had been collected, it was 'published' – that is to say, it was made available to the advocate and to the defender of the bond to study. Each was then free to call for more witnesses or for the re-interrogation of witnesses already heard. Ultimately, the presiding judge declared that the evidence stage of the case was 'concluded'. The advocate was then given time to prepare his pleadings, showing why the marriage should be regarded as null and void. A copy of these pleadings went to the defender of the bond, who then prepared his reply showing why, in his opinion, the evidence proved that the marriage should be regarded as valid.

Copies of all the evidence, documents and submissions of the advocate and defender were then handed to the three judges in the case. Each of these had to make up his own mind, individually, before the three judges met to announce their decision. At this joint meeting there was time and opportunity for discussion, and the judges were free to change their minds if they wished. However, everything comes to an end. The meeting finished with a vote and decision.

That, however, was not the end of the affair, for both the advocate for the petitioner (Princess Michael) and the defender of the bond had the right to appeal to another tribunal. Before a decree of nullity is issued, there must be two agreeing decisions in favour of the petition. In Princess Michael's case there were three hearings: one at the Westminster tribunal, a second at the Birmingham tribunal and a third at the Portsmouth tribunal. This helps to explain why eighteen months elapsed between the first application and the issuing of the decree of nullity in April 1978. Only then was Marie-Christine free to go ahead with plans for an engagement and, ultimately, her wedding to Prince Michael.

If she thought that her path would now be a smooth one, she was soon to be disillusioned. 1978 may have been the year in which she was freed by her Church from the bonds of her first marriage but it was also the year in which she found herself at the centre of a series of constitutional and ecclesiastical problems.

6

The Queen and the Engagement

'We are very lucky that the Queen has given her consent for us to marry' – Marie-Christine in *The Times*, 1 June 1978

'The announcement ... that Prince Michael is to renounce the right of succession to the throne ... draws attention to the ... problems which are likely to beset further moves towards intercommunion between the Anglican and Roman Catholic Churches' – *The Tablet*, 1 July 1978

'A princely marriage is the brilliant edition of a universal fact, and as such it rivets mankind.' So wrote Walter Bagehot, author of *The English Constitution*. Perhaps it is so. Prince Michael and his fiancée might have wanted to add a footnote to Bagehot, for in 1978 they found themselves entangled in a maze of con-stitutional-religious problems. Marie-Christine could have done without the burden of these extraneous problems; she considered that she had enough to contend with as it was. She quickly discovered that she 'wasn't received with open arms in some sections of society'. There were influential people who made it clear that they wished that Prince Michael 'had chosen one of our girls'. That social coolness was made the harder to take because of public debate and disagreement over the question of the engagement and marriage.

Despite speculation about a marriage between Prince Michael of Kent and Mrs Thomas Troubridge during the winter of 1977–8,[1] the Queen insisted that they put off the announcement of their engagement until Princess Margaret's divorce had been finalized and become public knowledge. But it was accepted by everyone involved that one day they would be married. Prime Minister James Callaghan had to be informed because at some time the Privy Council would have to exercise its constitutional role and advise the Queen to give, or withhold, her consent to the marriage.

Various authorities were put to work to search Marie-Christine's background – she might, after all, have been the impostor that *Private Eye* was to allege she was. There might have been, as there was in her father's case, an earlier and undisclosed marriage. Among the authorities which delved into Marie-Christine's background was the Royal Society of Genealogists. By chance Prince Michael was President of this society – in succession to his kinsman Lord Mountbatten. Officers of the society worked in co-operation with colleagues in Europe to draw up Marie-Christine's family tree. Until they had done so, neither Prince Michael nor his future wife was aware of their existing relationships.

Security and intelligence authorities were also employed to seek out any possible skeletons in Marie-Christine's ancestral cupboards. It was their research, in 1977 and 1978, which unearthed the truth about the Nazi past of her father, including the findings of the Bavarian de-Nazification courts.

Marie-Christine's family had access to most, if not all, of the documentary evidence. Among those who knew the whole story were her mother, her brother Frederick and some of her relations on the Continent. In 1985 they made this material available to her so that she could rebut the wild allegations that were being made about her and her father. Why did they not reveal this information to her while she was growing up? Or when she was preparing to marry Prince Michael? Who knows why a mother, an elder brother, guardian-like relatives and others would not wish to burden Marie-Christine with what they saw as relatively unimportant information about the past of the father who had left the Nazi Party before she was born and who, in any event, had had little, if any, influence on her upbringing?

A variety of genealogical societies and organizations were also provided with the Baron's history. In April 1985, when the *Mirror* headlined the information (or some of it), Harold Brooks-Baker, publishing director of *Burke's Peerage* said that genealogists had known about this 'for some years'. Certainly people working in the genealogical field had had the information available to them since 1978, and some two or three hundred, at least, had used the material in one form or another.

How much of the information was known, in 1977 and 1978, to the Queen and her advisers? We may never know the answer to that question. The Palace surrounds itself with a wall of secrecy which sometimes has unfortunate results. It is difficult, if not impossible, to believe that the security and intelligence services, and their political masters, including the Prime Minister, hid this information from the Queen. It is certain that the Palace knew of Marie-Christine's family tree and agreed that it should be published. It is equally certain that, at the very least, someone would have asked, 'What did he do in the war?' when the name of Baron von Reibnitz cropped up in the tree. It is reasonable then to assume that the Palace knew of von Reibnitz's Nazi past. If so, we may ask why did the Palace not allow the publication of that information alongside the well-publicized family tree? Here we are again in the field of conjecture.

There are at least four possible excuses for Palace silence. Firstly, the Royal Family was already preparing itself for the publicity that would surround Princess Margaret's divorce. It might be that the Palace did not want to provide the tabloid Press with an additional potentially harmful story. Secondly, the Palace knew that Prince Michael's proposed marriage was already surrounded by a thicket of constitutional-religious problems – as we shall see in subsequent chapters. It might be that the Queen's advisers felt that publication of von Reibnitz's story would add another – and avoidable – problem. Thirdly, and rightly, the Palace may have thought that the father's past had little, if anything, to do with Marie-Christine and her future. We have seen that she knew little of him and that he had played almost no part in her upbringing. Why visit the (doubtful) sins of a father on his daughter?

But perhaps the main reason for Palace silence on von Reibnitz's story was the fear that its publication might have led to other, perhaps more damaging revelations. While Lord Mountbatten and his nephew Prince Philip were helping to fight the Axis Powers, some of their close relatives were equally involved on the German and Italian side. All four of Prince Philip's sisters had married German aristocrats. The youngest, Sophie, was the wife of Prince Christopher of Hesse, a Nazi who, in the 1930s, was head of an important espionage network and a close aide of Heinrich Himmler, head of the SS and Gestapo. Although Christopher joined the Luftwaffe at the outbreak of war in 1939, he remained head of the Forschungsamt, the secret eavesdropping service, until his death in 1943. While he never reached more than the rank of major in the Luftwaffe, he was a brigadier-general on Himmler's staff. He died in an air-crash in 1943.

In 1977 and 1978 it is possible that the Palace thought that revelations concerning the Duke of Edinburgh's in-laws might be

used by the tabloid Press to embarrass the Royal Family. Lord
Mountbatten knew all too well how his father had been driven
from public life by a disgraceful anti-Battenberg campaign in
1914. He and Prince Philip had been made to suffer from the
crude campaign waged by the Beaverbrook Press against 'Phil the
Greek' and the Battenberg connection. One may judge that they
had every right to believe that the popular Press was well capable
of waging a 'Prince Charles's uncle was head of a Gestapo agency'
campaign.

It may be, then, that the decision not to publicize von
Reibnitz's limited Nazi past was motivated by fears of what that
minor revelation would do for the good name of the family as a
whole. More perceptive commentators might well wish to draw
attention to Lord Mountbatten's major contribution to the Allied
victory in 1945, others might point to Prince Philip's wartime
record, but, in the quest for a headline, the popular Press could
well ignore such records. And, as it was to do in 1985, the
headline-seekers would not ask whether it was fair to visit the
sins of relatives on Lord Mountbatten and Prince Philip.

Throughout 1977 and the early months of 1978 Marie-
Christine was being introduced to the Royal Family. Some people
may think that she had no need for 'introduction', that she did not
have to find out 'what sort of family' she was thinking of
marrying into. After all, the Royal Family is so visible; everyone
knows about them. She found that this popular view was an
erroneous one. She had 'a jolly good look and thought long and
hard'. She quickly discovered that most of the members of the
family were 'so busy' that she never felt free to ask anyone for
help and guidance. In particular, she felt the absence of a future
mother-in-law. Prince Michael's mother, Princess Marina, had
died in 1968. Marie-Christine regretted the absence of 'a
mother-in-law to help me'. She was to think, later, that if she had
been able to discuss things with such a relative-to-be, she might
have avoided 'some of the mistakes I made out of ignorance'.

In February 1978 Marie-Christine went with Prince Michael to
visit Dr Coggan, the Archbishop of Canterbury. A Church House
representative said: 'Prince Michael and Mrs Troubridge have
seen the Archbishop but it was a private meeting and we are not
prepared to discuss it further.'[2] In spite of this ecclesiastical
discretion, we may assume that discussion centred on the
constitutional and religious problems arising from a marriage
between a member of the Royal Family and a Catholic divorcée.
Clifford Longley, the Religious Affairs Correspondent of *The
Times* wrote: 'The legal and ecclesiastical complications of the

marriage ... are enormous. Five distinct hurdles had to be over-come.'[3]

The first of the hurdles was the annulment of Marie-Christine's 'former marriage'. The second consisted of the provisions of the Royal Marriages Act of 1772 (passed because George III was angered and alarmed at the sexual adventures of two of his brothers). This decreed that '... no descendant of His late Majesty King George II (other than the issue of princesses married or who may marry into foreign families) shall be capable of contracting matrimony without the previous consent of His Majesty, his heirs and successors, signified under the Great Seal.'

Because of the 1772 statute, the Queen was obliged to consult the Prime Minister and there had to be a special meeting of the Privy Council at which Her Majesty signed a document which began, 'Now know ye that we have consented and by these Presents signify Our Consent to the contracting of Matrimony between His Royal Highness ...'.

Subsequent research suggests that Prince Michael need not have asked for the royal permission. Since the Act does not apply to 'the issue of princesses married or who may marry into foreign fam-ilies', not one of the modern royal family, it is argued, is covered by the Act: they are all descended from Alexandra of Denmark, wife of Edward VII, who was herself descended from George II. As a foreign princess, she was not covered by the Act – and so nor are her descendants!

That the Queen gave her cousin Michael permission to marry a divorcée might seem, *prima facie*, surprising. Since the Queen is Head of the Church of England, which opposes the remarriage of divorced people, she might have been expected to demur. After all, it was the wish of her uncle, Edward VIII, to marry the twice-divorced Mrs Simpson which had caused his abdication in 1936; in 1953 Princess Margaret had been persuaded not to marry the divorced Group Captain Peter Townsend. Since then, however, the Queen had taken a softer line towards divorce and the people involved. First she had accepted as her Prime Minister the divorced Anthony Eden; then in 1967, she had given her permission for her cousin the Earl of Harewood to make a second marriage after his divorce. In 1976 her sister, Princess Margaret, formally separated from her husband, Lord Snowdon, and her divorce went through in the spring of 1978, almost coinciding with Prince Michael's application for permission to marry the former Mrs Troubridge, thus overcoming the third of Longley's 'hurdles'.

Even more surprising, to constitutionalists, was Her Majesty's permission for a prince to marry a Roman Catholic. In 1701 an Act had been passed excluding from the royal succession any member of the Catholic Church and anyone who married a Catholic – a reasonable enough provision since the British monarch is also Head of the Church of England: it would be absurd to have a Catholic Head of the Anglican Church. Thus implicit in Prince Michael's request for permission to marry Marie-Christine was his renunciation of his place in the royal succession. (Prince Michael has the most distant prospect of ever succeeding to the throne; the Prince of Wales, on the other hand, is heir apparent – when there seemed a likelihood of his marrying the Catholic Princess Marie Astrid of Luxembourg, there had been hot debate about the Anglican/Catholic position, in which the 1701 Act was decried as an anachronism, an insult to Catholics etc; at the time, there was talk of disestablishing the Church of England, so that a Catholic could become monarch without being Head of the Anglican Church.)

Despite Prince Michael's renunciation of his place in the succession, the Queen announced that, after the marriage, Baroness Marie-Christine von Reibnitz (as she was known since her annulment had gone through) was to be known as 'Her Royal Highness Princess Michael of Kent' – a special mark of royal approval: there had been no 'HRH' for the divorcée wife of the former King Edward VIII, Duke of Windsor, in spite of his constant demand for such a title.

Now that the fourth hurdle was overcome, on 30 May 1978, within days of the annulment of the Troubridge marriage, Baroness Marie-Christine von Reibnitz and Prince Michael of Kent announced their engagement, with the blessing of the Queen and the approval of the Privy Council and the Catholic Church. Or so it seemed.

There remained only what some saw as a minor hurdle – the dispensation from the Catholic authorities which, once obtained, would allow the wedding to take place in a Catholic church abroad. While congratulating the newly engaged couple on having overcome several hurdles, *The Times* pointed to the question of the dispensation, noting that 'in Roman Catholic circles yesterday [30 May 1978] ... opinion was generally optimistic in Prince Michael's favour.'[4] That optimism was unjustified.

7

The Churches and the Marriage, 1978

'I think it fair to say that the marriage will cause some
controversy. It would perhaps have been easier if the
circumstances had been different' – Prince Michael at a
news conference, 31 May 1978

Prince Michael and Mrs Marie-Christine Troubridge went to see
the Archbishop of Canterbury, Dr Coggan, in the spring of 1978.
The visit heightened speculation about a marriage between the
Anglican Prince and the Roman Catholic divorcée who was in the
process of having her marriage to Tom Troubridge annulled.

At this meeting in Lambeth Palace, the Prince and Mrs
Troubridge, 'obviously now blissfully in love'[1], heard the
Archbishop spell out what, in fact, they already knew. First, the
Anglican Church would not recognize the nullity decree which
Mrs Troubridge was going to get from the Roman Catholic
Church. In spite of her Church's decision, she would be, in
Anglican eyes, merely divorced according to civil law. As such,
she would not be allowed to remarry in an Anglican church. She
might well have wished to have her marriage to Prince Michael
take place in one of the country's prestigious churches. She had,
after all, been allowed to marry Troubridge in an Anglican
church. She might want her marriage to the Prince to be
celebrated in, say, St Paul's, St Margaret's or Westminster Abbey.
However, an Act of Convocation of 1957 expressed the Anglican
Church's total opposition to the remarriage of divorced people in
church.

Dr Coggan was later to explain the Anglican argument to the
Catholic authorities at Westminster. He was unwilling to
disregard the Act of Convocation; for him to have done so, or for
him to have allowed one of his clergy to do so, would have been a
major cause for scandal in the Anglican community. However,
the Archbishop did suggest that the Catholic Church might

celebrate the marriage – possibly at Westminster Cathedral, which Anglicans might have seen as a sort of 'Catholic Royals' church'. If not there, then perhaps the Jesuit Church in fashionable Mayfair? And if the Catholics were minded to have such a ceremony, Dr Coggan would welcome an invitation to take part in it – to be allowed, for example, to give a blessing to the now-married pair. Such a participation in a remarriage would not, it seems, be a cause of scandal in the Anglican community.

Denied a wedding in an Anglican church, the couple might have sought to marry in a register office; but even this way was closed to them: under the 1949 Marriage Act members of the Royal Family are specifically exempt from all other citizens' rights to have a civil wedding.

Thus Prince Michael and Baroness Marie-Christine were compelled to plan for a wedding in a Catholic church – which was, in any case, what the prospective bride desired.

To have such a wedding, Prince Michael (as the non-Catholic party) had to seek a dispensation for a 'mixed marriage'. This had been foreseen even before the couple went to visit Dr Coggan in the spring of 1978. In the report of that visit, *The Times* noted: 'It was authoritatively stated yesterday that there are no circumstances in which a Roman Catholic marrying a member of the Royal Family would be excused from the obligation to ensure that their children were brought up as Roman Catholics; no means exist for releasing or dispensing from that obligation and therefore the Roman Catholic authorities could not take part in any advance arrangement, so that the children could be brought up as Anglicans.'[2]

Lord Mountbatten had spoken to Prince Michael about the problem of his future children's religion, reminding him that if they became Catholics they would automatically be debarred from the royal succession. This might not matter to Prince Michael, or to Marie-Christine, but did they have the right to settle the children's royal position?

More influentially on the couple's decision, Sir Martin (now Lord) Charteris, then Private Secretary to the Queen, telephoned to ask the Prince to give a written assurance that his children would be brought up as Anglicans. Prince Michael was, at first, unwilling to accede to these requests. Charteris then wrote explaining that, without such an 'Anglican assurance', the Privy Council would be unable to give its assent to the marriage (under the terms of the Royal Marriage Act, 1772). Prince Michael assumed that this letter had originated with the Queen herself: he handed his written undertaking to the Queen personally. No one is willing to name the person who 'leaked' the news of the arrival of this letter, whose publication was to make it impossible, in 1978, for the Vatican to issue the dispensation. A Palace spokesman was willing to go as far as to explain that the political situation made it imperative that the 'Anglican assurance' had to be made to appear as the decision of Prince Michael and his fiancée: Catholic opinion in Britain, Northern Ireland and the Commonwealth might have been angered if the 'Anglican assurance' had appeared to be (as in effect it was) imposed on the couple. The Vatican, however, failed to appreciate the nuances of British politics: officials there took the Prince's 'leaked' letter at its face value – and assumed that he and his fiancée had, as it were, gone out of their way to publicize their determination.

Unfortunately, at the news conference which followed the Queen's consent to the marriage, Marie-Christine made a gaffe on the subject of her future children's religion. When asked about their religious upbringing, she stated clearly that they would be brought up in the Church of England: 'I think it is a matter of who is the head of the family and in this case the head of the family happens to be an Anglican.' She went further, perhaps, than she meant when she commented: 'With this new ecumenical spirit I think it is Christians versus the rest, and it does not matter which club you belong to.'[3]

Marie-Christine had long assumed that she would obtain the required permission from the Catholic authorities. She was aware, from recent cases on the Continent, that the Church was willing to reach an accommodation with non-Catholic princes whose consciences and/or particular positions in their Churches made it impossible for them to agree to a Catholic upbringing for their children. Among those who informed her of these precedents was Archbishop Heim, Apostolic Delegate since 1972 and Apostolic Pro-Nuncio since 1982. In October 1977 Archbishop Heim raised with Pope Paul VI the question of the dispensation for the marriage of Prince Michael and Marie-Christine. On his return he told them that the dispensation would be granted but that it could not be formally applied for until the engagement had been officially announced. It was then that they learnt that they would have to wait to announce their engagement until Princess Margaret's divorce had been announced.

A further difficulty was that the Catholic code of canon law insists that, where members of royal families are concerned, dispensations must be issued by the Vatican itself. This is not some royal privilege: on the contrary, the purpose of the law is to make it even harder for the 'high born' to get the permission they seek. (It is easy to see that a local bishop might feel under some pressure if he were known to head the court of appeal empowered to adjudicate on a royal application for a dispensation.) Thus Archbishop Heim explained to Prince Michael and the then Mrs Troubridge that he had no power to issue or deny the dispensation: it was only the Vatican that could do it. He, as Apostolic Delegate, would serve only as an 'ecclesiastical postmaster', transmitting the various communiqués.[4]

Monsignor Ralph Brown would act as Cardinal Hume's adviser throughout this period, as a canon law expert on marriage problems. From the outset, Brown fully understood the limitations which Prince Michael's undertaking about future children imposed on Marie-Christine's freedom of action to declare – as her Church required of her – that she would 'do all in her power' to ensure that her children would be brought up in the Catholic faith. If she was allowed to marry without having given such a declaration of intent, there might, it was argued, be a flood of applicants for dispensations who would demand the same liberty, using the royal case as a precedent. But if the dispensation were refused, it would go against the already established Continental precedents. Besides, at this late stage, a refusal of the dispensation might be seen as a rebuff to the British Royal Family – even to the British nation as a whole.

One 'let-out' might have been the use of the ancient, but now unused custom by which the sons of a 'mixed marriage' followed their father's religious practice, the daughters their mother's. (This was a device which Prince Michael had offered to Charteris and which had been refused.) The Catholic Church had outlawed this custom back in 1908, decreeing that in all mixed marriages there would have to be the promise concerning the Catholic education of all the children before a dispensation could be awarded. It refused to withdraw its decision now.

Prince Michael's declaration to the Privy Council was unfortunately 'leaked' to the public in May 1978, during the delay while the couple waited, as requested, for the furore over Princess Margaret's divorce to die away. By then Marie-Christine, her annulment 'through', had already made firm arrangements for the wedding to take place in the Schottenkirche in Vienna. But the publication of Prince Michael's 'Anglican assurance' declaration radically altered the position. Formerly the Vatican might have hoped to 'fudge' the issue (despite the fact that they had known of the declaration and of Marie-Christine's doubts as to the possibility of bringing up her children as Catholics); now both the Cardinal and the Archbishop had to re-think the position.

In October 1977 Archbishop Heim had given the couple a verbal assurance that the dispensation would be granted. Now he knew there was little, if any, chance of the Vatican's awarding it. His appeal to the bishops of England and Wales to act in collegiate fashion, to issue a joint statement containing the dispensation, was refused. The ball was back in the Vatican's court.

In the event, the Vatican rejected the appeal, and no dispensation was issued.

The news of the Vatican's rejection of the request was broadcast on the radio within two hours of its reception by Archbishop Heim. Prince Michael was annoyed by this: he asked how the information had been leaked and was told by the Delegate's secretary that the leak had taken place in Rome. When the Church authorities issued a public statement and formally announced the Vatican's refusal, the press had a field day. Typical of the comments was the report which appeared on Monday 19 June:

Christian Disunity
The decision of the Vatican to refuse permission to Prince Michael of Kent and his fiancée, Baroness Marie-Christine von Reibnitz, to marry in a Roman Catholic church will strike many people, both inside and outside the Catholic Church, as being both unfair and cruel, even if it is the strict interpretation of the Church's rules. Many thousands of mixed marriages have taken place inside Catholic churches; they are allowed as long as the Catholic partner promises to make every effort to see that the children of the marriage are brought up in the faith. Prince Michael's unusual position has prevented this; as a member of the British Royal Family he is constitutionally bound to state unequivocally beforehand in what faith his children will be raised and, understandably enough, he has said it will be in the Anglican faith. It is this that has led to the Vatican's refusal, in effect discriminating against the Prince because of his position. If he had been anything other than a member of the Royal Family, he and his fiancée would be pressing ahead with their church wedding plans, rather than having to book a Viennese register office for the ceremony. This papal pronouncement will not help the ecumenical movement.[5]

This begged a number of questions and also forecast events which we will examine in the next two chapters. *The Times* was to explain what might have happened if the Prince had been better advised: 'Authoritative opinion appears to be that had he simply said it out loud, had he expressed it as a hope rather than a foregone conclusion, or had he declared even that he would do all in his power to secure the Anglicanism of his children, there would have been no difficulty. The Roman Catholic Church has moved a long way since it demanded from the non-Catholic partner a writen undertaking about the religion of the children of a mixed marriage.'⁶

Some Catholics, notably some of the Baroness's clerical friends, took up the argument that the Vatican's decision had done the ecumenical case a deal of harm. They claimed that, if the Vatican had given a willing agreement to the marriage – in spite of the Prince's statement – Anglicans would have been drawn nearer the Catholic Church. This clashes with the Anglican refusal even to allow the marriage to take place in an Anglican church. The Catholic weekly *The Tablet* also took a pro-ecumenical and anti-Vatican line: 'Prince Michael and the Baroness were said to be "very distressed after the Pope's decision" and that distress will be shared by many in both communions.'⁷ *The Tablet* somewhat weakened its case by arguing that the children's right of succession was a possibility 'so remote as to be only of academic interest'. Furthermore, it argued, 'We consider that he was ill-advised to make a formal written and signed declaration which the Vatican would not, according to present practice, require of him.' It was that declaration which left the Baroness 'burdened with a specific declaration from the other party'. As *The Tablet* noted: 'What would have been a significant sacramental event ... has fallen foul not of any high principles but of bureaucratic mismanagement. The Baroness ... will be cut off from the sacraments of her church; the Church of England ... is bound to regard the Prince as marrying a divorcée and so cut him off from its own sacramental life. Those who may be tempted to cheer for absolute standards ... should reflect whether this ... is really what God demands.'

On the couple's wedding day, 30 June 1978, Prince Charles, addressing the International Congress of the Salvation Army gathered in London, criticized Church leaders who seemed to lack 'an awareness of the things of the spirit'. He said that, in view of the general paganism of the contemporary world, it was 'worse than folly' for Christians to be arguing about doctrinal matters which caused needless distress to a number of people. It is hardly surprising that many people saw this as an attack on the Pope for refusing to give the dispensation.

A leader in *The Times* dealt with that refusal; 'There can ... be no criticism of the Pope for acting according to the tenets of his faith, though equally there can be no surprise that ... the Church of England should find this demonstration of Roman Catholic principle a set-back to ecumenical hopes.' The leader writer took the opportunity to condemn the 'apparent ease with which an annulment can be obtained as a 'more ambiguous' example of Catholic principle, but, trying to be all things to all men, condemned the constitutional exclusion of Catholics from either being the sovereign or marrying the sovereign as 'an absurd anachronism'.[8] The same edition of *The Times* carried a report of 'the annoyance and anger' felt by the Catholic Archbishop Winning of Glasgow. He attacked Prince Charles for 'advocating a woolly type of Christianity which is very prevalent these days, preferring it to another type of Christianity which seems to have clear-cut ideas about what it teaches and what it believes ... I would like to hear what Prince Charles has to say about the law of succession ... a terrible slight on Catholics. Prince Charles probably feels quite upset about his cousin, Prince Michael ... but I think he will recognize ... that if anyone is really committed to one's faith then it is a matter of conscience whether one carries on with that faith or not. You cannot have your cake and eat it ...'

The Anglican Bishop of Worcester, the Right Reverend Robert Woods, a former Dean of Windsor and Chaplain to the Queen said: 'There are far too many people whose marriages have broken down and who wanted to make a fresh start in marriage but have suffered real anger and distress because of the intransigence of the churches.'[9] This point was repeated by the Labour MP Leo Abse; 'The despair expressed by Prince Charles with the doctrinal preoccupations of all the churches is shared by all who worked to bring about changes in our divorce laws.'[10]

The Press kept the argument going for some two weeks or so. Catholics praised and condemned the Papacy for its hard line; Anglicans condemned their leaders for their woolliness as well as for their attitude towards the remarriage of divorced people. There were, it seems, no ecclesiastical winners. What was certain was that both Prince and Princess Michael had every reason to regard themselves as losers. She was to strive to get matters rectified – as we shall see in Chapter 9.

And what did the Queen and other members of the Royal Family think of all this controversy? I am indebted to a leading Church official for the following account of a royal reaction. He found himself placed next to the Queen Mother at a function. 'I told her how sorry I was that things were not easy between our Church and the family.' The Queen Mother did not refer, as *The Times* had done, to 'a tactical error' nor, as *The Tablet* had done, to 'bureaucratic mismanagement'; more down to earth than the leader-writers and, perhaps, more experienced in the ways of the political world, she simply said that Prince and Princess Michael were 'very silly ...' to have made public their determination to flout Catholic requirements. It seems that the Queen Mother did not know of the Charteris letter and its apparently royal command for 'the Anglican assurance'.

—

8

The Royal Wedding, 30 June 1978

'Vienna ... a city of devout Catholics ... very much soft pedalling the marriage ...' (BBC report, 30 June 1978)

If all had gone as Marie-Christine had planned, the high spot of her wedding week-end would have been the Mass, with its blessing on the marriage, which was to have been celebrated in the Schottenkirche.

This church, in the most aristocratic district of Vienna, once belonged to the Schottenhof, a Benedictine monastery founded by Irish monks in 1158. At that time, Ireland was known as *Scotia major* and was the 'holy isle' which sent out 'saints and scholars' to civilize much of Europe. It has been left to modern and more sophisticated British travellers to decide that 'Schottenkirche' means 'the Scottish church'.

The church was reshaped in 1638–48 but the present building dates only from 1826–32. It contains the graves of Duke Heinrich Jasomirgott (d.1177), the patron of the initial foundation, and of Count Rudiger von Starhemberg (d.1701), who led the defence of Vienna against the Turks in 1683. It was the church in which Marie-Christine's grandmother and great-grandmother were married. It must have pleased her sense of history to plan her own wedding in what could be seen, with only slight exaggeration, as 'the family church'.

It was to have been a glittering occasion. The Vienna Boys' Choir was engaged; ecclesiastical dignitaries were enrolled; European royalty was to be present, along with a string of Szapáry-Windisch-Graetz related aristocrats. It is easy to understand the excited interest with which the Baroness planned the wedding while she waited for the annulment, for the Queen to give her consent and for the Vatican to issue the dispensation. 1977 and the early months of 1978 must have been akin to the 'golden days'.

One of her closest friends commented on the anxiety with which she pursued certain ends – ends which, desirable in themselves, take on, for her, almost an obsession. He listed some examples. In the Troubridge marriage, he says, she pursued money, which was more than ordinarily important to her (as indeed it still is, as we shall see). The child of an aristocratic mother, the Sydney-based girl who seemed ashamed of the modesty of her home, she had sought a compensation for what she may have seen as 'history-laden deprivation' in a marriage into a solidly based county family. Her determination to marry Prince Michael, in spite of constitutional-religious difficulties, was due, at least in part, to her desire to gain recognition for her 'roots deep in Europe's royal families'. None of her European relatives was immediately related to royalty, although, like her, they could trace their ancestry into a complexity of royal roots. It pleased her, I am told, to be *the* member of the family who would have this immediate intimacy with royalty. And with such royalty! Not with some ex-monarch or his descendants, not with some relative of a deposed member of a petty dukedom or electorate, but with the British Royal Family. Jumping ahead of our story, her friend makes the point that her constant search, after 1978, for a Catholic validation of her 'irregular' marriage was part of that 'recognition obsession'. We shall see in the next chapter how anxious she was to gain the validation in time for the visit of Pope John Paul II in 1982. She would then have been able to play the part of the Catholic royal representative. More importantly for this chapter, her friend says that the desire to have a glittering ceremony in the aristocrats' church in Vienna was due, in part at least, to that obsession for recognition. She wanted to play a leading role before an important audience in a fitting (for her) arena with an outstandingly royal leading man.

The family had engaged 'Party Planners' (Lady Elizabeth Anson) of London to prepare guest lists for the various functions associated with the wedding. The firm had issued an itinerary for 30 June:

1.30 Family lunch at Imperial Hotel
15.15 Horse-drawn carriage rides for those who would like to. (The ride lasts for approximately one hour.)
16.00 Civil marriage ceremony at the Rathaus (for close family only)
20.00 Dinner at Schwarzenberg Palace (Dress: white tie and decorations)

The peculiarity of one of the quoted times, 1.30, may be seen as evidence of British insularity failing to come to immediate terms with the twenty-four-hour clock. Similarly, the ambiguity of the instructions for the 'Horse-drawn carriage rides' reveals a last-minute rush to adjust to a new situation following the papal decision. There is no evidence as to how many showed that they 'would like to' take a ride in a horse-drawn carriage. In the days when Vienna was the imperial capital, the nobility, including Marie-Christine's ancestors, were accustomed to taking such outings, during which they would be gazed at by the multitudes.

About twenty close relatives attended the wedding ceremony in the Town Hall. These included the Duke of Kent and his sister, Princess Alexandra, her husband, Angus Ogilvy, Lady Helen Windsor, daughter of the Duke of Kent, and two whose attendance was most significant, Princess Anne and Lord Mountbatten of Burma. At that time Princess Anne was earning for herself the reputation of 'a rebel'. It may be that her presence at the Kent-von Reibnitz wedding was the act of a rebel, anxious to support anyone who was cocking a snook at all sorts of authorities, Anglican, Catholic, British and Austrian. Lord Mountbatten, frail but in good spirits, was there as the 'Grand Old Man' of the Royal Family. Sir Peter Scott, Prince Michael's Private Secretary, had done a good deal of work to help smooth the path of the couple in 1977 and 1978. He had once been British Ambassador to Norway, and his diplomatic experience stood him in good stead during his seemingly endless round of visits to Rome and Vienna, to cardinals and archbishops, as he tried to arrange a church wedding. It was he, in the last resort, who was called on to negotiate with the Viennese authorities who agreed to rent a room in the towering black neo-Gothic Town Hall for the wedding ceremony – for £210. It was, as Sir Peter said, 'the first register office wedding in the royal family apart from Mrs Simpson'.[1] Here, in the simple civil ceremony, Baroness Marie-Christine von Reibnitz, became Her Royal Highness Princess Michael of Kent.

It is worth noting that this civil ceremony would have taken place even if the Catholic Church had issued a dispensation and allowed a Catholic wedding on the Saturday. Such a civil ceremony is obligatory in most countries where the Church is separate from the state. Marie-Christine's friends are at pains to point out that this civil ceremony had always been planned; it was the church ceremony which had had to be altered. It is, then, a little misleading for a Central Office of Information hand-out to say that, because of Prince Michael's 'Anglican assurance', 'a civil ceremony had to suffice'.

Following the ceremony there was the dinner at the Schwarzenberg Palace. The menu showed the intertwined initials 'M' and

'MC' surmounted by the princely coronet. The guest list for the soirée reads like a rollcall of minor royalty and distinguished aristocracy:

HRH The Princess Anne, Mrs Mark Phillips
HRH The Duke of Kent
The Lady Helen Windsor
HRH Princess Alexandra, The Hon. Mrs Angus Ogilvy
The Hon. Angus Ogilvy
The Earl Mountbatten of Burma
Mr John Barratt
Prince and Princess George Galitzine
Sir Peter and Lady Scott
Sir Geoffrey and Lady Elizabeth Shakerley
Lt-Col. and Mrs Blair Stewart Wilson
Sir Philip Hay
Apponyi, Count and Countess Alfred
Apponyi, Graf und Gräfin Rudolf
Apponyi, Graf und Gräfin Alfred
Babington Smith, Miss S.
Batthanyi, Graf und Gräfin Laszlo
Batthanyi, Fürstin Antoinette
Bavaria, Duke and Duchess of
Baden, The Margrave of
Baden, Prince and Princess Ludwig of
Colleredo, Graf und Gräfin
Charles-Roux, The Rev. Father Jean
Dockerill, Lt-Colonel
Eldon, Lady
Esterházy, Count Andreas
Esterházy, Princess
Esterházy, Prince
Von Eichstedt, Baron und Baronin
Geddes, Mrs Andrew
Goess, Graf und Gräfin Franz
Von Haymerle, Baronin
Von Haymerle, Baron Franz Josef
Hanover, Prince and Princess George of
Kyburg, Countess
Koerfer, Mr and Mrs Patrick
Koczorowska, Countess

Kasterine, Mr Dmitri
Lockwood, Mr and Mrs John
Morgan, HE, The British Ambassador and Mrs Hugh
Nostitz, Graf und Gräfin
Von Reibnitz, Baronin Renate
Reneaud, Madame Pierre
Von Reibnitz, Baron Günther
Von Reibnitz, Baron Friedrich
Rasper, Fräulein Monika
Von Ratibor, Herzog und Herzogin
Schwarzenberg, Erbprinz und Erbprinzessin zu
Szapáry, Graf Nicholaus
Szapáry, Grafin Laszlo
Szapáry, Mr Peter
Szchenyi, Graf und Gräfin
Szapáry, Graf und Gräfin Stephan
Schwarzenberg, Fürstin
Schwarzenberg, Prinz Friedrich
Szapáry, Countess Katalin
Szapáry, Countess Christina
Trauttmansdorff, Gräfin Tanya
Thun Hohenstein, Graf und Gräfin
Thurn und Taxis, Prinz und Prinzessin
Toerring, Count and Countess
Von Varnbueler zu Hemmingen, Baronin Ellen
Vitetti, Count
Windisch-Graetz, Prinz Alfred
Windisch-Graetz, Fürstin
Windisch-Graetz, Prinz und Prinzessin Vincenz
Windisch-Graetz, Prinz und Prinzessin Franz
Windisch-Graetz, Prinzessin Natalie
Yugoslavia, Prince and Princess Alexander of
Yugoslavia, Princess Elizabeth of
Yugoslavia, Princess Margarita of
Yugoslavia, Princess Paul of

In passing we should note the presence of Marie-Christine's father in Vienna. In April 1985 the *Daily Mirror* remarked 'He was not at Prince and Princess Michael's wedding in Vienna in 1978.' As with much else, the *Mirror* simply had it wrong – again.

The Vatican's rejection of the application for a dispensation had been announced long after the arrangements had been made, guests invited and itineraries published. The original arrangements for Saturday 1 July were:

10.40 Departure from the Schwarzenberg/Imperial Hotels for those guests who have been invited to the Mass at the Schottenkirche
12.00 Departure from the Schottenkirche for luncheon at the British Embassy Residence
12.15 Departure from the Schwarzenberg Palace Hotel for those guests who did not attend the Mass, for British Embassy Residence for luncheon
12.30 Luncheon at British Embassy Residence
       Dress: Lounge suite and day dresses, hats optional
15.00 Return to hotel

You are asked to make your own arrangements re your departure to the airport.

How would these arrangements be affected by the Vatican's decision? Marie-Christine was said to have been 'very distressed after the Pope's decision'.[2] If she had followed Archbishop Winning's advice, she would have called the marriage off. Winning argued that she and Prince Michael were free to consider that their respective faiths were more important to them than mere earthly considerations; having failed to obtain the requisite dispensation, she might, as 'a loyal daughter of the Church', have decided to cancel the arrangements and to wait until the Vatican could be persuaded to change its mind. But, as Winning had indicated, she wanted to have her cake and eat it. The arrangements would stand; the marriage would go on – and the problem of the Church would be tackled later, if at all.

That decision angered Church representatives in Vienna, 'a city of devout Catholics'. On the day of the wedding, BBC radio reported that the city was 'very much "soft pedalling" the marriage'.[3] This was an understatement, due probably to a lack of understanding of the Church's teaching on marriage. If a woman wishes to hold her marriage ceremony away from her own parish church, she is obliged, by Catholic canon law, to obtain a 'release' from her parish priest. This 'letter of freedom' has to be handed to the priest who has agreed to take part in the ceremony. It tells him, in so many words, that the woman's parish priest is aware of the ceremony and that he has carried out the Church's regulations – by having the banns called in his church. Marie-Christine had no such 'release'. Nor, in view of the Vatican's refusal of the dispensation, could she have obtained one from a priest in Britain.

Under Catholic law, she was, quite simply, unable to have her Catholic wedding in Vienna.

Without a 'release', Marie-Christine could not receive the Church's blessing on her marriage. It was not, as has been claimed by one critic, 'the left-wing Koenig who refused to help her'.[4] Cardinal Koenig was bound by the laws of the Church. The publication of the itinerary, with its reference to Mass at the Schottenkirche, appeared to the Cardinal and his advisers a deliberate flouting of law, a challenge to the Church. This, I am assured, was not how Marie-Christine saw things. She appreciated that she would not be allowed a Nuptial Mass – this ceremony is available, normally, only when two Catholics are getting married – but she did hope that she would be allowed to attend Mass with the husband to whom she was 'civilly' married and that, at that Mass, a friendly priest would give his blessing and that of the Church to their marriage, which, within limits is what happened.

Prince Michael, Marie-Christine and those close to them were fully aware that, because of the failure to get a dispensation, there would be no Mass in the main church, on the Saturday, for the people whose names appeared on the original guest list. However, they had been told that there could be a Mass in a small oratory attached to the Schottenkirche. They had gone two days earlier to look at this oratory, make out a seating plan, organize floral decorations and the like. Because of the restricted size of the oratory, only members of the immediate family would be able to attend that Mass.

At the dinner at the Schwarzenberg Palace Hotel on the Friday night, Sir Peter Scott read a letter sent by Cardinal Koenig. This made it clear that there would be no music allowed at this private Mass; it also seemed to indicate that no Holy Communion would be distributed. Sir Peter announced the change of plans for those who would be unable to go to Mass the following day. Prince Michael followed his secretary: in what were described for me as 'a few words of noble and moving apology', he hoped that everyone would understand the position. The proposed reception at the British Embassy would take place as planned, and Prince Michael looked forward to seeing everyone there.

I am obliged to one of those present at the dinner for an account of what the letter said and for the description of the way in which its contents were received. Princess Michael 'showed no emotion'; the majority of the other guests also displayed 'a very English calm', although it was evident that everyone, Princess and all, felt the hurt very deeply. Once Prince Michael had sat down, dinner carried on, and in the event it turned out to be, said one who was there, 'a particularly happy and brilliant evening'. After dinner, Prince and Princess Michael opened the dancing. When she was interviewed by Roy Plomley, Princess Michael told him that if she were on his desert island, she would have with her a recording of Lehar's 'Gold and Silver Waltz'. This, it transpired was the tune to which she and Prince Michael had opened the dancing. And, as she explained to Plomley, it was far from being the 'gentle one-two-three' that Prince Michael had expected. She claimed that he was 'dizzied' by the time the whirling and turning had finished.

Later the Prince and Princess led their guests to watch a floodlit performance by the Royal Opera Ballet Company in the park of Prince Schwarzenberg's Palace. Dancing was later resumed, and at midnight the lights were dimmed to draw attention to a huge trolley laden with an assortment of sorbets and sweets.

Princess Michael still hoped, in spite of all, that she would be allowed to receive Holy Communion on the Saturday – 'for the last time' in the inept and incorrect terminology of a reporter.[5] For this reason, the newly weds spent the Friday night apart. Cardinal Koenig's advisers did not accept this gesture of good will as any sign of repentance. She had, in their eyes, broken Church law, by the act of going through with a civil wedding while she knew that she was not going to be able to have her marriage blessed by her Church. Shortly before breakfast, she rang one of her priest friends to ask whether she would be allowed to receive Communion. Reluctantly, he had to tell her that there would be no distribution of Communion at the private Mass which they were going to celebrate.

It was, then, a saddened Princess Michael who prepared for the Mass on what ought to have been her 'glittering' Saturday, Prince Michael and members of the Royal Family went to morning service at the Anglican Church before joining the Princess and a small, intimate party. The Duke of Kent and his daughter, the Princesses Anne and Olga (Prince Michael's aunt, Princess Paul of Yugoslavia), Sir Peter and Lady Scott and three members of the Szapáry family were the only ones who went to a private Mass in a small chapel of a convent attached to the Schottenkirche. Princess Michael wore the same Hardie-Amies cream suit which she had worn at the civil ceremony. When they got to the Schottenkirche, they found the main church locked – 'like a Good Friday', said one who was there. This was one outward sign of the Cardinal's determination not to be seen to be supporting Princess Michael. This was much more than the 'soft pedalling' to which the BBC referred.

The small party entered the convent through a side door. My informant described what might have been a grim procession through a series of passages – hot-water pipes, used as well as disused chests and wardrobes, turning after seemingly endless turning – until, I was told, 'We went into what seemed almost like a cupboard.' It was, in fact, 'a room about this size', he said, waving his arms to indicate the simple room in which we were sitting, some eighteen foot square.

It is not surprising that the small oratory seemed overcrowded, even though there was only a handful of people present. A friendly priest said Mass, during which he preached a sermon in which he said that the predicament in which Prince and Princess Michael found themselves was 'not their fault'. It was, he claimed, the fault of 'bureaucracy' and of 'authority gone mad'. However, in obedience to that authority, he did not attempt to distribute Holy Communion. Throughout the Mass, the onlookers received a distinct impression of the strong support which Prince Michael provided for Marie-Christine. The Mass ended with the priest saying prayers for all those present and for the British Royal Family. He also asked for the Lord's blessing on the marriage which had taken place on the Friday. When, later, he was asked why he did this, in view of the Cardinal's ban, he explained that he had received instructions on what he could and could not say during Mass. Some official at the Cardinal's house had gone through the order of the Mass, carefully crossing out any prayers in which there was a reference to the newly-weds present. But, carelessly, he had forgotten to cross out one such prayer. 'So, I took them at their level. I left out what they crossed out and I left in what they left alone.'

Prince and Princess Michael came out of the church holding hands. They were followed by the Duke of Kent and his daughter. Lord Mountbatten was there to watch them drive away to the British Embassy for the luncheon with their many guests.

While they waited for their guests to arrive at the Embassy, Lord Mountbatten took Princess Michael for a walk in the Embassy garden. It was then that, once again, he urged her to try to see how much easier her life would be with the Royal Family, with the Establishment (including members of the Privy Council) and, in particular, with the Royal Household, if she would only change her religion. He argued that she owed her Church nothing in view of the 'shabby' way in which she had been treated. She disclosed this conversation to several people and she was to show by her subsequent behaviour that she had no intention of following Mountbatten's advice.

At about 3 p.m. the guests waved Prince and Princess Michael off from the Embassy. The couple made their way to the airport to fly off on their honeymoon, which was spent in Iran and India, then back to Vienna. After that it was back to Britain for the start of life as a royal princess and, above all, to the struggle to obtain a Catholic validation of the marriage.

As a number of correspondents pointed out, this marriage left both the Prince and the Princess in unsatisfactory positions *vis à vis* their respective Churches. Prince Michael offended the Anglican Church by his marriage to a divorced woman. She, on the other hand, while legally married in the eyes of the State, was not validly married in the eyes of the Catholic Church. There had been no clerical 'essential witness' at the ceremony because of the papal refusal to grant the dispensation. The Princess, therefore, had cut herself off from the sacramental life of the Catholic Church.

Among the guests at the celebrations on Friday and Saturday was Countess Rogala-Koczorowska, – Princess Michael's mother, Marianne, who had married a former Polish diplomat and volunteer French Army war hero. She had been back to Europe several times since she took her children to Australia ' for four of five years' in 1950, but this royal wedding provided an opportunity for a gathering of the extended family in a very special way. It may be that it was this which determined Countess Marianne's subsequent decision to tell Baron Frederick about his father's Nazi past. Perhaps, surrounded by her wider family, many of whom knew the truth, she felt better able to talk about her first husband and the failure of that marriage. Perhaps it was the tinge of unhappiness surrounding Princess Michael's wedding which stimulated the Countess. Perhaps it was the evidence of her daughter's happiness which served to remind her of her own unhappy marriages – for her marriage to the Polish émigré had not been a success,

It was thus in Vienna, in 1978, that Marie-Christine's brother learned of his father's past. Despite the Countess's account of the Baron's disillusionment with the Party, and his distancing himself from it – and his dangerous support of her own stand against Nazism, her son was initially shocked by these revelations about the eighty-four-year-old man who sat across the table from him at the various celebrations surrounding the wedding. He had, after all, grown up in Australia; he had learned that Nazism was the great evil which Australians had helped to defeat; he knew of the holocaust engineered by the SS and Nazi leaders.

It is clear from conversations with members of the family that Countess Marianne did not tell her daughter of the father's unhappy past. Nor, indeed, did her brother share that secret with her. 'Why should I say anything?' Neither the mother nor the brother thought that one day the story would come out. Said the mother, 'I didn't think it mattered so much. It wouldn't have served much purpose.' In April 1985, after the story had been publicized, misinterpreted and made the subject of a deal of misreporting and wild allegations, Countess Marianne admitted, 'I should have told her ... Now, of course, I'm terribly sorry.'[6]

9

A Catholic Marriage – At Last, 1983

'Have you any news about "Our Great Hope?" Now the second baby is on the way and the years drag on ... Let's hope this Pope finds a way to let us marry in church at last' – letter from Princess Michael, 10 November 1980

Princess Michael had been badly hurt by her Church's mishandling of the dispensation question in June 1978. Many others who have suffered in a similar fashion have ceased to be members of a seemingly uncaring Church. She could have conformed to the Church of England, the Established Church, as Lord Mountbatten suggested. Instead, she persisted in her hope that the Catholic Church would be able to find a way to solve the problem which it had helped to create in June 1978.

The Princess wrote letters on her own behalf to Monsignor Ralph Brown, Cardinal Hume and Archbishop Bruno Heim. One Church official remembered that she seemed 'always to be saying; "You would put it right for some Mrs O'Donnell around the corner. Why not for us?" '[1] To many, still suffering because of their remarriage problem, this may seem a sweeping generalization. However, it is clear that in 1980 the Catholic Church was providing ample evidence of its willingness to help people with marriage problems. There was a greater pastoral concern for such people than there was some years ago. We have seen in Chapter 5 something of the work of the marriage tribunals and of the tug-of-war between the canon lawyers, concerned with the letter of the law, and the pastoral clerics with their concern for 'people as they are'. Cardinal Hume and the Archbishop of Liverpool, Derek Worlock, have on more than one occasion asked the Vatican to take a fresh look at Catholic teaching and practice on marriage and divorce. (I would stress that these approaches had nothing to do with the particular case of Princess Michael but were concerned with Church teaching in general.) Some Catholics see this as a sign of weakness, as evidence that 'Modernism' has gained more than a foothold in the Church, but the Catholic politician Norman St John Stevas is too harsh in condemning such people as 'theologically crabbed and bigoted':[2] they are, after all, the product of years of Catholic education – in schools, from pulpits, by books of varied levels of learning.

Even on the day of the wedding in June 1978, Cardinal Hume let it be known, publicly, that he had extended an invitation to the royal couple to visit him after their marriage. This was only one of many signs that the Catholic authorities in Britain were anxious to put things right. They hoped that their task would be made easier by Prince Michael, that he would take the edge off the 'Anglican assurance' by acknowledging his wife's equal rights in the matter of the children's religious upbringing. Such an acknowledgement would make it easier for the Church to recognize the marriage *post factum*.

Meanwhile, the Princess considered that she was barred from receiving Holy Communion. She thought/that/in the eyes of the Church/she was 'living in sin' with a man whom the Church did not recognize as her husband. This is how some of the 'crabbed and bigoted' saw her case. While I was writing the book, I met a priest who had been in Vienna at the time of the wedding in June 1978. He was there as a holidaymaker; he had nothing to do with the wedding – before, during or after the sad events of June. When I said, in conversation, that I had read that Princess Michael had gone to Communion 'for the last time' on 1 July, the otherwise kind and friendly priest attacked me. 'She never did,' was his first statement. When presented with alleged evidence that she had received the Eucharist on the Saturday morning, he exclaimed; 'She shouldn't have. It was a wicked thing to do.' With this experience in mind, I have read with some caution the opinion of the Religious Affairs Correspondent of *The Times*: 'No one in authority appears to regard her "sin" as a particularly grave one. Couples in uncanonical marriages are sometimes advised to follow their consciences about Communion, but not to make too much of a fuss. The Roman Church has a way of being very tough in theory, very lenient and understanding in practice. There is a whole grey area between immoral liaisons on the one hand and cast-iron canonically sound marriage on the other, and the tendency has been growing to treat cases in the grey area on their merits.'[3] My own experience with a priest in 1984 suggests that he, for one, regarded 'her "sin" as a particularly grave one ...' I do not know whether he would have advised all concerned 'to follow their consciences about Communion'. And if some priests, somewhere, are advising some people in one way, while other priests elsewhere are advising their people otherwise, it becomes easy to understand why many Catholics believe, wrongly, that there is 'one law for the rich and another for the poor'.

While the Archbishop of Canterbury was unable to allow their wedding to take place in an Anglican Church, he had been ready to participate in a ceremony if it took place in a Catholic church in Britain. On 30 October 1978 he held a Service of Prayer and Blessing for the couple at Lambeth Palace. The Anglican Church was, in a sense, recognizing the marriage *post factum* in its own way. For the Princess this was, relatively speaking, a minor recognition, but it was important to Prince Michael and to her sense of what was publicly appropriate. For her, the main thrust had to be to obtain her own Church's recognition of her marriage.

The Princess and some of her friends would argue that the main, if not the only, reason why she wanted a Catholic validation was to enable her to get back to the sacraments again. She was, and is, a through-and-through Catholic even if, as one of her friends says, 'in a European sense'. In the matter of her marriage, she behaved, as Norman St John Stevas once wrote, 'with punctilious regard for the rules of her Church'.[4] She got an annulment of her first marriage; she accepted the Church's ruling as regards her second marriage; she did not listen to the influential but siren voice of Mountbatten when he urged that she change her religion; she did not go to Communion on or after 30 June 1978, because of her regard for the rules of the Church, until her marriage was finally recognized by her Church. She imposed this self-denial on herself in spite of a suggestion that she should go to Communion, if needs be after Mass had ended and in the privacy of the sacristy. She had, in this regard, an attitude that was, at one and the same time, more traditionally 'rigid' and better attuned to the susceptibilities of Mass-going Catholics who might well have been scandalized (in the Church sense) if they had seen her going to the altar. She also pointed out that, if she had accepted the offer of Communion in the sacristy, she might have given the impression that she had to be ashamed of receiving it or that she was not worthy to take Communion in full view of the public.

Some, among them some of Princess Michael's friends, are prepared to play the part of the Devil's Advocate against her 'Catholic' claim. They cite, for example, her statement that 'it does not matter which club you belong to'. Was this, they ask, the remark of a devout Catholic? Maybe not. But perhaps it was the remark of a not too-clever woman, under pressure of a crowded Press conference, saying the first glib thing that came into her head. Certainly her subsequent practice – attendance at Mass, refusal to get some compliant priest to give her Holy Communion, constant search for validation – shows her to be fully aware of the importance of the Catholic 'club'. If she had really meant that 'it does not matter', she would have slid easily into Anglicanism, as Mountbatten urged her to do.

Her 'friendly critics' argue that among the main motives behind her campaign for a Catholic validation were 'worldly' considerations. She wanted, they say, public recognition for its own sake. This, it is evident, is the sort of value judgement which is neither provable nor unprovable. In this regard, she is in her own form of Catch-22. If she had not sought to have her marriage put right in the eyes of her Church, her critics would have claimed that she was not a good Catholic. When, on the other hand, she campaigned for validation, they claimed that she is a publicity-seeker.

It happened, but not because she made it so, that the initial years of her campaign (1978–82) coincided with the plans for, and the actuality of, the papal visit to Great Britain. Her critics claimed that she was anxious to obtain the Church's blessing on her marriage so that she could play the role of the Catholic princess who would welcome the Pope. As a contrary argument, why did she continue the campaign into 1983, the year after the papal visit? If, in fact, the main motive for her campaign had been a desire to meet the Pope in 1982, it can be argued that she ought to have suffered an anti-Catholic reaction when she failed to gain her objective. She gave no evidence of such anti-Catholicism. Indeed, she continued to work for a recognition – as she had done before the visit.

Why, in 1983, did the Church accept her argument and give that recognition which it had denied in 1978? Some canon lawyers were prepared to argue that, in spite of the papal decision of June 1978, her marriage in Vienna was valid. They cite Canon 1098 in their favour. If they are right, it is clear the Church was not being asked to 'change its mind'. It was merely being asked to recognize the true position which had existed since 1978.

We have seen that in the 1960s the Church amended its teaching on mixed marriages (p. 55). There was, for example, an *Instruction of the Sacred Congregation for the Faith, Matrimonii Sacramentum* (18 March 1966). While acknowledging the existence of divine law, the Instruction asked that, in the new spirit of ecumenism, 'the rigour of the present legislation be mitigated – not as regards divine law but in regard to certain norms of ecclesiastical law'. By this time, Catholic thinking was in the process of making a major 'jump'. An American canonist, Father Charles Curran, wrote a learned article in which he called for 'the suppression of the promises'. He argued that ' ... it seems difficult to sustain a divine law obligation to raise all the children in the mixed marriage in the Catholic Faith' with 'the principle of religious liberty and the so-called ecumenical principle'. Curran called for the 'suppression of the promises'. If, in 1978, there had been no call for 'promises' in whatever form, there would have been no problem in getting a dispensation.

Many canon lawyers, as well as many of the clergy who took part in the Second Vatican Council, saw that the Church's 'traditional' position was no longer tenable. Ecumenism, the liberty of conscience of the non-Catholic partner, the liberty of that partner as regards his/her practice, the rights of that partner in decision-making as regards the religious upbringing of children, all these considerations threw a new light on the question of promises. In 1984 some canon lawyers, such as Curran, were prepared to argue that the demands for promises in 1978 might well have been either invalid, *ultra vires* or unnecessary. It was this sort of thinking which came to influence the Church authorities as they came under pressure from the Princess and her friends.

Why, if the Church's position was untenable, did the authorities make the demand for promises? Why did they not recognize the marriage in June 1978? We have seen that Archbishop Heim wanted the British hierarchy to issue a dispensing statement. I asked various Church officials why, in their opinion, his pleas had fallen on deaf ears. The answer, almost invariably, was that the bishops were afraid of the effects which a publication of such a dispensation would have on their people. It seems to me that this is an unhappy state of affairs, for if a dispensation was merited, the bishops' fears of their people's unwillingness to accept it reflected their own failure to teach properly and effectively. It also begs the question: 'What was different about the expected reaction in 1983 (when recognition was finally granted) and expectations in 1978?' The normal response to this legitimate question is a raising of eyebrows and a shrug of shoulders. Without saying as much, the canonists were apparently accepting that in 1978 the human beings who make up the teaching Church had got it wrong.

Some, who defend the position taken in 1978, argue that the hierarchy was anxious not to get involved in a possible constitutional-religious argument. At that time, there were strong rumours that Prince Charles was considering the Catholic Princess Marie Astrid of Luxembourg as a marriage partner. It is argued that an accommodation for Marie-Christine might have appeared as an attempt to influence the Charles-Marie Astrid 'affair'. The unhappy intervention by a Catholic peer did not help. He raised, in the Lords, the thorny problem of the constitutional position that would arise in the event of the Prince's marriage to a Catholic princess. What would happen to the Act of Succession? Would the children be brought up as Catholics? While this raised more dust than it settled, it did not make life easier for the British hierarchy. They did not want to appear to be trying to influence the Royal Family. Hence their reluctance to grant the dispensation in June 1978.

On 6 April 1979 the Prince and Princess celebrated the birth of their first child. He was born at St Mary's Hospital, Paddington. The infant and his parents met 'throngs of cameramen and reporters' on the steps of the hospital when they left on 11 April to return to Kensington Palace. The Princess told reporters that they had set no date for the baby's christening. She did not tell the Press that the birth of the child was one more reason for her campaign to get a Catholic recognition of her marriage. For if that marriage was, in Catholic eyes, invalid, it was at least arguable that, in those Catholic eyes, the child was 'illegitimate' in an ecclesiastical sense. This question is dealt with in Monsignor Brown's definitive study, *Marriage Annulment in the Catholic Church*: 'The rule about illegitimacy is that where a child is born of a union that is known to be invalid by the partners at the outset [as it may be argued was the case with the Kents' marriage in 1978], the children are indeed regarded as illegitimate. Illegitimacy is used here, of course, in the canonical sense and has no relation to civil illegitimacy.'[5]

Princess Michael did tell the assembled reporters that, 'Our child will be definitively Church of England.'[6] However, one of her priest friends was present at the christening of Frederick Michael George David Louis Windsor, which took place in the Chapel at St James's Palace in the presence of the Queen and other members of the Royal Family. Royalty-watchers noted that three of the infant's godparents were Catholics. They also pointed out that he had 'Lord' at the beginning of his style and 'Windsor' at the end. His title of 'Lord' was both an echo of a controversy of 1917 and a style which ensured him a small place in constitutional history. Titles descend in the male line: HRH Princess Anne's children are not Royal Highnesses; HRH Princess Alexandra's children are plain James and Marina Ogilvy. The style of 'Lord' is commonly held by the younger son of a duke or marquess; Prince Michael is neither. Princely sons of a king or queen are normally made dukes in adult life, and eldest sons succeed to the ducal titles (as in the case of the present Duke of Kent) – but only eldest sons in the next generation assume such titles, not other sons. In 1917, when George V gave the Royal Family the name of 'Windsor', he also laid it down that the third generation through younger sons should take the new family surname and should have the rank and precedence of younger sons of dukes. Because of that decision, Princess Michael's son was both 'Lord' and 'Windsor'.

In the early months of 1980 preparations were being made for the Queen's visit to the Vatican (October 1980) and for the papal visit to Britain planned for 1982. Princess Michael's friends hoped to use those visits as levers in their approach to the Catholic authorities. In February 1980 one of them wrote to Cardinal Hume to ask that the wedding be validated before the Queen went to the Vatican. He felt that it would be an embarrassment to the Queen if she were to visit the Pope while one of her relatives was publicly at odds with the Church. He was told that the Cardinal preferred to leave the matter in the capable hands of Monsignor Ralph Brown and that he certainly would not wish to approach the Pope through the Queen. To do so would place both of them in an impossible position.[7] The Princess's friend's comment on this response was, 'I did not suggest that the Queen should be "used" but that the matter should be settled before the Queen went to Rome.'

Perhaps the Cardinal's misinterpretation of the appeal is understandable. He was, after all, concerned with the plethora of committees that were planning the first visit to Britain by a reigning pope. This was small consolation to the Princess. In November 1980 she wrote to an influential friend: 'Have you any news about "Our Great Hope"? Now the second baby is on the way and the years drag on ...' [her stops]. Let's hope this Pope finds a way to let us marry in church at last.' There are two interesting points in this letter – apart from the evident wish to get her marriage recognized.

The use of the word 'this' in reference to Pope John Paul II is a reminder that the Pope who had refused the dispensation in June 1978 was the sick Paul VI – who was to die on 6 August 1978. Earlier in his career he had been a Vatican expert on foreign affairs. As Cardinal Montini, adviser to Pope Pius XII (1939-58), he had won the reputation of being 'soft'. Later, as Archbishop of Milan, he had worked for an understanding with the increasingly influential Italian Communist Party. As 'the Red Archbishop', he played an influential role at the Vatican Council called by Pope John XXIII (1958–63). When John XXIII died, Archbishop Montini was elected to succeed him. Some observers thought that Paul VI hoped to catholicize Russia: certainly he wanted to normalize relations with Communist governments throughout the world. Critics saw him as the Pope who supported anti-Franco guerrilla movements in Spain and left-wing parties in Latin America. He was, they argued, the Pope who looked benignly on Castro's Cuba and who allowed 'Marxist' bishops and priests to say Mass in the 'progressive' Church in America, the Third World and Asia. They noted that he never said a word publicly about the suppression of the Church in Hungary, Romania and Czechoslovakia.

Some of Princess Michael's friends had their own contacts with Paul VI; one or two of them had worked with him since 1962. Fully aware of his political views, they allege that his rejection of her appeal for a dispensation in June 1978 was clouded by his anti-aristocratic prejudice; they point out that the same Pope had refused to grant a similar dispensation for the 'mixed marriage' of the daughter of ex-King Umberto of Italy. One such friend, a priest and ex-diplomat, wrote to the Vatican on 28 June 1978 – well after the wedding – outlining the position. He has been kind enough to allow me to reproduce the reply which he received from the Secretariat of State at the Vatican.

Reverend Father,
The Secretariat of State has learned of your letter of 28 June last addressed to His Excellency Cardinal Jean Villot, relative to the reaction in certain circles in England excited by the refusal of Pope Paul VI to grant, in present conditions, the dispensation of canonical law as to a mixed marriage of Prince Michael of Kent and the Baroness Marie-Christine von Reibnitz.

The Secretariat of State is surprised to note that you seem to take into account all the arguments advanced in favour of the couple, and even the accusations of 'blindness' on the part of the Holy See, without balancing them with the serious reasons which the Supreme Pontiff had to take into consideration and which you could have presented.

I confine myself to observing to you that your remarks do not reflect the conviction of Cardinal Hume, of the bishops of England, Wales and Scotland, and of the Apostolic Delegate in London, who, you must appreciate, in such a serious affair have been consulted by the Holy See with the greatest care, to take into account all the elements of the case and also the exact context of the situation of the Church in England ....

The recipient of that letter remains dissatisfied with its general tenor. In particular he still cannot understand what is meant by certain of the key phrases in the Vatican's reply. What, exactly, is meant by 'in present conditions'? Whatever they were, it seems that it was these that forbade the Pope issuing the dispensation. What were 'the serious reasons' which the Pope had been obliged to take into account?

Reference to the advice of the Cardinal and the British bishops, as well as that of the Apostolic Delegate, and to 'the situation of the Church in England', is a classic example of the passing on of responsibility. On the one hand, the Cardinal and his advisers were free to protest that responsibility for the adverse decision lay outside their control: 'It's all down to the Vatican.' On the other hand, the Vatican claims that it has acted in compliance with the conviction of the Cardinal and the bishops ...

In what may seem to be a surprising defence of the Vatican's position, my diplomat priest points out that in June 1978 Paul VI was a very sick man; he was to die on 6 August 1978. This may have affected his reaction to the 'English problem'. My informant also points out that, while he was ill, the whole matter may have been handled by officials at the Curia; their minds may well have been more on the question of the succession to the papal throne than on what, in fairness, must have seem to be 'a little local difficulty'. It is also argued that the Curia was not aware of the impact which the marriage question would have on Britain. Neither did they seem to appreciate the amount of Press coverage which the religious question would receive.

By November 1980, when Princess Michael wrote about 'Our Great Hope', certain external factors had changed. Cardinal Koenig, for example, no longer believed in the 'window to Marxism' which had once influenced both his and Paul VI's outlook. (The latest experience in, for example, Poland, had shown that there was little prospect of the Communists and the Church arriving at much more than an uneasy form of co-existence.) The accession of the Polish Pope, John Paul II, had led to further changes of attitudes in the Curia; it is doubtful if the 'anti-aristocratic and pro-Communist' attitudes of the past found many supporters in John Paul II's entourage.

The November letter also mentions the 'new baby'. That baby (for whose canonical legitimacy she feared?) was born in St Mary's Hospital, Paddington, on 23 April 1981. Like her older brother, she was christened in the Chapel of St James's Palace, where she was named Gabriella Marina Alexandra Ophelia. Present were the Queen Mother and Princess Michael's priest friend. It may be seen as a sign of the development of the ecumenical spirit that, at this ceremony, he was robed as a priest would be at a Catholic ceremony (i.e. with cope and other vestments) and that he was asked to share in the prayers of the christening liturgy.

It may have been the birth of Lady Gabriella or, as some of Princess Michael's critics see it, it may have been the approaching papal visit which led to an increase in the intensity with which she pursued her campaign to have her marriage validated by her Church. Monsignor Ralph Brown had been charged with the task of preparing the bishops' response to her appeals. From various correspondents he learned of her practice of her religion – for example, that she went to Mass while living in the country home in Gloucestershire and that, while she went to Anglican services with Prince Michael every other Sunday, he accompanied her when she went to Mass. Neither of them, it was noted, went to Communion in the other's church, while the Princess, in deference to her conscience, did not receive Communion in the Catholic church.

In one letter Monsignor Brown noted: 'I appreciate that in town it isn't at all possible for her to go to Mass.' Many people condemn this as 'special pleading'. Not at all possible to go to Mass when living in Kensington Palace? Difficult, perhaps, if she were to go *à la Princesse*, to a High Mass at Westminster. She is, after all, a well-known and distinctive person, and she might be right in thinking that for her to appear as a Mass-going Catholic in London would have been a cause of scandal or, at least, of embarrassment to fellow-Catholics. But, as others have pointed out, there are churches other than the Cathedral in London and there are Masses other than a High Mass. It is doubtful if she would have attracted any attention if she had slipped into any one of a dozen nearby churches at, say 8 a.m. of a Sunday morning for Mass.

Monsignor Brown was aware that his questioning of her practice sounded 'rather censorious'[8] but pleaded that 'this is not the intention. In order to put together all the facts of the case for the bishops, these are the details which I know they are bound to ask ...' In April 1981 the Princess's appointment of a Catholic nanny for Lord Freddie Windsor was 'a fact with a number of implications' favourable to the Princess's campaign.[9] I am tempted to ask the authorities what 'implications' are involved, in

1984, of the appointment of a Methodist as current nanny?

In July 1981 the papal visit looming large, Cardinal Hume received several letters asking for the matter to be resolved. However, it was clear that he had little, if any, room for manoeuvre. There was, in the first place, the 'Anglican assurance' given to the Privy Council, with which Marie-Christine had publicly associated herself. There was, too, the publicity which surrounds royalty. It would have been easier, if only because of the absence of publicity, for the Church to have come to terms with the pastoral reality of some 'Mrs O'Donnell' than it was for it to have announced an agreement on the Prince and Princess Michael case. Many Catholics may well have been scandalized (in the theological sense) by such an agreement; certainly the Press would have ensured that any such agreement received the widest (and most probably the most unfavourable) publicity.

The Cardinal let it be known that the resolution of the problem would depend to some extent on how the marriage developed. It was all very well for Marie-Christine to have signed a note in which she promised to do her best about the religious upbringing of her children, but the Church was entitled in 1978, to share generally held Catholic opinion that there was little chance that she would be able to or, indeed, prepared to carry out those promises. Now, said the Church officials, in time, as the marriage went on, it was possible to see whether she was trying to 'do her best'.

Having failed with the Cardinal, the Princess's friends turned once more to the Apostolic Delegate. This correspondence lends credence to the arguments of those who link the Princess's campaign for recognition with the papal visit. One letter from the Apostolic Delegation, written in the absence of the Delegate, dealt with 'the plans for the visit of the Holy Father next year and the case of the marriage of Prince Michael'.[10] But in spite of the Cardinal's 'very serious thought' and the Apostolic Delegation's gratitude 'for your concern in sharing your views' about the papal visit and the marriage, no action resulted. The Pope came and went and the situation remained as it had been.

At least, so it must have seemed. In fact, there had been a good deal of movement. I am assured that the question was discussed by the Cardinal and the Pope as they journeyed from Gatwick Airport to London. That would have pleased the Princess: among the first issues raised at the start of this historic visit was her marriage. After the Pope had departed, the English and Welsh hierarchy at one of their meetings said, 'Put it right', to quote one who was involved in the discussions. How far was this due to papal urging? How far was it due to regret for having erred in June 1978? How far was it a modern illustration of the Lord's teaching that 'persistence will be enough' to make the lazy man get up to find loaves for a friend in need?

Little, if any, of these discussions was known to the Catholic public. It came as a shock, therefore, when on 25 July 1983 the Pope announced his recognition of the five-year marriage of Prince and Princess Michael. He sanctioned a dispensation allowing them to renew their marriage vows in the Roman Catholic Church. The majority of Catholics were 'surprised and bewildered ... by the announcement'.[11] Monsignor Brown said: 'Of course, criticism will come because of this decision. But there was criticism in 1978 from Catholics and non-Catholics when dispensation was refused.'[12] He was speaking at a Press conference where the question was raised: 'Why, if the Anglican upbringing of the children was an obstacle to the Church recognizing the marriage in 1978, is it no longer so?' In answer, he said that the Pope's decision suggested that the question of the children's upbringing was not the reason why the dispensation was refused in the first place. He was then asked to suggest the reasons for that original refusal. He had to admit that he did not know precisely why the dispensation was originally refused, nor why Rome had now agreed to validation. In defence of the Church's general position, he pointed out that there had been 174 validations in the Westminster Archdiocese in 1982, including cases where the children were not being brought up as Catholics.

The service of validation is virtually the same as the marriage ceremony. It includes the blessing of the rings, prayers, readings from Scripture and a blessing for the couple. Monsignor Brown was unwilling to say when and where the service would take place. However, Archbishop Heim's secretary told Prince and Princess Michael that the Pro-Nuncio would conduct the ceremony. He gave that statement to the Catholic Information Office, which said that, 'The service will take place shortly, probably in London, and will be conducted by Archbishop Bruno Heim, the apostolic Pro-Nuncio.'[13] The rank-conscious Princess hoped that, as a matter of protocol, the ceremony would be conducted either by the Pro-Nuncio – the Pope's representative in Britain – or by the Cardinal, the head of the Church in England and Wales.

Before she could fix a date for the validation ceremony, Princess Michael consulted the Duke of Kent and Princess Alexandra – the only two people who were let into the secret. Their diaries, like those of all the members of the 'royal firm', were already quite full. It was not easy to fit in what one friend referred to as 'an unscheduled occasion'. By the time that a mutually agreed date had been fixed, Cardinal Hume's diary had already been filled and he was away from Westminster. (This explanation will, I hope, suffice to give the lie to the cynical comment which I was given: 'Cardinal Hume insisted that the validation ceremony should take place only when he was unable to perform it.') Archbishop Heim, along with the authorities of the Westminster Archdiocese, wanted the ceremony to be as private as possible; recovering from a serious operation, he was unable to take an active role in it himself.

It was Monsignor Brown who conducted the simple, private ceremony in a private chapel in Archbishop's House, Westminster. It was he, too, who had to cope with the seventy-nine letters which arrived at Archbishop's House, mainly written by Catholic mothers, asking why their children's marriages could not be put right in the same way. In 1984 he took a good deal of pleasure in telling how forty-three of these 'irregular' marriages had been put right in less than a year, while the other thirty-six were in the process of being re-examined in the hope that the Church's pastoral concern should be shown in action. Thus some good (to many others) had come from the well-publicized validation of the Princess's marriage. The spate of criticism had, by then, died away; the happiness of the many families who had been 'regularized' was a result of the validation which had brought about that short-lived criticism. And the Princess? The more cynical noted that she had now got the recognition that she felt due to her. The obsequious noted that, 'Catholics should rejoice that the highest-ranking Catholic in the land is now in good standing with both Church and State.'[14] She herself may simply be glad that, once again, she can participate in the sacramental life of her Church, the reward of her fidelity to her religion and her determination to get what even the Church now admits are her just desserts.

As I pursued my research into this complicated marriage question, I repeatedly asked, 'Why the refusal in 1978 and the convalidation in 1983?' I have suggested earlier in this chapter some of the responses to that question. Perhaps, however, the truth lies in an answer which was given in 1985 by one of Cardinal Hume's officials: 'In 1978 there were already too many problems facing Marie-Christine and us – the annulment, the constitutional row, the "Anglican assurance" and so on. By 1983, we hoped, the fuss had died down and we felt better able to go ahead with the convalidation.' Little, if anything, here of 'serious reasons' or canon law, merely, it seems the actions and reactions of very human people.

By 1983 Monsignor Brown and other Church officials were able to consult a good deal of evidence, observing that Prince Michael had allowed Princess Michael opportunity to influence the religious upbringing of their children and that she had taken full advantage of such opportunities. Attendance at Mass on alternate Sundays was merely the outward sign of the parents' sincere attempts to provide their children with an ecumenical upbringing. The intention is that when they are old enough (say, eighteen years of age), they will be allowed to choose whether to follow their father or their mother in religious practice. Looking to the future, the plan is that Lord Frederick will attend Eton, but, I was told, 'his name is down for the only house which has a Catholic housemaster.'

Church officials stressed that whereas in 1978 the Church was faced with a theoretical situation, in 1983 it could examine a real situation. Hundreds of cases of convalidation are celebrated every year, evidence of the Church's pastoral concern and of her unwillingness to exclude Catholics from the sacramental life of the Church. Princess Michael's case was treated in exactly the same way as would have been the case of the mythical 'Mrs O'Donnell'.

Was the Catholic body outraged by the convalidation? Was there, in the theological sense, the 'scandal'? The officials patiently answering my questions reminded me of the many letters which had been received at Archbishop's House. However, I was told, the reaction was not as great as many had feared. It seems that Catholic indignation was deflected from the Kent convalidation because of the more widely publicized blessing which Father Michael Hollings gave to the non-sacramental and (in Catholic eyes) invalid marriage of David Frost to one of the Duke of Norfolk's daughters. In this instance, at least, the Princess may have reason to be grateful to the tabloid Press, which devoted many column inches to the Frost-Norfolk affair and almost ignored the convalidation.

10

The House of Kent

'Prince Michael? Which one is he?' – Viscount Linley

In 1978 Princess Michael was working on a biography of an ancestor, Elizabeth of Hungary. It is not surprising that she should be interested also in the name and origins of the family into which she married in 1978. She may have been disappointed to find that Prince Michael is only in the second generation of the modern House of Kent. His father, Prince George, was named Duke of Kent in 1934, immediately prior to his marriage to Princess Marina of Greece.

However, in her researches, Princess Michael would have found ancient and royal connections with the name Kent. There was once a kingdom of Kent which, while being of interest to historians, has also been the subject of a good deal of romanticizing mythology. Early in the fifth century, after the Romans' departure, parts of Britain came under the control of invading Picts, Jutes, Angles and Saxons. These invaders had no written language; they have left no records of their attacks or their successes. Only after the arrival of Augustine and his monks in 597 were written records produced.

Bede's *Ecclesiastical History*, a major source of information for the period following the collapse of the Roman domination of Britain, shows that the kingdom of Kent was the most stable of England's seven kingdoms, or Heptarchy. Later historians, seeking to please their royal masters in Kent, named two brothers, Hengest and Horsa, as the kingdom's founders. They were said to have led the Jute invasion of the southern part of Roman Britain. Furthermore, they were alleged descendants of the great god Woden. Bede was careful to note 'It is said ...' whenever he recorded something of which he was uncertain. He did so when recounting the tale of Hengest and Horsa. In Old English, Hengest meant 'gelding' and Horsa meant 'horse', giving some force to the arguments of modern historians that the two brothers did not exist outside the realms of Kentish-based myths.

In time, the kingdom of Kent was subsumed into the extended kingdom of Wessex which, under Alfred and later kings, became the unifying force which helped create the kingdom of England. After the Norman conquest the Grey family were created Earls of Kent. In 1710 Henry, the eleventh Earl of Kent, was named the first Duke of Kent. He died without leaving a male heir and most of the family titles died with him.

The next person to be entitled Duke of Kent was Edward Augustus, the fourth son of George III, born in Buckingham House (*sic*) on 2 November 1767. After receiving military training, he took part in the campaign in the West Indies where, in 1794, Britain was trying to seize the French-occupied islands. In 1799 the King named this fourth son Duke of Kent. Unlike two other royal dukedoms, Lancaster and Cornwall, that of Kent was not a territorial title; Edward Augustus derived no income from his dukedom as such, for there was no 'duchy' to go with it. He relied on his allowance from the Civil List – the £12,000 a year which Parliament voted to grant him in 1799.

Kent was a wild and extravagant member of a dissolute family, friendly with and a supporter of his brother the Prince Regent and future King George IV. If the latter married Mrs Fitzherbert invalidly, the Duke of Kent went further, for he maintained one Madame St Laurent as his mistress for many years, taking her with him when he was Governor of Gibraltar (1802) and when he joined the throngs in Brussels in 1815. One wonders what Princess Michael's Schwarzenberg and Windisch-Graetz relatives thought of this section of the British royal family whom they met during their diplomatic manoeuvres of the time.

Madame St Laurent ended her liaison with the Duke of Kent in 1818 because of a crisis which had its origins in the parlous state in which the Royal Family found itself. Only three of George III's sons were validly married. The Prince Regent's only child had died in 1817, by which time he was long separated from his wife, Caroline, whom he abhorred and from whom he would have no more children. Ernest, Duke of Cumberland, had married a twice-widowed German princess who was rumoured to have murdered one of her previous husbands. Ernest was described as 'vicious, incestuous, perverted, disgusting, tyrannical, reactionary and un-British.'[1] No one could have regretted that by 1817 their marriage had not been blessed with children. Nor had that of Frederick, Duke of York. Fearing that the family of George III was heading for extinction, Parliament turned to the four unmarried dukes. For many years they had been receiving incomes from the public purse. Parliament demanded a return on the investment. They would all have to get married. Only Augustus, Duke of Sussex, refused; he would not become 'unfaithful' to Lady Cecilia Underwood, his long-serving mistress.

The other three dukes complied. William, Duke of Clarence married Princess Adelaide of Saxe-Meiningen; Adolphus, Duke of Cambridge, married Princess Augusta of Hesse-Cassel; Edward, Duke of Kent prepared himself to marry Princess Victoria of Saxe-Coburg-Saalfeld, the sister of Leopold, the future King of the Belgians. Various approaches had been made during 1816 and 1817 before the death of Princess Charlotte, the Regent's daughter, deepened the crisis of the royal succession and forced the Duke of Kent to take this need into consideration. Madame St Laurent learned of the lay of the land by accident: 'The exiled pair were sitting over their Sunday breakfast table like any Darby and Joan. In answer to a casual request the Duke passed Madame the London paper; a minute later an extraordinary noise brought him to his feet. Madame was on the floor in convulsions, the newspaper lying open at an editorial recommending the Duke of Kent and his brothers to get married forthwith.'[2] In January 1818 Kent became engaged to his Princess on the promise of an additional £25,000 a year from Parliament. Madame St Laurent retired to a Paris convent to which the Duke sent emissaries asking for her forgiveness and continued friendship. She refused to receive any such reminders of 'the happy times of our intimacy'.

The Duke's wedding to Princess Victoria was held at Kew on 11 July 1818, and his elder brother William was simultaneously united to Princess Adelaide of Saxe-Meiningen. The Kents' married life was burdened by financial anxieties which were not lifted by the 'mere £6,000' by which his allowance had been raised. They complained continually that they were 'pigging it' at Kensington Palace while hoping for better things. Within two months the Duchess of Kent was pregnant.

The four royal dukes seemed to be engaged in a child-production race. In 1819 there were four royal births. In March the Clarences and the Cambridges produced children. William, Duke of Clarence, had already fathered ten healthy illegitimate children, but he was much less successful as a married man. His two weakly girls did not survive infancy. Adolphus, Duke of Cambridge, produced a son in 1819 and later two daughters.

In May came the second pair of succession babies. The younger, born on 27 May was George, son of the Duke of Cumberland. He went on to become the sad, blind King of Hanover. The Kents' daughter was born on 24 May. It seemed that she would not make a significant difference to the succession problem, for it was confidently expected that she would be only the first of a string of boys and girls who would be born to the healthy and young Duchess. The Duke, the potential father of this string of putative children, had never had a day's illness in his life. 'The best laid plans' were misplaced. The Duke of Kent died eight months after the birth of his daughter, Victoria, who as Queen was to rescue the British monarchy from its low ebb. She was also to provide sons and daughters for several of the thrones of Europe – and to further her family intertwine with that of Princess Michael's ancestors.

Princess Michael may well be interested in the Duke of Kent who fathered Queen Victoria. Like him, she lives in Kensington Palace; like him she complains of being short of money; like him she often finds herself at odds with other members of the Royal Family. She would also find that the Duke of Kent had played a significant role in the history of Freemasonry, a 'brotherhood' with which the Royal Family has had active contact since 1782 when Ernest Augustus, Duke of Cumberland and George II's fifth son was installed as Grand Master.

Princess Michael's research would also bring out the importance of Queen Victoria's second son, Alfred. Born in August 1844 at Windsor Castle, he was old enough to have played with aristocratic refugees from Austria-Hungary who arrived in Britain in 1848 (while Schwarzenberg and Windisch-Graetz were suppressing rebellions). Prince Alfred did not become Duke of Kent until 1866. Before that, his name had featured in a significantly important Greek negotiation. Otto, son of King Ludwig of Bavaria, had come to the Greek throne in 1832 when the country won its independence from the Turks. During the Crimean War he had approved a Greek invasion of Turkey, hoping to take advantage of that country's difficulties to enlarge his own borders. Russia, Britain, France and Austria had united to force the Greeks to withdraw. The unfortunate Otto was blamed for this humiliation and in 1862 ardent nationalists drove him from the throne. They then set out to look for another king. They offered the throne to Prince Alfred, by then Duke of Edinburgh. The Queen refused to allow her son to risk Otto's fate. Instead, she and her Prime Minister, Palmerston, suggested that the throne be offered to Prince William of Denmark, whose sister Alexandra had recently married the Prince of Wales. Prince William's candidature was supported by Tsar Alexander II and by Britain.

On 30 October 1863 Prince William of Denmark ascended the throne of Greece as King George I. His youngest son, Prince Andrew of Greece, married Princess Alice of Battenberg and fathered Prince Philip. Another of King George's sons, Prince Nicholas, married a Russian princess. Among their children was Princess Marina of Greece, who was to become the wife of another Duke of Kent and the mother of Prince Michael.

By this time Princess Michael would have delved deeply into the history of the British Royal Family. She would have found many proofs of that complex interweaving of royal relationships. She would have been able to follow Prince Philip's description of his relationship with the earlier Duke of Edinburgh, Prince Alfred. He was, said Prince Philip, 'my great-grandmother's brother ... my grandfather's sister's brother-in-law, my brother-in-law's grandfather and my grand-uncle's father-in-law'.[3]

Prince Alfred became Duke of Coburg in 1894 and left Britain for Germany. When he died in 1900, his title of Duke of Kent died with him. It was resurrected in 1934 for Prince George, the fourth son of King George V, who was about to marry Princess Marina of Greece. Between his birth in 1902 and 1918, the future Duke of Kent was brought up in the harsh climate prevailing in the home of his father, King George V (after 1910), and mother, Queen Mary. Their failure as parents is now a matter of record, evidenced in the lives of Edward VIII, the Duke of Windsor (who sought solace in the arms of older and married women), George VI (who was rescued by the present Queen Mother) and Prince George, described as 'gifted, wild and charming, handsome, with wavy brown hair and bright blue eyes ... the tallest and largest of the brothers ...'[4]

In May 1920 he 'kept up the best traditions of my family by passing out at Dartmouth from the bottom, the same place as I did!!!' noted an older brother, later King George VI. As he developed, Prince George showed that he had inherited Queen Mary's love of furniture and paintings, books and bibelots. The *Diaries* of 'Chips' Channon, a close friend, are full of references to the Prince's homes – in Belgrave Square and at 'The Coppins' in Buckinghamshire. Channon was impressed with his 'expensive toys, his lovely bibelots, his books, his paintings, his Meissen ...'.[5] But there was a darker side to George's character. Like his eldest brother, 'he was shallow and frivolous ...', according to Mrs Dudley Ward, one of the Prince of Wales's mistresses.[6] His allowance from the Civil List of £10,000 a year (increased to £15,000 when he married in 1934) enabled him to enjoy the social whirl in which royalty and aristocracy mingled with leading figures of the world of entertainment. In his biography of *Edwina, Countess Mountbatten of Burma*, Richard Hough describes 'the fevered fantasy world' as 'decadent, meaningless and self-indulgent ... but its worst evil was its wastefulness'.[7] Novelists such as Michael Arlen and Evelyn Waugh wrote about that world in which real persons were used as models for decadent characters such as Margot Metroland, Paul Pennyfeather, Lottie Crump, Peter Pastmaster and Lily Christine. In his memoirs, the novelist Anthony Powell described the moral tone of the 1930s as being set by the 'homintern' – the homosexual group which dominated British social life much as the Comintern controlled Communist affairs. It was, wrote Powell, a society indifferent to moral values.

Another frequenter of this *demi-monde* was the Prince of Wales. The two brothers had, in fact, a good deal in common, apart from their notable good looks and charm. Both were rebels, in a way that their other brothers were not; both seemed unable to control their wildness. There are many accounts of the unorthodox behaviour of the Prince of Wales, of his drinking habits, ill-temper and misalliances with a variety of older women. Prince George's misbehaviour and social offences were 'more extreme, more frequent, more alarming, as Wales realized'.[8] In her autobiography, the Duchess of Windsor remembered; 'I had a distinct feeling ... that the older brother was at times a little worried, even anxious, about the younger, perhaps because he was too lighthearted'.[9] Prince George had more serious defects than lightheartedness. In their study *The Windsor Story*, where Bryan and Murphy quote a series of men and women who had known both the Princes, Prince George is described as having 'a clear tinge of narcissism', 'more brains than any of the other brothers ... but a scamp. He was always in trouble with girls. Scotland Yard chased so many of them out of the country that the Palace stopped counting.'[10] One of those women, an American, seduced him into taking drugs and so corrupted him that he was led to the brink of suicide. It was the Prince of Wales who persuaded his younger brother to take a cure. He took Kent down to his country home, Fort Belvedere, staffed it with experienced attendants and made him stay there until he had conquered his addiction. Prince George remained grateful for his rescue and redemption which he knew he owed only to the Prince of Wales.

In November 1934 Prince George was created the Duke of Kent when he married Princess Marina of Greece. King George V welcomed to 'the royal firm' the newcomer whom he hoped would bring some stability to the life of his erstwhile wayward son. 'She has not a cent,' the King told Prime Minister MacDonald. But, as was pointed out, 'she had other qualities; grace and beauty and intelligence, a practical interest in the arts and a sense of style that was to inspire a generation of couturiers.'[11]

Princess Michael never knew Princess Marina, who died in 1968. She would have helped Princess Michael in her work of researching into the history of the Kent family. She would have told her of the Duke of Kent's anger when Edward VIII informed his brothers that he was going to abdicate so that he could marry Mrs Simpson. The Duke of Kent was consumed with anger. ' "Besotted." That was what the Duke of Kent called it over and over again,' Stanley Baldwin remembered. 'He is besotted on the woman ... One can't get a word of sense out of him.'[12] Princess Marina would also have been able to provide the inside story of the week-end which began with Saturday 5 December 1936, the day on which Edward VIII made up his mind to abdicate. Prime Minister Baldwin asked him not to discuss the matter with his family immediately. The government needed a few days to discuss whether the Duke of York (the future George VI), and, after him, Princess Elizabeth would be capable of restoring the tattered image of the monarchy. We have it on the authority of Dermot Morrah that: 'It was certainly considered at this time whether, by agreement among the royal family, the crown might not be settled on the Duke of Kent, the only one of the abdicating King's brothers who at that time had a son to become Prince of Wales, and so avoid laying so heavy a burden on the shoulders of any woman';[13] ' ... the draftsmen preparing the Abdication Bill at least tentatively considered what to do if his two elder brothers asked to stand aside in favour' of the Duke of Kent.[14]

Here we have one of history's 'might have beens'. If the Duke of Kent had succeeded to the throne in 1936, Prince Michael would have become the younger son of a ruling monarch. It is alleged that the Establishment rejected the idea of having the Duke of Kent, with his recent problem of drug addiction, as King.[15] There had not been time, yet, for Princess Marina to prove to be what she became, the stabilizing factor in the Duke's life.

On 1 September 1939 the Duke of Kent and his brother the Duke of Gloucester were in the House of Commons to hear Prime Minister Chamberlain inform MPs about the ultimatum that had been sent to Germany following the invasion of Poland. The Duke was, at that time, Governor-General designate of Australia. Once war was declared, he asked for a more active role in the national war effort. He had the titular rank of Air Marshal, which made it difficult for him to be employed. He solved that difficulty by resigning his rank. He became an Air Commodore and for some time performed the duties which that rank entailed, taking special interest in the welfare and comfort of the RAF at home and abroad. In the summer of 1941 he made a wide tour of inspection of the Empire training scheme in Canada. He visited the USA, where he met President Roosevelt, renewing memories of their first meeting in 1935. The President wrote to King George VI of 'the great affection' he had for the Duke. That affection was mutual. When his younger son was born on 4 July 1942 – Independence Day in the USA – it was natural that the President of the USA should be among the godfathers. That baby was christened Michael George Charles Franklin. Prince Michael was to be the first member of the royal family to have the name Charles since the departure of the ill-fated Stuarts. He was also the first to be named Franklin – in honour of his President-godfather.

Prince Michael was christened at Windsor on 4 August 1942. Three weeks later the Duke left for a further tour of inspection of RAF establishments. On Tuesday 25 August he took off from Invergordon in Scotland for Iceland. A low mist, rain and an east wind provided the very worst flying weather. After half an hour's flying, the Duke's Sunderland Flying Boat crashed into a mountain at Morven. He was killed along with his crew, only one member of which survived. If Princess Michael had ever known Princess Marina, she would have learned how the Duke's death affected King George VI. She would also have learned how it had affected the Duchess personally, with three young children to bring up. She had no place on the Civil List, and the Kent family were brought up in relative poverty, relying on the generosity of relations and money received from the sale of some of the Duke's earlier acquisitions.

The eldest of the Kent children was Prince Edward George Nicholas Paul Patrick, born in 1935. He was christened in the Chapel Royal in St James's Palace. 'All the Royal Family, including Princess Elizabeth and Margaret Rose, were at the lunch (in the Kent home) in Belgrave Square afterwards.'[16] As a sixteen-year-old, the second Duke of Kent walked with three other royal dukes (Edinburgh, Gloucester and Windsor) in the funeral procession of King George VI, at the start of the reign of Queen Elizabeth. After training at Sandhurst, he was gazetted to the Royal Scots Greys and started a twenty-one-year career as a professional soldier. He passed out in the top ten from the Staff

College and served with his regiment in Hong Kong, Germany, Cyprus and Northern Ireland. He had advanced to the rank of Lieutenant-Colonel by the time he left the Army in 1976. Then he became a busy civilian who represented the Queen on many occasions. As Vice-Chairman of the British Overseas Board, he has visited several countries, including China, to promote British technological skills and exports. He has a practical interest in and experience of electronics, which fits him to be chairman of the National Electronics Council. He is a devotee of fast cars and, by contrast, opera. He is an active sportsman, best known perhaps as the President of the All England Lawn Tennis and Croquet Club which operates the Wimbledon Championship each year.

Prince Edward followed in his father's footsteps as a Freemason. The first Duke had been Grand Master between 1939 and 1942. In 1966 the second Duke, then a major in the Royal Scots Greys, was initiated into Masonry. In June 1967 he was installed as Grand Master at the greatest masonic spectacular of all time – the 250th anniversary celebrations at the Royal Albert Hall, when Masons from all over the world attended in full regalia.

Prince Edward was seven years of age when his father was killed. He has his own memories of his tall, handsome and active father. Not so Prince Michael, born only six weeks before his father's death. Like his brother, Prince Michael became a regular officer in the Army after leaving Eton. He was gazetted to the 11th Hussars, which, like many other famous regiments, was later subjected to mergers. Prince Michael was a major in the Royal Hussars when, in 1968, he was first appointed to serve in the Ministry of Defence. In 1971 he went with his regiment to serve with the UN forces in Cyprus. Between 1974 and 1976 he was back at the Ministry of Defence where he served as an Intelligence Officer, in which post his ability as a Russian-speaker was invaluable. Between 1976 and 1978 he served with the Army Recruiting Directorate following which he returned to serve as a member of the Defence Intelligence Staff.

Like his elder brother, now the Duke of Kent, Prince Michael is a sports car and motor-racing enthusiast, an aviator (like his father), a very expert skier and a bobsleigh champion. As President of the Institute of the Motor Industry, Prince Michael plays a part in that industry's concern for standards, for programmes and for the recruitment of personnel.

Although he has shown some of the Windsor males' ill-temper and ability to be 'frosty', Prince Michael is also 'the least pushing of men', hence, perhaps, the Linley jibe. When he sported a beard, he bore a striking resemblance to his great-grandfather King Edward VII, but he lacked the jovial monarch's confidence as well as his ability to get on with women. We have seen that the then Mrs Thomas Troubridge felt sorry for him when she met him after the collapse of a friendship. Though there are signs that marriage has increased the Prince's self-confidence, Princess Michael dismisses talk about her having to 'push' her husband as so much 'rubbish'. On the contrary, she admits that, 'He has done an enormous amount for me. He has tried to teach me tolerance and patience and has taught me to take a deep breath and think before I speak – not that I always do. He is such a wise and underestimated man.' As to the gossip that she 'brought him out': 'When a man marries, he changes, he has responsibilities and when he has children he changes again. It was all in him just waiting to come out. It wasn't me. I just turned the key, he opened the door and came out into the light.'[17]

11

Princess Michael and Other 'Ladies of Kent'

'They have always been fortunate in their choice of
women' – a commentator on past and present choices
made by men of the House of Kent
'I know how to be a Princess' – HRH Princess Michael
of Kent

Younger readers who may not have known of Princess Marina
(who died in 1968) will have seen, and read of, the present
Duchess of Kent and her sister-in-law, Princess Alexandra. Most
readers will agree with the favourable judgement which appears
at the head of this page. In this chapter we shall see how Princess
Michael compares with these three 'ladies of Kent'.

Many royalty-watchers have compared her with Princess
Marina. One report noted; 'The indisputable fact remains ... that
not since the arrival of Princess Marina ... during the early 1930s,
had any royal spouse cut so great a dash in the popular
imagination. For like her late mother-in-law ... Princess Michael
of Kent possesses all the glamour and magnetism people expect of
their princesses but had, for so long, been without.'[1]

Princess Marina (born in 1906) was the youngest daughter of
Prince Nicholas of Greece and Grand Duchess Helena of Russia.
She was the sister of Princess Olga who married Prince Paul of
Yugoslavia and a first cousin of King George II of Greece and of
Prince Philip, the then future Duke of Edinburgh. She had been
brought to Britain as a prospective bride for the Prince of Wales,
but he preferred older and already-married women. It was Prince
George who fell in love with her.

Their engagement evoked a wave of national sentiment: the
wedding of the dashing thirty-two-year-old Prince to the
glamorous foreign Princess provided a welcome gleam of light
amidst the encircling gloom of the economic depression which

still gripped Britain. The Royal Family welcomed the marriage, hoping that it would prove to be the stabilizing factor so badly needed by the Prince. Their hopes were to be fulfilled in full, which helps explain the affection in which Princess Marina was held in the family.

Prince Michael is, in many respects, the antithesis of his father. 'The quiet Prince' seems to appreciate that he is the younger son of a junior branch of the Royal Family. He does not seek, or get, any of the 'perks' that people assume goes with being a member of the 'royal firm'. Princess Michael has not had to cope with any wildness or tendency to misbehaviour. On the contrary, her friends claim that/ if she has been 'Princess Pushy', her 'pushiness' has been on behalf of an over-quiet husband. It is claimed that, in this respect, she plays a role not unlike that of the present Queen Mother in regard to her husband. (When Lady Elizabeth Bowes-Lyon married the Duke of York, he was a shy, retiring, stammering younger son. It was she, more than anyone, who helped 'bring him out', who helped his confidence to grow. Her success was seen by the way in which the shy Duke matured into the much-loved King George VI.)

Reports in the Press in the 1930s, and comments in contemporary diaries, provide historians with the source material for their studies of Princess Marina. 'Chips' Channon was one such diarist. He was also a close friend of the Kent family. He thought that Princess Marina and her sister Princess Olga were 'surely the two most beautiful Princesses, if not women, in the world'. At the lying-in-state of King George VI, she 'as ever, managed to look infinitely more elegant than the others; she wore violets under her veil and her stockings if not flesh coloured were of black so thin that they seemed so'. On 19 May 1943, when she attended the service held at St Paul's to celebrate the British victory at El Alamein she was a widow but 'in black and pearl, as ever, the cynosure of all admiring eyes'.

And the praise goes on into the 1950s and after. At the Coronation of Queen Elizabeth II in 1953: 'The Duchess of Kent was fairy-like, and there was a well-bred gasp as she walked in with her children.'[2] Family photographs taken on Coronation Day show her as 'looking elegant and withdrawn', thinking perhaps of her dead husband, the new Queen's uncle, while she watched 'Princess Alexandra joking with her brothers, Prince Edward and Prince Michael, all in irrepressible high spirits'.[3] In 1967 even the Socialist Richard Crossman, taking part in the State Opening of Parliament, was driven to write of 'the elegance of the Dowager Duchess of Kent' whom he compared with the 'goofy

Duke of Gloucester, looking terrible with his very dull wife'.[4]

In a sense, Princess Michael took over where the 'Dowager Duchess' left off. Princess Marina died in 1968; Princess Michael joined 'the royal firm' in 1978. Immediately there were comparisons of the elegance, dress sense and glamour of the two. However, there were critical undertones in some of these comparisons. Princess Michael was sometimes described as 'flashy' as distinct from 'elegant'. An Establishment which had become accustomed to the ageing of the leading ladies in the Royal Family took unkindly to the introduction of this tall, good-looking foreigner. As long ago as August 1957, Lord Altrincham had gained a deal of publicity for an article he wrote for a magazine which he owned, the *National and English Review*, in which he described the Queen's entourage as 'almost without exception the "tweedy" sort'. In a subsequent article he described the Royal Family and the Court as 'not imaginative, a second-rate lot'. By 1978 little had changed – except that the participants were older. Princess Michael's glamour stood out all the more because of the relatively poor background against which she appeared. The introduction of Lady Diana Spencer into the family in 1981 changed things. The Princess of Wales brought her own freshness of ideas and of dress sense and her own glamour into royal life. In one way she was a competitor to Princess Michael; in another she provided Princess Michael with some relief, for here was another and younger glamour-princess. Princess Michael no longer stood out quite so vividly, and her glamour no longer looked quite so unroyal as it had done before Prince Charles's marriage.

Princess Michael also resembles her mother-in-law as regards tastes and friendships. Like Princess Marina, she is an accomplished linguist and has a highly developed artistic sense and a love of beautiful things. In the 1930s Princess Marina was a member of the demi-monde in which minor royals rubbed shoulders with leading figures in the world of entertainment. Singers such as Florence Mills, film stars such as Douglas Fairbanks, playwrights such as Noël Coward figure in the lists of guests at parties given by or attended by the Duke and Duchess of Kent. Princess Michael has also revealed a taste for the company of people involved in the world of entertainment, but she has been more at home in the company of the conductor Karajan and the critic Bernard Levin than in the modern counterparts of Coward and Mills. It is not surprising that the descendant of the Esterházys should have such taste: her ancestors had employed Haydn and Mozart, had their own orchestras and opera houses and, in general, were patrons of 'the arts' in the widest sense. Some, but few, of the British aristocracy have acted in a similar fashion, but the Royal Family have not been noteworthy for their support of 'culture'. 'More at home, perhaps, with Flanagan and Allen and the Crazy Gang than with Mozart,' observed one friend. Indeed, there is a national trait best described as a suspicion of things of the intellect. Even in the world of politics, the British, unlike the Europeans, seem to hold 'cleverness' as a mark against someone. In Germany, for example, Chancellors such as Adenauer and Erhard did not fear to put their doctorates before the public. In Britain, on the other hand, Prime Minister Harold Wilson seemed almost to want to hide his academic ability; he preferred to be known as 'a fervent supporter of Huddersfield Town' and the patron of the Beatles. Princess Michael's taste for the arts and theatre mark her down as 'one of those intellectuals' held in suspicion by the 'tweedy' sort surrounding the Royal Family.

It is, perhaps, too soon to compare Princess Michael and Princess Marina as mothers. Princess Marina brought up her three children in as normal a way as was possible for members of the Royal Family. Godfrey Talbot wrote of the present Duke and Duchess of Kent: 'It is a natural and uninhibited family, as indeed the Duke and his brother and sister were as children, for Princess Marina's children were attractively integrated, "mixing" as royal youngsters had never done before. Probably some of their happiest memories are of cycling round the village shops in Iver and of spending gregarious bucket and spade holidays on South Country beaches.'[5] A friend of Princess Michael who also knew Princess Marina drew my attention to the latter's influence on her children. From her, he says, they got their artistic taste, their ability at languages, their deep spirituality, their 'naturalness' and love of family. Time alone will tell whether Princess Michael will be as successful a mother. We do know, already, that she has said that, 'I want to spend as much time with the children as possible.'

If Princess Michael were able to compare notes with her late mother-in-law, she would find that they both beautified their homes. In London, Princess Marina and the Duke of Kent had a home in Belgrave Square which Channon described as 'a houseful of treasures'. A frequent visitor to their country home, Coppins, near Iver in Buckinghamshire, he was there on 1 May 1942, some three months or so before the death of the Duke: 'How *gemütlich* Coppins is, and how full of rich treasures, and gold boxes, *étuis* and pretty expensive objects always being exchanged or moved about. The Duke adores his possessions. Her, I am completely devoted to. Her loyalty, her gentle sweetness and charm, which equals her beauty and her saintly character, making her an outstanding woman.'[6] In Chapter 12 we shall see how Princess Michael has done her best, in limited circumstances, to follow Princess Marina's example as home-builder.

Those 'limited circumstances' provide another matter on which the two Princesses would have found common ground. After the wartime death of the Duke of Kent, the family did not feature in the Civil List; it had no allowance from the public purse. It is a tribute to the widowed Princess Marina that she was able to maintain her elegant appearance and bring up her children in spite of her straitened circumstances. It may seem strange that the Kents' allowance from the Civil List ended with the tragic death of the Duke, but that is how the system worked and, apparently, works. The Duke's fortune of around £150,000 was left in trust for his eldest son. Princess Marina could have claimed the widow's pension due to her from the RAF – some £398 a year, but she refused, she said at the time, to 'humiliate' herself to that extent. She sold the lease on their much-loved home in Belgrave Square along with its contents and rented out some of the land surrounding their country home. She came to 'arrangements' with a variety of clothiers, by which she was allowed to take away clothes 'on approval', only to return them once she had worn them at some function.

The Duchess was helped by Queen Mary and, later, by King George VI, both of whom were grateful for what she had done for the late Duke and, in the crisis of 1936, for the monarchy as an institution. In spite of their generosity, she and her children lived frugally: simple seaside holidays, well-worn clothes, cheap – indeed, second-hand – bicycles, these are among the memories dear to Princess Alexandra and her brothers. This, in turn, may help to explain the unostentatious way in which Princess Marina's children have continued to live.

Another and more important reason for the manner of their lives is the nature of their religious belief. In 1984 I talked to a priest who had known Princess Marina well and who has remained a close friend of her children. He spoke of the Princess's 'almost mystical spirituality ... very Russian in its way ... other worldly ...'. We have seen that Marie-Christine's mother exercised a major influence over her – partly because of her father's absence from her life; since Prince George, the Duke of Kent, died while his three children were very young, Princess Marina was the dominant influence over their children. In particular she gave them this 'very Russian' attitude towards religious and spiritual affairs. One of those closest to Prince and Princess Michael assured me that 'Prince Michael is much more deeply religious than she is ... something which Marie-Christine freely admits ... inherited from Princess Marina.' It was this deeply held other-worldly religious attitude which helped Princess Marina cope with the problems of bringing up her children in straitened circumstances.

There is a reminder of that relative poverty in a conversation which took place in 1976 between the ageing Duchess of Windsor and her life-long friend Lady Monckton. When they were discussing the Duchess's will, Lady Monckton told the Duchess, 'Princess Alexandra and the Duchess of Kent are loyal, hardworking girls, both of them, and they haven't many jewels. Unless you've made other plans, you might remember them.' The gentle request was turned down, as 'Everything is going to Prince Charles ...'[7]

Princess Michael may have been surprised at the relative poverty of her husband, but marriage into the Royal Family provided her with other problems which had nothing to do with money and which others who have married into the family have also faced.

Lady Elizabeth Bowes-Lyon, the future Queen Mother, was fully aware that marriage into the Royal Family would bring not only 'big responsibilities' but a wholesale change in the pattern of her own life. But, as we know, she agreed to marry the shy Duke of York, was welcomed into the family by King George V and went on to be a popular and supportive wife.[8] Philip of Greece experienced hostility before and immediately after his marriage to Princess Elizabeth, and the young, thrusting, ambitious and able naval officer found himself at odds with the Establishment which in 1952 surrounded the young Queen and tried to exclude him as far as was possible.[9]

Princess Marina had been more fortunate than her younger cousin, Prince Philip. King George V, who ill-treated his sons, went out of his way to make her welcome into the family. Queen Mary, who accepted her husband's dislike of her sons, also imitated him in the welcome she gave to Princess Marina in 1934. She spent many hours with the elegant twenty-eight-year-old Greek Princess, explaining to her the duties expected of the British Royal Family. In subsequent years Princess Marina and the Queen drew very close, the older lady appreciating the effect that her daughter-in-law had had on her handsome son's life.

Princess Marina repaid some of that kindness during the Abdication crisis of 1936. She joined with Queen Mary, Queen

Prince and Princess Michael of Kent, photographed in one of the drawing rooms at Kensington Palace before flying out to represent the Queen at the independence celebrations in Belize on 20 September 1981. The Princess wore a long evening dress of pure silk and jewellery of sapphires and diamonds; Prince Michael wore the uniform of the Royal Hussars – from which he retired only in March 1981.

Barnwell Manor, the house of the Gloucesters, where Prince and Princess Michael first met.

Lord Frederick with proud parents, 1979.

Prince and Princ[
Michael with their gro[
ing family: L[
Frederick and La[
Gabriella, and two b[
mountain pigmy goat[
the gardens at Net[
Lypiatt, June 1983.

A photograph taken at Nether Lypiatt for Princess Michael's 40th birthday, 15 January 1985. Pet labrador, Sponge, got into the act.

Princess Michael perfectly poised in the saddle at the Mayfield Horse Trials in East Sussex, 13 August 1983, when she presented the prizes.

The descendant of tennis champions: Princess Michael on her way to play.

Princess Michael's many public engagements: presenting the Women Mean Business Award to business woman, Mrs Luella Tills, at a ceremony in London on 14 February 1984.

At the Chelsea Flower Show, May 1984, the keen gardener felt 'at home'.

Showing the signs of strain, following the *Daily Mirror*'s attack on her father, 16 April 1985, Princess Michael on her way to the state banquet at Windsor Castle after she had recorded the TV-am interview which went out on the following morning.

At the Badminton Horse Trials a few days after the *Mirror*'s attack, Princess Michael walked happily in the crowd – unnoticed for the most part. She told well-wishers who did spot her: 'I feel great'.

Looking pale and gaunt, her hair swept severely back, Princess Michael leaving King Edward VII Hospital in Marylebone, 5 July 1985. She had entered the hospital some ten days before, suffering from nervous strain brought on by the crisis inside the Royal Family over the allegations concerning her father.

At Men's Final Day, Wimbledon, Sunday 7 July 1985, the day on which the *News of the World* carried reports linking her name with that of the Texan billionaire, Ward Hunt. She was given a standing ovation by the Centre Court crowd as she took her seat; the supportive Kent family had deliberately changed the seating arrangements so that, instead of being at the end, Princess Michael sat in the centre of the row, her husband's relatives gathered around her.

In July 1985 Prince and Princess Michael were at Monte Carlo harbour, guests of Argentinian arms' dealer, Carlos Perdomo, on whose yacht, *Jessica*, they hoped to find some rest after the recent controversies.

Elizabeth and the other women in the Royal Family in condemning the infatuation of Edward VIII with Mrs Simpson. After the Abdication she maintained her hostility. When the Kents were on holiday in the Tyrol in the summer of 1937 and Prince George wanted to see his brother, Princess Marina refused to go with him. He telephoned to tell the Duke of Windsor that he would come alone; his wife, he said, unfortunately had a previous and unbreakable engagement with her parents. Windsor told him; 'Well then, if you can't bring your wife, don't you come. Wait until she can come too.' Even when, later, King George VI suggested that Marina should go with Prince George to visit the Windsors, she refused. Prince George went alone. The Duke of Windsor wrote: 'When he showed up without Marina, the Duchess properly refused to see him, and I gave him a brotherly lecture he wouldn't soon forget.'[10] The Duke of Windsor never forgave her. He did not send a message of condolence to the widowed Duchess on the death of the brother of whom he had been particularly fond.

Princess Marina's entry into the Royal Family was not as traumatic an experience as it might have been. She was, after all, related to the family already. The daughter of Prince Nicholas of Greece, one of her aunts was Princess Andrew of Greece, the sister of Lord Mountbatten, and the mother of Prince Philip. Even more directly and immediately than Princess Michael, she was related to 'most of the royal houses of Europe'. We have an indication of that relationship in the story of the courtship of Prince Philip and Princess Elizabeth. They often used Coppins as a meeting place before their engagement, for it was sufficiently remote from London to enable them to meet in a degree of privacy. Princess Marina was very popular with the younger members of the Royal Family, as indeed, she was with the public at large. In the spring of 1944 Prince Philip discussed with her the possibility of his marrying Princess Elizabeth. After their marriage, he and the Princess were frequent visitors to Coppins, where the ubiquitous Channon was a fellow-guest in May 1948: ' ... for the dance at Coppins for the Edinburghs, who were enchanting. She was in black lace, with a large comb and mantilla, as an Infanta ... Philip ... as always extremely handsome and pleasing ... His charm is colossal, like all Mountbattens ...'.''

Princess Michael's entry into the Royal Family was not as smooth as that of Princess Marina. There was no welcoming father-in-law – Prince Michael's father had died in 1942 – or helpful mother-in-law – Princess Marina had died in 1968. Nor was Mrs Thomas Troubridge, Baroness Marie-Christine von

Reibnitz, so closely related to the family as Princess Marina; there were no immediate Mountbatten links to draw her in. Also, Marina was obviously 'fit for the job' and accepted into the extended family. Did the same family consider Mrs Troubridge 'fit for the job'? Her roots might be deep in European royal houses, her family tree might show her to be a distant cousin to Prince Michael, but to Establishment representatives of the 'tweedy' sort she was somewhat suspect.

Divorced, Catholic, of German origin and Australian education, the extrovert and intelligent Marie-Christine provided something of a 'culture shock' to the Court surrounding the Queen. One who knows the family well reports: 'They are not given to talking things out ... They would talk about shooting, the weather, a friend's marriage, the shocking behaviour of the French' but not about things intimate or cultural. Channon reports the games they played when *en famille* – building towers of matchboxes until the lot fell down. He and others tell of the 'Game', as charades is known in the family. What room was there in this family for the interior designer with an interest in history, opera, theatre and intelligent conversation?

Some people suspected that the glamorous divorcée was too obviously self-seeking with her 'off the old and on with the new' marriage. No one had levied such an accusation against Prince Michael's grandmother, Queen Mary when after the death of her fiancé, Prince Albert Victor, she married his brother, the future George V.

There was no such generous kindness towards Mrs Troubridge. She was seen as a dominant character who would overwhelm the gentler, more retiring Prince Michael. Even in 1984 some of her admiring friends considered that, in accepting his proposal of marriage, Marie-Christine was self-seeking. From Troubridge, they say, she got money and entrée into British society. From Prince Michael, they say, she got an entrée into the Royal Family. If her friends see her second marriage in this light, how much more so do those who know, or knew, less of her?

There has never been a 'self-seeking' finger pointing at the present Duchess of Kent. Katharine Worsley was born in 1933, the only daughter of a Yorkshire landowning family. Like the present Queen Mother, she took a long time before she agreed to marry into the Royal Family. Her wedding to Prince Edward, the Duke of Kent, was celebrated at York Minster on 8 June 1961 and provided opportunities for comment on the radiant beauty of the Yorkshire girl, 'the personification of the English rose'. She was described as having the 'smooth unpompous good humour and exquisite courtesy peculiar to a species of aristocrats'. It was this lack of pomposity which helped explain her popularity.

Having agreed to become a member of the family, the Duchess of Kent fully accepted the responsibilities that went with the honour. She followed the Duke abroad during his military career and at home and overseas played an active public role. She became patron of a number of organizations, being especially interested in the welfare of older people. She accepted many invitations to 'do the royal thing' – opening fêtes and buildings, shaking hands on countless occasions which are memorable to most participants but which may well become a bore to the royalty involved. Her sense of humour and her 'exquisite courtesy' save her from showing any such boredom – and from hurting the people involved in 'their' royal day. In this she has followed the model of the Queen Mother. Although she admits to being happiest in country life, she has accepted the inevitability of having to live much of her time in town.

There has been widespread concern for the Duchess's health in recent years, but Wimbledon-watchers have noted that, in spite of hospitalization and ill-health, she is a constant attender at the Lawn Tennis Championships. Here, as elsewhere, she shows that concern for everyone – the ballboys, umpires, referee and so on – and does not appear to be, in any way, self-seeking.

How does Princess Michael match up to the image projected by her sister-in-law? Some claim that, in contrast to the simple beauty and charm of 'the English rose', Princess Michael appears 'gaudy'. She wears 'diamonds as big as greengages on her fingers'[12] which reminded some observers of the 'tiara rule' invented by David Williamson, chief contributing editor of *Burke's Peerage*: '*I have a theory that the size of a tiara worn by a princess is in inverse proportion to her importance. In other words, if you see a princess with a tiara about a foot high, she's likely to be the most minor member of the most minor former ruling family. Whereas the princess with a very modest single band is probably the highest princess you could ever expect to meet.*'[13]

The Duchess of Kent seems, to the public eye, to be as shy and retiring as Princess Michael appears thrusting and ambitious. The Duchess does not claim, in speech or in writing, any 'royal' position; Princess Michael seems constantly to do so. The Duchess does not appear as a publicity-seeking guest on radio programmes such as *Desert Island Discs* or television programmes such as the once-popular chat programme chaired by Maria Aitken on which Princess Michael appeared. The Princess welcomes chances to appear thus publicly, and when she does so she provides, as it were, visible and verbal examples of the 'tiara rule'. In an off-shoulder style which is 'slightly outrageous', she seems to be eager to provide a 'sense of adventurousness'[14] which, said the reporters, was 'very different from the usual royal pattern'. Her ambition 'to make the cover of *Horse and Hound* in my own right' may be laudable but hardly in keeping with the 'exquisite courtesy' of real aristocracy. She may, indeed, be more royal than the royals but it is less than modest to state: 'I know how to be a Princess ... to give people good value for money'[15] – a boastful claim which carries an implied criticism of other princesses.

Some who know both the Duchess of Kent and Princess Michael well contrast the reluctance of the former to enter the Royal Family with the seeming haste and eagerness with which Princess Michael went ahead with her second marriage – and that in spite of the problems involving her Church. They ask, and sometimes answer, the question: 'What makes Marie-Christine run?' They are only amateur psychologists, but as her friends they are well placed to gain insight into her behaviour. They suggest that her 'pushiness' is due largely to an attempt to compensate, to herself, for the years of under-privilege, the days in that modest suburban home in Sydney when schoolfriends mocked her 'I am a baroness' claim. The Duchess of Kent, on the other hand, does not have this urgency to gain acceptability. Paradoxically, she gains wider public acceptability than the more thrusting newcomer.

The youngest of her generation of 'ladies of Kent' is Princess Alexandra. The only daughter of Princess Marina, she was the first British princess to have a normal schooling – at a boarding school in Ascot. She went to a finishing school in Paris before returning to take up a nursing course in London. On 24 April 1963 she married the Hon. Angus Ogilvy, younger son of the twelfth Earl of Ogilvie. His father had been Lord Chamberlain to Queen Elizabeth the Queen Mother for many years; his grandmother, Mabell, Countess of Airlie, had been a close friend of Queen Mary's for over fifty years. Princess Alexandra respected Angus Ogilvy's request that, after marriage, he should be allowed to remain a private person; he wanted no part in the royal 'scene', agreeing to accompany Princess Alexandra only in circumstances which would be normal in other married couples.

Princess Alexandra has been in many ways the least 'royal' of the family. She has the tall grace of her mother and the handsome looks of her father. From one or both she inherited a spontaneous zest so that she is full of fun. Brought up in an uninhibited fashion by Princess Marina, she is unaffected and has a deliciously natural manner which helps make her one of the most popular of royal personages. She combines a charming manner with an infectious enthusiasm and a willingness to work as a member of the 'royal firm'. She has often represented the Queen, particularly on overseas missions, has accepted a large number of patronages and is particularly involved in societies concerned with music and musicians. Even in these 'open' days, there is never any criticism of this princess; the public seem to appreciate her integrity, her loyal service to the throne and nation and her ability to keep a fine balance between being a working 'royal' and a private mother.

Princess Alexandra and her husband have their home in Thatched House Lodge, Richmond Park – sufficiently far from London to be 'in the country' but sufficiently convenient for Angus Ogilvy to reach his office in Old Broad Street. We have seen that Prince Michael used the Princess's home as a base from which to ride in the park while he was seeking out the then Mrs Tom Troubridge. Princess Alexandra's affection for her brother – and her innate goodness – explain her loyalty to Princess Michael through the difficult years which were to follow. In June 1978 she (like the Duke of Kent) was in Vienna for her brother's wedding: in July 1983 she (and the Duke) signed the handsome book (now lodged in the archives at Westminster Cathedral) which registered the convalidation of the marriage. It is not surprising that Princess Michael looks on Princess Alexandra as a loyal ally and close friend.

12

The Princess and Her Homes

'We hope to have bought a country house by Christmas
which is full of ghosts and will need your boundless
blessings and exorcisms' – letter from Princess Michael
from Kensington Palace, 10 November 1980

Princess Michael's interest in history has provided her with some
knowledge of the various palaces which serve, or have served, as
royal homes: Whitehall, the former royal palace with the Inigo
Jones' Banqueting Hall and its historic links with the Stuart
family, the Palace of Westminster (the Houses of Parliament),
Buckingham Palace, St James's Palace, still the 'Court' in
diplomatic terms, across a narrow road from Clarence House, now
the home of the Queen Mother, and near Marlborough House,
once the residence of the Dowager Queen Mary, now a set of
royal and governmental offices.

Buckingham Palace is both 'home' and 'shop' for the Queen,
who has other official homes at Windsor and at Holyrood in
Edinburgh. She also has two private homes at Balmoral and
Sandringham. These were purchased and developed by the astute
Prince Albert, the Consort of the Queen Victoria. From her Civil
List of some £385,000 a year, he managed to save enough to
provide the £300,000 needed to buy the estates and build these
two homes. He also bought Osborne House on the Isle of Wight
as a third private home. (Edward VII gave Osborne to the Royal
Navy when he came to the throne.)

As Mrs Tom Troubridge, Marie-Christine visited some of the
private homes of members of the Royal Family. We have seen
that she first met Prince Michael while visiting the Gloucesters in
their country home at Barnwell Manor, some five miles
south-west of Peterborough in Northamptonshire. The late Duke
of Gloucester bought the 2,000-acre estate in 1938. Barnwell is a
Tudor manor house which has the remains of the thirteenth-

century Barnwell Castle in its grounds. The present Duke of Gloucester plays an active part in the managing of his estate, driving tractors as well as handling the paperwork.

Prince Michael's brother, the Duke of Kent, has a London home at York House, part of the complex at St James's, but he also has a country home at Anmer Hall, near Sandringham. Parts of it were built in Elizabethan times but the main structure is Georgian. Princess Michael, the trained and professional designer, has a particular interest in the interiors of seventeenth- and eighteenth-century houses so that she has a special liking for this Kent home. Anmer Hall became part of the Sandringham estate in 1898, when the Prince of Wales, the future Edward VII, was the local 'squire'. The Duke of Kent bought the Hall in 1973 with its ten acres of parkland and gardens. The Duke and Duchess find that its four bedrooms and nursery wing provide them with an agreeable country retreat.

Princess Michael's sister-in-law, Princess Alexandra's home, Thatched House Lodge, stands on a knoll in the southern corner of Richmond Park and is a royal property. It started life as a keeper's house and became a hunting lodge in the royal deer park in the seventeenth century. It gets its name from the little gazebo, thatched and beehive-shaped, which stands in the grounds. The Lodge itself has the appearance of a good-sized, comfortable eighteenth-century home. Sir Robert Walpole, Prime Minister to George I and George II, when given the Rangership of Richmond Park, had the Lodge built as his residence, and he employed Sir John Soane to design it. The Princess welcomes the privacy which the lodge provides.

In 1979, shortly after they were married, Prince and Princess Michael were given a home at Kensington Palace. The urbane and civilized brick of the palace is at the top of the rising ground at the west of Hyde Park where it joins the 275 acres of Kensington Gardens. It was acquired by William III in 1689, the year after he arrived from Holland and triumphantly ousted the unpopular James II. He made it the principal residence, wanting to get away from the plague-ridden and low-lying palaces at Whitehall and St James's. Part of the building was designed by Sir Christopher Wren, and in the 1720s Kent was employed to develop other parts. William was careful to demand a relatively simple structure. He seemed determined to provide the outward sign of his opposition to all the works and pomps of Louis XIV with his palace at Versailles. His puritanical background helps to explain his determination to provide this relatively simple base from which to launch his campaign against the overweening Catholic ambitions of the French King in his baroque palace.

Between 1689 and 1760 Kensington Palace was the main royal residence. Queen Anne lived and died there; George I loved it; George II laid out Kensington Gardens and opened them to the public. With the help of Queen Caroline, he designed the many avenues, including the Broad Walk which is, today, less impressive because of the felling of the great elms which once bordered it. The present Walk is now pleasantly bordered with limes. The long Flower Walk links the Broad Walk with Rotten Row. This was originally the *Route du Roi*, the royal way to the new palace.

Kensington Palace has been described as 'almost middle class' in appearance. Certainly it has no grand entrance; it is set amongst a domestic, almost cosy, layout of stables, yards and, behind it to the west, a stretch which resembles a village green. To the north is the Orangery, designed by Wren as a sun-trap, an ordered arrangement of space and light. The palace is fronted on the west by the hedge running along the Broad Walk which contains a marble statue of Queen Victoria made by her daughter Louise. The public entrance leads past the Sunken Garden and its herbaceous borders, formal basins and lead tanks and the bleached lime tunnel.

The first floor of the palace contains a long suite of state rooms open to the public. These house some of the royal collection of pictures, furniture and tapestries, part of the richest private collection in the world. Not surprisingly, among the portraits and statues are those of some of the past inhabitants; William III is represented by a portrait and by a statue outside the south front, a gift from Kaiser William II to King Edward VII. There are portraits of Queen Anne and of her son, the Duke of Gloucester, the only survivor into boyhood of her many children, and of George I and George II, who did so much to enhance the house and gardens. Among the most beautiful rooms is the cupola room, built in 1717 to Kent's design. Its coffered vault and gilt statues in their niches provide a contrast to the pale relief over the mantelpiece, made by Rysbrack.

King George II was the last monarch to live there for any length of time. He preferred to live in the redesigned and enlarged Buckingham House at the end of the Mall. Kensington Palace then became what it remains, a home for a number of minor royals and for members of the Royal Household. A Duchess of Kent lived there and gave birth to a Princess Victoria. One of the rooms open to the public is the one in which the eighteen-year-old Victoria received the news of her accession from the Archbishop of Canterbury. Almost immediately, she moved out of the 'minor' palace to Buckingham Palace. Princess May of Teck, the future wife of George V, was born in that 'accession' room some thirty years later. In 1883 the sixteen-year-old Princess was forced to leave the Palace and go into exile in Florence, her mother having run up debts of nearly £70,000 so that Queen Victoria insisted that the family go abroad to live more quietly. Princess Michael, with her concern for money, would appreciate the hardship facing the Tecks.

Prince Philip, too, knew years of poverty. He was taken to Kensington Palace when he was just over one year old, when his mother, Princess Alice, brought him from Corfu for the wedding of her brother Lord Louis Mountbatten to the rich and glamorous Edwina Ashley. While his four sisters went to the wedding as bridesmaids, Philip was left in the nursery at Kensington Palace. He was back there again in less than a year, this time with his exiled father and mother, refugees from a junta-controlled Greece. Kensington Palace housed, at that time, Princess Alice's mother, the Dowager Marchioness of Milford Haven, the widow of His Serene Highness Prince Louis of Battenberg and mother of that Lord Louis who was to play a decisive role in Marie-Christine's life in the 1970s.

Prince Philip came to Kensington Palace again in 1947, prior to his marriage to Princess Elizabeth, to stay with his grandmother. His valet, John Dean, who went with him, was appalled at the state of the palace; 'their rooms were astonishingly poor and humble – not at all what one would expect in a palace. The floors were scrubbed boards, with rather worn rugs and the stairs creaked badly ...'[1]

When Princess Michael moved into the palace in 1979, she was merely one of a number of royal residents. The oldest was the nonagenarian Princess Alice, Countess of Athlone – a seventeen-year-old girl when her grandmother, Queen Victoria, died at Osborne in the arms of the Kaiser. Her husband was Prince Alexander of Teck, Queen Mary's younger brother, who was created the Earl of Athlone. The next oldest resident was the unobtrusive Dowager Duchess of Gloucester, widow of Prince Henry, the third son of Georve V. She was born in 1901 on Christmas Day, as was her niece, Princess Alexandra – although thirty years later. In 1972 she suffered the tragic loss of her elder son, Prince William, killed while piloting his own aircraft in a race. When the Duke of Gloucester died in 1974, he was succeeded by his younger son, Prince Richard, a professional architect. He had to give up his career when he inherited the dukedom and became responsible for running the Barnwell estate. He is one of the busiest members of the royal family and officially represents the Queen both at home and overseas. In 1972 he married a Danish girl, Birgitte van Deurs, whom he had first met while she was a student at a language school in Cambridge. The Duke and Duchess now live, with their three children, in one of the suites at Kensington Palace.

So, too, do Princess Margaret and her children, Viscount Linley and Lady Sarah Armstrong-Jones. Relations between Princess Margaret and Princess Michael are said to be 'strained'. They have not been helped by comments made by Viscount Linley, who has been publicly critical of both Prince and Princess Michael. Princess Margaret and her children live in the Clock Court of the Kensington complex, sufficiently removed from the Kents' appartments to avoid immediate contact. However, it cannot be pleasant to have such 'difficult' neighbours.

Princess Michael and her family live at Number 10, Kensington Palace. Some reporters have referred to it as 'a doll's house'. No. 10 Kensington Palace has eight bedrooms. The Nursery occupies the top floor with a bedroom for each child and the nanny, a large open area of wide passage and a room with two walls removed to make a kitchenette and eating area, a large playroom and two bathrooms. Leading off from the children's bedrooms is the roof garden, (built by Princess Michael before her daughter was born). It is often incorrectly said that this was built in defiance of the Wales's opposite, but in fact it was built before they moved to Kensington Palace.

The floor below consists of a large study which spans the width of the house, overlooking their beautiful courtyard on one side and also their private garden, a large master bedroom, their individual dressing rooms and bathrooms. The main floor is a 'piano nobile', reached by a stone double sided staircase leading to the front door, has their formal drawing room, dining room, cloakrooms, kitchen, pantry etc. The basement is the largest area, with several offices for staff, ladies-in-waiting, protection officers and another large staff room where officials dealing with functions can be received. There is also a flat for Princess Michael's Portuguese cook-housekeeper, as well as a butler's pantry, and the laundry.

Prince Michael inherited all the contents of Princess Marina's apartments at Kensington Palace, including even the chimney-pieces and door furniture. As her apartments were roughly twice the size of No.10, Prince Michael had enough furniture not only for his apartment at Kensington Palace but also for his country house. Prince George, Duke of Kent, was a known collector of furniture, pictures and *objets d'art*, a passion much encouraged by his mother Queen Mary. Queen Mary also loved this foreign Greek Princess who married her favourite son, and after his tragic death during the war, took special care of Princess Marina and even more so, her six week old son, Prince Michael. This 'special care' included leaving her and Prince Michael a fabulous Fabergé collection and a great many other of her treasures.

Princess Michael has put her own stamp on the house. She designed the drawing-room with its blue moiré walls hung with works of art, and furnished it with modern sofas set around a low, glass-topped display table, containing some of the Fabergé collection.

She runs the house with the help of a number of staff – many fewer than would have been employed by her ancestors in imperial Austria. Nor does this small army of staff have the white gloves, family uniform and powdered wigs which her ancestors were accustomed to and which Princess Michael sees when she is at Buckingham Palace.

Princess Michael in fact has a cook-housekeeper both in London and at her country house, two 'dailies', a dresser who looks after her clothes, a valet for Prince Michael (who also sees to the silver); when she entertains she calls on a regular team from Buckingham Palace who come in their time off. She has a full-time nanny and a part-time nanny, who are both also trained teachers and nurses. She has only changed nannies once when her first, a Canadian Norland trained girl, returned home after four years. As for office staff, the couple have a Private Secretary, Colonel Michael Farmer, a Personal Secretary each and a typist. Princess Michael also has two official ladies-in-waiting who deal with official correspondence and fan-mail. As well as these, there are also two protection officers in their Household Office who deal with organizing the security of their public and private lives. Then there is a full-time chauffeur, a part-time chauffeur and a gardener for the London garden.

Few people realize how many staff are needed to run what is, in fact, only a small Royal household. Nor are they aware of the expense involved, all of which has to be borne from the incomes of Prince and Princess Michael – there being no assistance provided for them from the Civil List. Prince Michael is on the boards of several City companies: he also enjoys a private income because of his inheritances from both his grandparents, his father and his mother – who knew that he would never receive a Civil List allowance and so left him the bulk of her fortune. The

Princess, too, has been a 'working' wife. She has kept her interior design company in being — although she now works only as a consultant in the company. She has several business involvements in Britain and in the United States and hopes to finish the first of her two historical biographies in the summer of 1985. Negotiations are in hand for the first of these to be made into a television series.

In April 1984 the Princess spoke of the biography of one of her ancestors, Elizabeth, The Winter Queen, on which she was working. At that time, her friendly adviser was the distinguished historian, Sir John H. Plumb. She had contracted to write this work of love in autumn 1981 and a company was engaged to handle the sales of what will be, without doubt, a book of some interest. There are all too few royal authors of royal biography. In October she was reported as having just finished what she called 'a happy chapter' and in a radio interview in January 1984 she said that she was still 'working on the book'. The book had had an interrupted history. The company that commissioned it went into liquidation and the contract was dissolved. At the same time, following a long journey in the footsteps of her heroine, Elizabeth of Bohemia, to Heidelberg, Prague and The Hague, Princess Michael was flown back to London for an emergency gall bladder operation. In the rush, somehow all her research material was mislaid. On her recovery, Princess Michael returned to The Hague in the hope of finding her papers. Before deciding to do the whole trip again, visit all the archives etc, two things happened. Her most important contact regarding the Bohemian section of the book, died in Prague, and she was offered another contract to write six articles on a subject of her own choice by a German magazine. While researching *The Winter Queen*, she became fascinated by this Jacobean princess's cultural and social influence on the countries and people over which she and her husband lived. This led her to decide to write about six princesses who became queens of another country and the influence they brought to bear on their newly adopted people, whether it was in fashion, food, interior design, gardens, the arts, their pets and in general, all the details that most history books left out. A well-known publisher and friend of the Princess was so taken with the idea that he asked her to add another six princesses and she would have a book. In return she was given the assistance of a researcher who could take some of the burden off her limited time. It is this book on the princesses which is due to be finished this summer. In the meantime, to her great relief, all the Princess's research material from her trip about *The Winter Queen* was found, so she intends to move back to this book on completion 'of the Princesses. Princess Michael very much sees her future in the field of historical biography and takes her writing extremely seriously.

In Chapter 13 we shall see that the Princess also undertakes a number of public duties. However, she points out that she is unable to accept every invitation and request because of lack of money and time. Her domestic and business interests take up an 'unroyal' amount of her time both in London and in the Kents' country home near Stroud in Gloucestershire.

At the time of their marriage in 1978, Prince Michael was still a professional soldier. He had reached the rank of major but further promotion was dependent on his serving in a command capacity in Northern Ireland. When his brother, the Duke of Kent, had commanded a squadron of armoured cars in Northern Ireland early in 1971, the news of his posting roused protesting voices. It was said that the Queen's cousin was too tempting a target for terrorists; it was alleged that the politicians had made a mistake in allowing him to become involved in a delicate situation; observers noted that, by taking part in what was almost civil war, the Duke would be the first modern Royal Highness to be in the 'firing line' since another Duke of Kent, Queen Victoria's father, fought the French in the West Indies in 1794. The upshot was that the Duke was recalled after having served in Ulster for three weeks. He was very bitter: 'The fact that I am a member of the Royal Family makes no difference whatever. I have a job to do, like anyone else in the Army.'

The War Office was not going to get itself involved in a second public controversy; there was no likelihood that Prince Michael would get a command posting to Ulster. In 1978 Lord Mountbatten, already the couple's committed friend and supporter, advised Prince Michael that he had no future in the Army. In spite of his twenty or so years of training and his experience at the Ministry of Defence and in the field, promotion would come only after a period of service in Ulster. He was not going to be allowed to serve there. As Mountbatten pointed out, this was a royal version of the Catch-22 situation. Reluctantly, Prince Michael resigned from the Army. This forced him to make a new career in industry and commerce. In 1981 he became a director of Standard Telephones and Cables and in 1982 a director of Aitken Hume Bank.

As an income-earning civilian, the Prince had to provide for his family without any assistance from the royal purse. Having been brought up at Coppins, he wanted to find a country home where he, the Princess and their children might enjoy an escape from life in London. He wanted his children to enjoy the freedom which he and his brother and sister had enjoyed with Princess Marina at Iver. Prince Charles was able to afford to buy a country home from the income he derives from the Duchy of Cornwall, which, in fact, is the legal owner of the·Prince's home, Highgrove. In 1977 the Queen helped Princess Anne to buy a home at Gatcombe Park, near Stroud in Gloucestershire, which cost £250,000. Subsequently the Queen helped her to buy an additional 600 acres to add to the 730 acres in the Gatcombe estate. Together the two estates cost the Queen about a million pounds. 'Very kind of her', Captain Mark Phillips remarked. But who was to provide the money for Prince Michael to purchase a country home? Some claim that Lord Mountbatten left him £500,000 in his will. 'Would that he had!' remarked Princess Michael who did not go on to suggest (and why should she?) the source of the £300,000 which the Prince was supposed to have paid for the Manor House, Nether Lypiatt. In fact, while the asking price was £300,000, they paid much less because most potential buyers disappeared once the owners candidly told the press that the house was haunted. As to the source of money: a friend of the family reminds me that Prince Michael has his own inheritance. 'Just the contents of the coffee table designed by Princess Michael to hold some of his Fabergé would be more than enough to cover the cost of buying their country house.'[2]

Nether Lypiatt Manor House is one of the most beautiful houses in Gloucestershire and is a listed Grade 1 residence. It has its own history as well as the more popularly accepted legends which are attached to the Manor. The right to the Manor was held by the Freame family from 1304 for thirteen generations. Around the time of the Restoration (1660) ownership passed to the female side of the family, and so to a Judge Charles Coxe of local legend. He was the son of a local gentleman farmer of Rodmarton and, in 1704 was the owner of Nether Lypiatt and the local MP. He was also the judge at the trial of a young blacksmith who was hanged for sheepstealing on 25 January 1704. Shortly after the young man's execution, Judge Coxe was found dead in the local Tradesman's Woods. One of the legends favoured by local people is that each year, on 25 January the gates of the courtyard 'burst open' and the young blacksmith's ghost rides three times around the yard on the ghost of Coxe's own white horse (to which he built a memorial which still exists). In another legend, Coxe himself is supposed to appear – on his horse – on the chestnut stairway of the house itself.

As with much of the journalistic speculation about Princess Michael, so too with the Nether Lypiatt legends, the truth is very different. The Manor was let for a very long period to tenant farmers who used only a few of the rooms and barricaded the rest. This gave the beautiful house a semi-derelict appearance which it retained until its restoration in the 1960s. It was this, says a local historian, which gave rise to the ghostly legends.

Shortly after going to live in the Manor House, Princess Michael invited the local Anglican canon and the local Catholic priest, then Father (now Canon) Tom Carter-Hayward, to visit the House to meet her and Prince Michael. As they were leaving, she asked them both to bless the house. The tabloid press were to learn about this blessing some three years after the event. In what a friend has called 'typical "gutter press" sensationalism', the traditional blessing was blown up into an 'exorcism' story and, as Canon Carter-Hayward told me, a simple house-blessing 'provided the media with an opportunity ...'[3] Not surprisingly, the press ignored the fact that Princess Michael had always had her different homes and offices blessed by a priest-friend; this is a normal custom in Catholic countries and one which is observed by Catholics and other Christians in this country, too.

There was firmer evidence of another death connected with the house. While Princess Michael was having a lawn dug up to provide room for a rose-bed, a skeleton was unearthed. This proved to be the remains of a soldier killed during the Civil War, during which John Stephens, owner of the much larger and neighbouring Lypiatt Park, took the side of Parliament. Lypiatt Park was attacked and captured by Royalist forces led by Sir Jacob Astley, and it is possible that the dead soldier was killed during this attack. (Princess Michael reported the finding of the skeleton just before she went off to the 1984 Chelsea Flower Show, where she was the guest of honour of the English Tourist Board. At this Show she saw a new yellow floribunda rose which had been named after her in 1979. She may see this as some compensation for the sometimes adverse comparisons made between her and the Duchess of Kent, 'the Yorkshire Rose'.)

One of the reasons why the Princess enjoys living at Nether Lypiatt is that it offers her the opportunity to do some gardening. As she says, 'I am, after all, a farmer's daughter', a reference to von Reibnitz's work in Silesia and Mozambique. The Princess is a very keen gardener and has almost completed the restoration of the gardens at Nether Lypiatt. In place of the walled vegetable garden she has planted a rose maze of her own design containing six thousand roses. The garden (as well as the house) was very run down when the Kents bought it. For the last three years, the gardens have been open to the public for one day a year in aid of local charities.

Nether Lypiatt also provides a chance for fishing on the Wye. Her brother, Baron Frederick, is an expert fisherman. It was he who first taught her to cast and to take an interest in fishing, a pastime which she enjoys in common with the Queen Mother. On Roy Plomley's desert island she would wish to be reminded of Nether Lypiatt and the peace of the Cotswolds by a recording of Mozart's violin concerto,' 'conducted by Karajan, who is a friend'. She explained that when they first moved into Nether Lypiatt, a tape-recording of the Karajan version of the concerto 'stuck to the machine', so that she and Prince Michael were forced to listen to it for seemingly endless hours. On her desert island she would want to remember those hours and her country home.

Another of the attractions of living at Nether Lypiatt is the local hunting. Princess Michael is a member of the Cotswold Hunt (although she has not been out with them for three years) and of the Beaufort and the Warwickshire Hunts with whom she goes out during the season. She is a very keen hunter and enjoys visiting different parts of the country to try out their hunting.

In the winter of 1983, the Princess took part in the annual point-to-point organized by the Beaufort Hunt. Of the fifty-odd starters, only twenty-odd actually came in. The Princess was ninth at the last fence when she and any riders behind her were pulled up as a horse lay stunned over the obstacle. The Princess and the other riders who had by this time caught up then decided to walk over the finishing line. Her horse was never quite sound again after this four and a half mile race and she did not want to ruin one of her precious eventers in it again. The race is run at the end of the hunting season to test the fitness of the hunters after a full season; however, as the eventing season begins when the hunting season ends, it would be unwise to take such a risk with precious eventers.

Ever the keen horsewoman, the Princess took part in the 1984 Army Horse Trials organized by the Tidworth Hunt. This Tidworth competition is eventing – i.e. Dressage, Showjumping and Cross-country – and the scores for all three disciplines are added together to decide the riders' final placings in the competition. The Princess was very successful in the Cross-country section, getting over the forty obstacles without fault, but her many faults in the Dressage section meant that she did not figure among the prize winners. Following these Trials, the *Daily Mirror* quoted the Princess as saying that she was determined to make the front cover of *Horse and Hound* 'in my own right' as a successful rider. The *Daily Mirror* was merely repeating something which she had once said in a radio interview. Today, in fact, the honest Princess admits to having 'too little talent and too many years' ever to be able to hope to emulate Princess Anne who, together with Mark Phillips and his sister, Sarah, has been very supportive of Princess Michael's efforts to develop her riding skills. She, in turn, has gratefully accepted the advice which these more experienced riders have offered.

And, in fairness to her, she applied as much effort to this end as one might expect after reading about her admitted 'ambition' in general. She rode in her first event in 1983 when she was thirty-eight years old. She has not, yet, taken part in high-class events such as the Badminton Horse Trials – although, she says, if she had taken up eventing earlier in life, this would have been her target. She explains her love for riding and for eventing in particular: 'For me, the fascination is the adrenalin running, and the challenge – particularly of the cross-country. I have trouble sleeping the night before and I shake in my shoes before I start. But when you're home safe after an exhilarating ride across country, it's a wonderful feeling.' She has been taught by Pammy Sivewright of the Talland School of Equitation, who has had to help restore the Princess's confidence after, for example, 'two crashing falls at Crookham'. In April 1985 she was riding with damaged shoulder ligaments – and against medical advice. But, as says her trainer, ' … she is determined.'[4]

From Nether Lypiatt the family go to local churches when they are in residence. Although the Princess insists that 'I shall remain a Catholic', she, Prince Michael and the children attend the Anglican and Catholic churches on alternate Sundays.

The very outspoken Princess has made no secret of her hopes for her children and the way she sees her role as their mother. She is honest enough to admit that she is 'not a natural mother. I am not good at the practical side, which I leave to my first-class nanny.' She was never 'an ardent nappy-changer' but enjoys the time she spends talking and playing with the children. She agrees that she does not spend much time with the children so that she sometimes feels 'consumed with guilt'. However, she argues that, although she does not spend a long time with them, they always have the security of knowing that she is around. In any event she claims, the important thing is not the quantity of time spent with the children but 'quality time. When I am with them, I focus, I zoom in on them. In those twenty minutes, I do believe we get an awful lot across to each other and they seem to me to be very happy, very easy children.'

Lord Frederick is a clever child: 'Imagine, he reads *The Times* to us at breakfast,' she says. Lady Ella ('very Kent but a bit more like me') appears to be 'a cool intellectual really – but full of mischief'. School reports show that both children are bright, intelligent, happy and well adjusted. They are more fortunate than some royal children: they are not pestered by the Press as are the children of senior members of the family. And Princess Michael has tried to ensure that, if they do sometimes have a 'public' image, they do not get carried away with a sense of self-importance. She has brought them to see that, as royal children, they have more responsibilities than the general run of children. She has taught them that they have to be 'that little bit more polite and take that little bit more trouble because I want them to understand quite early on that they have obligations. When they see their pictures in the paper, which they do sometimes, I say this is because you have a responsibility. You just don't get your picture in the paper because you're a good-looking child. You might see your picture in the paper because you belong to a family which has a great obligation to this country.'

In this respect she is trying to reproduce for her children 'the philosophy of life that I was brought up with. Good things happen and bad things happen, there are good people and bad people and you must just keep your head above water and go on the way you were brought up believing in and doing what you know to be right even if everything goes against you.' She hopes that her children will turn out to be like their cousins, James and Marina Ogilvy: 'They are the nicest children I know, charming, eloquent, studious ... fun, good tempered, well behaved, beautiful manners and enterprising, all-round human beings who will perceive life as a challenge and meet it with all their energy.' In this tribute to her close friend Princess Alexandra, there is also a tribute to 'the mother-in-law I never knew', for it was Princess Marina who taught Princess Alexandra and Prince Michael when they were young. Her influence is evident in the Ogilvy grandchildren, and if Princess Michael's hopes are realized, that same influence will be seen on her own children.

13

The Problem of the Civil List

'We have never asked for the Civil List, we have never
wanted the Civil List' – Princess Michael quoted in the
Daily Express, 15 January 1985

From time to time the question of royal finances becomes a topic
of public interest. It is discussed in newspaper reports and
debated in Parliament. Sometimes the matter is raised by critics of
the system such as the MP Willie Hamilton. Sometimes it is raised
by angry MPs. In December 1947, for example, the House of
Commons debated the amount that was to be allocated to Princess
Elizabeth and Prince Philip following their marriage in November
of that year. 'Chips' Channon noted in his diary: 'In the
afternoon there was a rumpus in the House of Commons and the
Royal Family had, I think, a deserved jolt ... the annuity to be
paid the Edinburghs was discussed and the Socialists were in
favour of reducing the proposed sum of £40,000. We then had
the unpleasant spectacle of the Royal Family's finances being
discussed in the House of Commons. Had they all been invited to
the wedding, this would never have happened, and the larger sum
voted immediately.'[1]

In November 1969 the question of royal finances was raised by
Prince Philip in an interview on American television. He was
asked about reports that the Royal Family were spending more
than the £475,000 annual allowance being made by the
government. His reply sparked off a controversy that went on for
several years.

We go into the red next year, which is not bad housekeeping if you
come to think of it. We've in fact kept the thing going on a budget
which was based on costs of eighteen years ago. So there have been
very considerable corners that have had to be cut, and it's beginning
to have its effects.

There's no question of we just get a lump sum and we can do what we like with it. The thing is that it's allocated for particular purposes. Now, inevitably, if nothing happens we shall either have to – I don't know, we may have to move into smaller premises, who knows?

We've closed down – well, for instance, we had a small yacht which we've had to sell, and I shall probably have to give up polo fairly soon, things like that. I'm on a different allowance anyhow, but I've also been on it for the last eighteen years.

Buckingham Palace tried to get the tapes cut before the interview went out on British television, but British journalists had been present at the original interview and to have doctored it would have been very unwise. So the interview was replayed on British television – and there was widespread comment under headings such as 'In the Red'. This was reminiscent of the furore that had broken out in 1845 when Queen Victoria had asked Peel that Parliament should grant her £150,000 to put Buckingham Palace in order. *Punch* printed a cartoon showing the Prince Consort, cap in hand and surrounded by his family, addressing the ragged poor of London:

Good people, pray take compassion on us. It is now nearly seven years since either of us have known the blessing of a comfortable residence. If you do not believe it, good people, come and see where we live at Buckingham Palace and you will be satisfied that there is no deception in our story. Such is our distress, that we should be truly grateful for the blessing of a comfortable two pair back, with commonly decent sleeping rooms for our children and domestics. With our slender means and our increasing family, we declare to you that we do not know what to do. The sum of one hundred and fifty thousand pounds will be all that will be required to make the needful alterations to our dwelling. Do, good people, bestow your charity to this little amount, and may you never live to feel the want of so small a trifle.

In 1969 comment was less forthright, but eventually it forced Prime Minister Harold Wilson to announce that a Select Committee would be set up during the next Parliament to examine the whole question of the Civil List.

The first Civil List Act was passed in 1697, when William III reigned. Parliament voted the annual sum of £600,000 to enable him to run the civil government. In 1727 George II persuaded Parliament that he would need £800,000. On the accession of George III in 1760 a new arrangement was made: the Crown handed over to the Treasury some of its lands, and in return the government took over the entire cost of running the government of the country. An annual sum, fixed at the start of each reign, was to be given to the monarch for running the Royal Family's part in the process of government. In 1777 this allowance was increased to £900,000 a year, but Queen Victoria's Civil List was set at £385,000 a year. This was a sufficiently large sum for the economy-minded Albert to save £200,000 to buy Osborne on the Isle of Wight and £300,000 to pay for the Sandringham and Balmoral estates.

Edward VII's Civil List was fixed at £470,000 a year, of which his Privy Purse, or private salary, was £110,000. It remained at this figure until 1936, when it was reduced to £410,000 as the monarch's contribution to the government policy of cutting public expenditure during the Depression. In 1952 Parliament fixed the new Queen's Civil List at £475,000, allocated, as Prince Philip said in his interview, 'for particular purposes':

		£ per annum
Class 1	Her Majesty's Privy Purse	60,000
Class II	Salaries of Her Majesty's Household	185,000
Class III	Expenses of Her Majesty's Household	121,800
Class IV	Royal Bounty, alms and special services	13,200
Class V	Supplementary provision	95,000
		£475,000

'The Privy Purse' is the historic name for the private spending by the monarch. In fact, the Queen uses this money for both 'private' and 'public' expenses. Some of it is spent on her private affairs – such as the estates at Balmoral and Sandringham. Some of it has been used to set up pension funds for employees not already covered. Some of it pays the official or public expenses of members of the Royal Family who do not get an allowance from the government.

In addition to the Queen's allowance of £475,000 a year, there were also provisions for other members of the Royal Family in 1952. Prince Philip, as we have seen, received £40,000 a year, the Queen Mother £70,000, the Duke of Gloucester £35,000 and Princess Margaret £15,000. There were also provisions for the Queen's children: princesses would receive £6,000 a year until they were twenty-one and £15,000 a year after marriage; princes, other than Prince Charles, would receive £10,000 a year until they were twenty-one and £25,000 a year after marriage.

Other 'working' members of the Royal Family – the younger members of the Gloucester and Kent families – had to rely on the money which the Queen could afford from her Class V provision.

It was agreed in 1952 that £25,000 of that allowance should be spent on paying the expenses of members of the family not otherwise provided for. The remaining £70,000 was to be set aside to build up a fund which, it was hoped, would provide against post-war inflation.

Until 1962 there was no problem; the allowance was always more than the expenditure, and by 1962 the inflation fund had built up to over £700,000. In 1962 for the first time spending was greater than £475,000 – due largely to inflation and increases in salaries of Household Staff. Each year after 1962 the family had to draw on the inflation fund. In 1970 the total spending was £1,235,000 – £760,000 more than the money provided by the Civil List. And to meet this massive deficit there was now only £30,000 left in the inflation fund. Hence Prince Philip's claim of being in the red.

The Conservatives won the election in the summer of 1970, and it was the Heath government which had to fulfil Wilson's promise of setting up a Select Committee. On 19 May 1971 the Queen sent a 'most Gracious Message' to the Commons asking for an increase in the Civil List because of the 'developments of the intervening years' since 1952. A Select Committee was set up after a Commons' Debate which showed that MPs, like the majority of the British people, knew very little about royal finances. The proceedings of the Select Committee were only the start of a public debate on the subject which still concerns an increasing number of people. The Committee met six times between 21 January and 27 July 1971 and made a thorough investigation of the official royal finances.

One of the few solid facts which emerged from the work of that Select Committee was that the money allocated in the Civil List is only a small fraction of the money spent on or by the Royal Family. There is what Robert Lacey called 'a hidden subsidy' amounting to about £3 million a year. The Department of the Environment maintains the royal palaces. In 1971–2 the Treasury set aside £385,887 for maintaining Buckingham Palace – paying for the fuel, gas, electricity and water, for maintaining the furniture and refurbishing the fabric of the building. The total cost for Windsor Castle was £377,584, with another £265,766 going on Hampton Court, £197,802 for St James's Palace and £101,104 on Holyrood house in Edinburgh. Here there was a total spending of over £900,000 a year. Today the figure is about £5 million a year.

The Ministry of Defence paid for the maintenance of the royal yacht *Britannia*, which first entered service in 1954 at a final cost to the taxpayer of £2.25 million. By 1974 the yacht had been refitted ten times. The refit of June 1974 cost £1.75 million – almost as much as she had cost in the first place. The annual running cost of the yacht rose from £29,000 in 1953–4 to over £75,000 in 1970–1, and to £2.7 million in 1982.

The Ministry of Defence also pays for the upkeep of the Queen's Flight, which consists of three light planes and two helicopters which are also used by Cabinet Ministers when necessary. In 1973 the cost of the Flight was £800,000; in 1982 it was £3 million.

British Rail pays for the maintenance of the royal train and meets other expenses of royal travel by rail – at a cost of about £36,000 a year. Other government departments make similar payments: the Post Office provides postal and telecommunication services estimated to be worth £52,000 a year, while the Treasury repays taxes paid on any goods bought for state or ceremonial purposes.

All in all, there is a hidden subsidy which the Select Committee of 1971 estimated to come to £2,932,000. Leading politicians seemed unaware of this in 1971. Jeremy Thorpe, for example, then leader of the Liberal Party, reckoned that the Commons was discussing 'fiddling little sums of money! The annual cost of the Monarchy is the same as that of the British Embassy in Paris.' This ignorance – shared by politicians and public alike – also extended to the income received from the Duchies of Lancaster and Cornwall.

George III handed over only a portion of the Crown lands to the Treasury in 1760. He held on to those lands which he owned as Duke of Lancaster. (This was a title which Henry IV retained after his accession in 1399, and since then all monarchs – male and female – have been dukes of Lancaster.) The Lancaster estates consist of coal mines, all of Lancashire's foreshore, agricultural and moor land, property in Pickering, the Strand in London and the City, in Aldershot, Bedford, Bristol and other cities and towns as well as residential property scattered throughout twelve counties. The Duchy estate is administered by a Cabinet minister, the Chancellor of the Duchy of Lancaster. He spends less than a day a week on the work of supervising Duchy affairs so that the Cabinet post is normally given by the Prime Minister to a colleague whom he wishes to have available to look after special duties. The income from the Duchy, however, is far from negligible. Between 1952 and 1974 the Queen, as Duke of Lancaster, received £3 million – and this income, like all her income, was tax free.

The Queen's tax position was revealed by the work of the Select Committee. In 1969 Norman St John Stevas, contributing to *The Monarchy and its Future*, asserted: 'It is sometimes thought that the Queen is not liable to pay income tax, but this is not the case.' In the same year the Central Office of Information published a pamphlet, *The Monarchy in Britain*, which stated that the Queen pays tax on her income from her private estates. But the Treasury informed the Select Committee that, 'The Queen is not liable to income tax or surtax and is entitled to claim repayment of any income tax suffered at source (e.g. on company dividends). She is not liable to capital gains tax.'

Until 1970 the Queen had not had to draw on any of her private income for private or public purposes. It was only when the 'inflation fund' had almost run out that there was a danger that she would have to spend some of her own money. And, as we have seen, at that point Prince Philip claimed that 'we go into the red', while the Queen and her Prime Minister, Harold Wilson, agreed to the setting up of the Select Committee with a view to increasing the allocations under the Civil List.

The Queen is the untaxed Duke of Lancaster. Her eldest son, as heir to the throne was, from the moment of birth, the Duke of Cornwall. The Duchy of Cornwall owns 26,000 acres of land in Cornwall, 100,000 acres in Devon, Dorset, Wiltshire, Berkshire and counties bordering on London. Included in the estate's property are Kennington Oval, where Surrey and England play cricket and, at the other end of the social scale, the prison at Princetown, Dartmoor. The net income from these various properties amounted in 1968 to £220,000 a year. This means that by the time he was twenty-one (1969) Prince Charles had received something like half a million pounds from the Duchy – the total income from the Duchy over the same period amounting to about £10 million.

Prince Charles, as heir to the throne, was not liable to income tax until in 1969 he decided that he would pay fifty per cent of his Duchy of Cornwall income to the Treasury and also agreed that because of the remaining income from the Duchy he would not need any provision from the Civil List. This led him to pay over about £110,000 as income tax – leaving him an after-tax income of £110,000. Since this was a voluntary decision, he could, presumably, decide not to pay tax – and so increase his income from £110,000 to something over £220,000. But even the decision to pay fifty per cent in tax made Prince Charles the most fortunate of tax-payers. If he were treated as an ordinary tax-payer, he would have to earn about £2½ million to have an after-tax income of £220,000. If on the other hand he paid the normal rates of tax on his Duchy income of £220,000 he would retain a little more than £22,000.

The Queen does not pay capital gains tax or the capital transfer taxes which have now replaced the former death duties. Balmoral was bought and rebuilt by Prince Albert from money saved out of Queen Victoria's Civil List. Sandringham was bought and improved from incomes received from the Duchies of Lancaster and Cornwall. Together they amount to about 47,000 acres – handed on intact from Victoria to Edward VII and so on to our present Queen. If the Sovereign had to pay the same death duties or, now, capital transfer taxes, these estates could never have been handed on.

What investments have recent monarchs made with surplus income? The simple answer is that no one outside the immediate family knows. The Select Committee pressed this question on the Queen's representative, Lord Cobbold, the Lord Chamberlain. He pleaded ignorance. 'The Officers of the Household, including myself, do not handle Her Majesty's private funds and are not conversant with the details of such funds. Her Majesty handles these matters herself, as did the late King and earlier Sovereigns.'[2]

This allowed wide speculation as to the size of the Queen's private fortune. A former palace spokesman, Sir Richard Colville, suggested in a letter to *The Times* that the true figure was probably about £2 million. Others suggested that the figure must be nearer £100 million. Lord Cobbold would merely state that the Queen wished it to be known that such suggestions were wildly exaggerated. This satisfied few of the members of the Select Committee. Roy Jenkins, a former Chancellor of the Exchequer and leader of the right-wing group inside the Labour Party argued: '... what we are concerned about is not the information given to us but the case we are going to be able to present to the House as a whole and to the public ... I wonder whether by going as far as that and by not being a little more precise there is not a possible danger of getting the worst of both worlds and approaching precision without really achieving it.'[3]

The staid *Financial Times* examined the work of the Committee and then claimed: ' ... the central question is, *how much is the Queen's PRIVATE income?*'[4] On Sunday 5 December the *Observer* took a similarly critical line, while the *Guardian* argued that, 'to say that the Queen's private income is irrelevant is altogether too deferential. There is a need for more openness and clarity. A constitutional monarchy needs to be democratic in form as well as in good intent.'[5]

But the furore died down and the Civil List was more than
doubled to £980,000 a year. This took account of the need to set
aside further provisions against inflation. There were also
additional and separate increases in the allowances paid to the
Queen Mother (£95,000 a year), Prince Philip (£65,000), Princess
Margaret (£35,000), the Duke of Gloucester (£45,000) and
Princess Anne (£15,000 to be increased to £35,000 after
marriage).

However, the runaway inflation which set in around 1973 made
even these generous provisions meaningless. By 1975 the Civil
List needed at least another half a million pounds if it was to stay
out of the red. In February 1975 the House of Commons
discussed yet again the question of royal finances, and once again
it was obvious that the question was being discussed 'in the dark'.
This time the unease was best expressed by Michael Stewart, a
former Foreign Secretary and, like Roy Jenkins, a leading member
of the right-wing section of the Labour Party. On 26 February he
said:

> The difficulty in discussing this question is that we do not know how
> much tax is being forgone [by] the nation. We are now living in a
> community where we are always exhorting each other to show respect
> for the law, to have some sense of national unity and to have a fair
> sharing of burdens ... The example of a Head of State who is immune
> from that part of the law that requires us to pay taxes is
> unfortunate ...
>   I am not talking about the size of the bill. I am saying that
> immunity from tax exposes the Monarchy to unnecessary criticism. I
> am saying that this way of paying for the Monarchy by granting an
> inadequate Civil List, because the Queen does not have to pay income
> tax, is slovenly and an undignified way of going about the matter.[6]

There is some indication in the most recent Civil List of the
continuing effects of inflation:

Class I	Her Majesty's Privy Purse		306,000
	from which are paid:		
	The Duke of Gloucester	83,900	
	The Duke of Kent	113,000	
	Princess Alexandra	107,000	
Class II	Salaries of Her Majesty's Household		2,330,000
Class III	Expenses of Her Majesty's Household		1,000,000
Class IV	Royal bounty, alms and special services		210,000

Other payments:

Queen Mother	306,600	
Duke of Edinburgh	171,100	
Princess Anne	106,500	
Prince Andrew	20,000	
Prince Edward	16,183	
Princess Margaret	104,500	
Princess Alice, Duchess of Gloucester	42,000	766,883
		£4,612,883

To this we should add the cost of:

Royal Flight	3,000,000	
Royal Yacht	2,700,000	
Upkeep of Buckingham Palace and Windsor	5,000,000	10,700,000
		£15,312,883

Prince Michael of Kent is the only one of the three Kents not to be 'in receipt of' an allowance from the Civil List. Fortunately, he inherited a trust fund at the time of his father's death and when he was only six weeks old. This was well invested and had become a large fund when he came of age. Prince Michael also inherited from his grandmother, Queen Mary, and from his other grandparents, Prince and Princess Nicholas of Greece. Finally, he inherited a great deal from his mother, Princess Marina, who was well aware of the fact that he would never receive a Civil List. As an army officer, Prince Michael had received the normal officer's pay; but, as a friend points out, this would not have paid for his Private Secretary or his valet, let alone allowed him to satisfy his penchant for fast cars. Since leaving the army, the Prince has become the director of several companies. Various attempts have been made to estimate his income from these City sources — some £40–50,000 a year seems to be the generally agreed figure.

From time to time there have been press reports that the Princess has expressed resentment at her husband's exclusion from the Civil List. Words such as 'unfair' and 'unjust' have been attributed to her. However, in the only interview which she has given, she was adamant that 'We don't want to be ...' on the List.[7]

Princess Michael is proud of the fact that, 'I know how to work.'[8] As evidence of her ability, she can quote the fifty or so public engagements, her work on her history books and her research for another projected book about *My 100 Favourite Rooms*. (She did not accept the commission to do this book because the cost of photography that would have been involved would have made the book too expensive.) She might also have referred to what may be described as her 'royal-public' work. She is Patron of the British Ski Federation, the Breast Cancer Research Trust, the Society of Women Artists, the British Digestive Foundation, the Royal Shakespeare Theatre Trust, the Ponies of Britain, the Arab Horse Society, the Horse Rangers Association and the Royal Society for the Prevention of Accidents' Tufty Club. Nor, as anyone knows who has seen her at work for these organizations, is she merely a sleeping figurehead. She attends functions, addresses gatherings, gives prizes and does the other work which makes her so welcome a Patron. Clearly, she would not have been invited to become Patron if she were not married to Prince Michael; no one, after all, asked Mrs Tom Troubridge to accept such positions. Clearly, too, there is a cost to being an active Patron. It would be understandable, therefore, if she and Prince Michael were to be in receipt of public money (from the Civil List) for this sort of public work.

In 1980 Princess Michael is alleged to have approached the Queen to ask that she and Prince Michael be given an allowance from the Civil List. 'The interview, reports said, was cold to the point of frigidity. The appeal fell on deaf ears. The Kents would have to fend for themselves.'[9] These reports reveal impressive ignorance of royal behaviour. No member of the Royal Family asks the Queen for anything directly; any such request would be channelled through Private Secretaries. The petitioner would only approach the Queen in person when it is already known that the answer will be in the affirmative. I am assured by people close to the officials who would have been involved if there had been any approach by the Prince and Princess that, in fact, Princess Michael has never asked or approached the Queen for any concession of any kind. I was reminded by one spokesman that only a born member of the Royal Family may be in receipt of an allowance from the Civil List; Princess Michael, knowing this, could never have dreamt of asking for an allowance for herself.

Princess Michael gives her support to a variety of charities and 'good works'. In May 1984, for example, she attended a Charity Performance at the Prince of Wales Theatre, Coventry Street, organized to provide funds for the Chiswick-based centre which houses and supports battered wives. In the same week she was at the London Coliseum for the Royal Gala Performance of the London Festival Ballet's *Onegin*. A week earlier she had been at the première of Peter Ustinov's film at the ABC cinema, Shaftesbury Avenue, which was devoted to getting funds for the United Nations' International Children's Emergency Fund (UNICEF). In March 1984 she joined the mayors of all the London boroughs in a campaign to replace diseased trees at

Queen Charlotte's College, Kensington. In June 1984 she was at the Opera House, Covent Garden, along with many stars of opera and stage to celebrate the memory of Sir Anton Dolin – and so on month after month.

Newspaper reports on the Princess's appearance at such charitable functions may be summarized in one which read: 'Simply stunning.' She has explained that, for each appearance, she takes a great deal of care – 'hair, clothes, jewellery – the lot', so that she may be seen to live up to her claim that 'I give people value for money.' She believes that if people have paid money to see, among other things, a princess, then they are entitled to see someone who lives up to whatever fairy-tale picture they have of a princess. But all this costs money – clothes, hair, travel and a lady companion – and that money has to come out of Prince Michael's private income, or from whatever money she herself may be able to earn from writing or lecturing. Most of the jewellery which she wears at public functions was left to Prince Michael by his mother, Princess Marina. Princess Michael also inherited some of the collection once owned by her grandmother, Princess Hedwig Windisch-Graetz. A knowledgeable friend of the Kent family assures me that the two collections have been conservatively estimated to be worth over two million pounds.

Members of the Royal Family who are on the Civil List receive their grant precisely to cover the expenses incurred on such charitable activities: Princess Michael has to find hers out of the family's income. Nor, contrary to popular belief, is such expenditure tax-deductible. The Inland Revenue does allow some people to claim some of their expenses against tax – self-employed people, for example, can claim expenses which they incur as a result of earning their living – but such self-employed people are not allowed to claim against tax any expenses they may incur when they are undertaking charitable and voluntary work.

Because Princess Michael does not earn an income from her charitable work, the expenses she incurs are not tax-deductible. They have to be added to the other living expenses which the family incurs. There are the staff at Kensington Palace and at Nether Lypiatt, there is the £5,000-a-year telephone bill and the postal charges (many of which are incurred in replying to 'well-wishers').

It is not surprising that Princess Michael has turned to lecturing as a means of earning a personal income. In the autumn of 1984 she gave a lecture on imperial Vienna to a conference of businessmen. Predictably it was a success. Few people can be better qualified – by family ties and by personal study – to bring home to people the society, traditions and culture of that long-ago society. Nor is it surprising that the extrovert Princess enjoyed the experience of talking to an intelligent audience. The upshot of that initial step into the world of lecturing is that she is now considering making such lectures into a profitable side line – another string to her bow. Even before the hurtful publicity to which she was exposed in 1985, Princess Michael had made it clear to her friends that she would be very particular about audience, location and subject matter, which explained why, even then, she had not accepted any of the many offers made to her. One suspects that she may be even more careful in the future.

In March 1984 ill-informed yobbos who saw her entering the jewellers Asprey's in Bond Street jeered at her. 'Kept out of the country's money' was among the printable comments they yelled.[10] If it had been true, it would have been bad enough. That it is untrue made the stupidity all the more objectionable.

14

The Princess and the Royal Family

If I had had a mother-in-law, I would not, perhaps, have made some of the mistakes I made out of ignorance' – Princess Michael, August 1984
'Princess Pushy' – *Daily Express*, 15 March 1984

Marriage into the Royal Family has almost always presented the newcomer with great difficulties. For one thing, Princess Michael had to learn to live in the the glare of publicity. 'Admittedly,' she said in 1984, 'we didn't realize that we would be so public. My husband never had been, so we didn't think that anybody would find us at all interesting. We thought we'd be able to slip in under the woodwork.'[1] Some may see this as a naïve and ingenuous claim by the foreign-born, divorced and glamorously elegant Catholic newcomer. Even her friends admit that she knew, or ought to have known, that she would be a magnetic newcomer in the 'goldfish bowl' in which the family lives.

Her advent into the family was, as we have seen, aided by Lord Mountbatten, described by some as 'surrogate father and guru' to Prince and Princess Michael of Kent. Prince Philip, too, had been a Mountbatten-backed newcomer. He could have told Princess Michael that to be backed by Lord Mountbatten was to invite critical comment from a section of the Press. The *Express* chain, for example, had maintained an anti-Mountbatten line since 1942. It warned the country in 1952 that, through 'Phil the Greek', Mountbatten had his eyes on controlling the new young Queen. Fear of Mountbatten's influence drew members of the Establishment to side with Beaverbrook; their anti-Philip attitudes and policies from 1947 to about 1960 were inspired by a desire to thwart what they saw as the danger of the throne becoming 'a Mountbatten property'. Others in the stuffy Establishment resented aspects of Mountbatten's lifestyle. He was unusually able and intelligent, a successful naval officer, popular

Viceroy of India and Chief of Defence Staff. This 'unroyal' ability was matched equally by 'unroyal' behaviour: as a friend of the high-living *demi-monde* of café society, and a flamboyant spender of his wife's great wealth, his conduct was at odds with that of the majority who formed 'the Court'.

By 1977, when Lord Mountbatten was helping to ease Mrs Thomas Troubridge into the family, much of this criticism had died down. Beaverbrook was dead, the *Express* chain less influential than it had been. Other old enemies had also died and the new 'Court' tended to take a more kindly attitude towards Mountbatten, the popular 'Uncle Dickie' to whom Prince Charles looked for guidance. But there was enough residual anti-Mountbatten feeling for it to have affected Princess Michael's chances of being readily accepted into the family and by the Court surrounding the throne.

The Princess did not improve her chances by her own well-publicized behaviour. There was her determination to carry off 'the royal bit' well: 'Why should I not?' she blazed angrily. 'I know how to be a princess.' She does indeed.[2]

But if she is, for some, 'Princess Pushy', for others she is the 'constant complainant'. 'I come very, very low in the pecking order,' she has said. When in this mood she has been known to 'hold her hand low, almost to the floor. 'I am here, I must not be thought ever to be trying to push my way up.'[3] Her critics argue that her behaviour has been at variance with her claim that she does not seek to 'push my way up'. One of her admiring friends argues that she has been 'Princess Pushy' only on behalf of her shy and retiring husband, that in this regard she has taken on the sort of role which the Queen Mother played in the development of the late King George VI. But even this friend admitted that, 'She has a German attitude towards rank; she has to be acknowledged.' Such a comment ignores the fact that Princess Michael has less German blood than any of our own Royal Family; her mother is half-Hungarian and half-Austrian; her Silesian father had a Russian mother. Prince Michael, by comparison, is more German, as even his Greek mother was of German origins.

We have seen that Lord Mountbatten played a major role in the lives of Prince and Princess Michael before and after their engagement. Shortly before the Queen was asked to give her official permission for the marriage, Mountbatten went to see her to tell her something about the ancestry of the potential newcomer. He rather overplayed his part which led the Queen to remark that, 'She sounds much too grand for us.' Mountbatten told some of his close friends this story – against himself – and of the Queen's other (now oft-quoted) remark that Marie-Christine was 'more royal than the royals.' There is no truth in the report that, having seen her 'in action' as a member of the 'royal firm', the Queen described Princess Michael as 'more royal than the royals'. A newspaper report featuring that 'quote' also described how, at Windsor Castle, the Queen curtsied when Princess Michael entered a room, while Prince Charles bowed as if to a superior.[4] There was no reporter present in the castle when this 'royal acknowledgement' was supposed to have taken place. Perhaps there is a royal 'mole' who talks to the royalty-watching reporters? Perhaps this is just one more example of newspapers inventing royal stories, secure in the knowledge that the family can take little if any action against such dishonesty.

Almost all newspapers have used, at one time or another, the story that the Queen refers to Princess Michael as 'Our Val'. Certainly we know that members of the Family use their *Private Eye* names in comic reference to one another. This capacity for self-mockery may be seen as one of the family's saving graces. It preserves its members from taking their public persons too seriously.

It is possible to see the use of the nickname 'Our Val' as a comic reference to the 'more royal than royal' manner of Princess Michael. Stunningly glamorous, strikingly tall, naturally blonde, she may well justify comparison with the Valkyries of Norse myth. If it was right to describe a young Philip of Greece as 'a dashing Viking', it is surely in order to see Princess Michael as a latter-day version of one of Odin's handmaidens. We do not know who, if any, she would wish to choose as the warriors who are to be slain in battle. Her list of such 'about to be slain' would make interesting reading.

Discussions with various people close to the Palace and with friends of Princess Michael confirm the truth that, inside the Royal Family, she is known as 'MC'. Her personal writing-paper carries the initials embossed one beneath the other, the 'M' being surmounted by a small crown. The notion that members of the Royal Family would use the term 'Our Val' is dismissed laughingly – along with the notion that, even if they had done so, they would have gossiped to prying journalists about it.

The Queen has, in her own 'career', been a most assiduous 'professional'. Both in Britain and abroad, she has never been slow to let people know when she feels that things have gone even slightly amiss. It is worth noting, therefore, her approval for the thorough, professional way in which Princess Michael has 'worked'.

Some journalists have reported that the Queen probably found Princess Michael 'too talkative and a bit flashy'. There is no solid evidence that this is so, although one may well believe that the Queen might not have welcomed Princess Michael's acknowledgement in May 1984 that, fresh from a flight from America, she was 'still a bit blotto' even before attending a party with Peter Ustinov.

In May 1984, the Queen was supposed to have been angered by Prince Michael's too close friendship with Peter de Savary, the millionaire financier. Prince Michael had gone to a rum-punch extravaganza at the St James's Club in London to publicize the development, by de Savary, of a St James's Club in Antigua. Photographs appeared of Prince Michael with a live python draped around him. 'The Queen was not amused by this circus act.'[5] Many reporters wrongly decided that Princess Michael must have been part of this event. In fact, she did not attend the launching of the Antigua club. It is true that she did launch de Savary's America's Cup boats, *Victory* and *Victory 83*. But de Savary was over-optimistic when, in May 1984, he told the Press that the Kents would be with him at the grand opening of his new Club in Antigua in January 1985. A spokesman for the Kents informed the Press; 'I'd no idea of such an invitation.' And, in July 1984, de Savary himself sadly admitted, 'I don't think Prince and Princess Michael will be coming. I don't think it's their scene ...'

The Press have described Princess Michael as 'the most amusing and amenable of royals'.[6] This is a far cry from the Queen's own understanding of her royal role. Elizabeth II has remained, even in a more relaxed later period, conscious of the need for her to remain formal and dignified, her main role being the maintenance of the royal mystique. As one of her staff has said: 'We don't exist to divert or convert people. We Are.' However, the Queen appreciates the public call for the monarchy to show other than formal and dignified faces. She has always approved of the geniality, outspokenness and informality of Prince Philip. She could do no other than admire the Queen Mother's ability to maintain an air of informality which seems to invite the public to draw near. She has welcomed the public adulation of Princess Diana and has sought to protect her from an over-intrusive Press. So she is not annoyed by the description of Princess Michael as 'amusing' and 'amenable'. For the Queen sees her extended family as making a team of individuals whose diverse personalities help to make the Monarchy more appealing to different ages, sexes, classes and interest groups.

But if she enjoys the approval of the Queen, Princess Michael remains at loggerheads with Princess Margaret. A close friend told me that 'She can't stand her', leaving me uncertain as to which Princess was the subject and which the object of that sentence. Perhaps Princess Margaret compared the royal welcome to the divorcée in 1977 with the way in which the family had treated Peter Townsend, whom she wanted to marry after he had obtained his divorce two decades earlier. Perhaps she has been upset by the success of the Kent marriage, compared with the failure of her own marriage to Lord Snowdon. It cannot have helped matters that her divorce came through as the Kents were planning the announcement of their engagement. It may be that Princess Margaret resents the attention which Princess Michael gets from a generaly favourable Press, compared to her own bad Press.

For reasons best known to herself, Princess Margaret made it known that she was bitterly opposed to the introduction of a Catholic into the Royal Family. In this she shared a hostility which was also expressed by the then Lord Chamberlain and other members of the Court 'establishment'. It may be that this bigotry has continued to colour Princess Margaret's attitude towards her cousin-in-law. If so, it has been yet one more reason for the coldness which has developed over the last twenty years between Princess Margaret and the Queen. There may be some truth in the allegations that the Queen has not always welcomed Princess Michael's extrovert behaviour; there is no doubt that she resented the adverse publicity which Princess Margaret earned before and after her divorce from Lord Snowdon. The unfortunate men friends, the over-publicized holidays, the lack of 'royal' acceptance of various public responsibilities, all these and more helped create a gulf between the two royal sisters. And, in a sense, Princess Michael was caught up in their estranging process.

Princess Margaret's attitude must be seen as the background to the several jibes which her son, Viscount Linley, has made at the expense of Prince and Princess Michael. Soon after their engagement, Linley asked: 'Prince Michael? Which one is he?' On reflection this may be seen as the 'clever-clever' remark of a brash young man. On the other hand it was much more likely a remark born of ignorance. When he met Princess Michael at the family get-together at Windsor Castle at Christmas 1978, he asked her what relation Prince Michael was to Princess Alexandra!

In November 1983 Linley was twenty-two and youthful inexperience could no longer be claimed for his behaviour when interviewed on behalf of an ephemeral magazine editor by one of his society friends. He was asked to name, among other things, the gift which he would make to his worst enemy. 'Dinner with Princess Michael', he answered. The Press rang Princess Michael's office to ask for her reactions to this remark. She put out a statement saying that she did not believe that Linley said such a thing and that she was extremely fond of him. As she told one of her friends, this was done to save Linley's face. He, on the other hand, when asked by the Press what he meant by his remark, did not take the opportunity to say that it was meant as a joke or that he took it back. He simply giggled and let everyone know that he thought it rather funny. A few weeks later, at Christmas 1983, Linley approached Princess Michael as if nothing had happened. She asked him not to speak to her, and she has not spoken to him since — because he has never apologized.

Initially, at least, Princess Michael enjoyed a much happier relationship with Prince Charles: he took the Kents to the opera, an indication of a common interest in classical music: both by his public condemnation of some aspects of modern architecture and by his work for various conservation groups, Prince Charles provided evidence of his interest in historic artefacts and of good design — things dear to the heart of the Princess. However, this relationship came under great strain in the aftermath of the *Mirror*'s attack on von Reibnitz and, by implication and name, on Princess Michael. That attack appeared on Tuesday, 16 April. Only two weeks later, the *Mirror*'s publisher, Robert Maxwell, was the host at an occasion when paratroopers of Prince Charles's regiment were doing a demonstration jump into the gardens of Kensington Palace. The world press saw charming pictures of little Prince William and his father and alongside them, none other than Robert Maxwell, with his hand on Prince Charles's back and shaking his hand in front of television. This cut Princess Michael to the heart that the person whom she admired most in the Royal Family, namely Prince Charles, should be seen apparently fraternizing with someone who had just so grievously hurt her. It is for this reason that she cancelled her attendance at any family occasion this last summer.

In the light of subsequent events linking Prince Michael and his Gloucester cousins, one might have expected to find that they had always been close to one another. After all, Prince William was born shortly before Prince Michael and Prince Richard in 1944; all three of them had been at Eton together. However, I am reliably informed that, when they were children, the Kents and the Gloucesters were not very congenial to one another. There are well-meaning and charitable reports that when Prince William died in an air crash in 1972, Prince Richard turned to Prince Michael for help and advice. As a close friend of theirs wrote to me; 'Alas, there is no truth in that at all.' Indeed, Marie-Christine, when still Mrs Tom Troubridge was more friendly with the Gloucesters than was Prince Michael. She and Tom Troubridge were regular guests of Prince William's at Barnwell Manor, the Gloucester's country home. We have seen that she first met Prince Michael at a week-end party at Barnwell Manor – Prince Michael having been invited, I am told, merely as 'a spare young man'.

Prince Richard, Duke of Gloucester since his father's death in 1974, has a foreign-born wife. In 1972 he married Miss Birgitte van Deurs, the daughter of a Danish lawyer. Again, one might have thought that the foreign-born Duchess and Princess Michael might have become friends. However, they see little of each other, because, apart from being foreign, they have little in common. They are very different in character and outlook and dedicate themselves to different activities and interests.

Relationships with the Gloucesters form an unfortunate postscript to the *Mirror*'s 'SS-Gestapo' stories concerning Princess Michael's father. Some two weeks after the story had appeared, the Duke and Duchess of Gloucester were due to attend a function for OXFAM at the Royal Albert Hall and be seen with Robert Maxwell in the Royal Box. When Prince Michael heard of this he tried to dissuade them from either going or having anything to do with Robert Maxwell's attendance at the function.

Princess Michael admires Princess Anne enormously, particularly her equestrian achievements – which she knows she can never emulate. She was grateful for Princess Anne's presence at the wedding in Vienna in June-July 1978, which was due to the affection which the Princess had and has for Prince Michael who, she thought, was getting a 'raw deal' from the family at large.

We are so used to seeing the members of the Royal Family 'on duty' that we may forget that they, too, have private lives. They have their close friends whom they entertain and by whom they are entertained. These friends are drawn from a fairly restricted circle to whom the gossip columnists of the popular dailies pay a good deal of attention – not always flattering.

Princess Michael herself makes the point that this closed society resents her foreignness. She appreciates that some of these people say, 'Why did he have to look abroad for a wife?' 'We wish he had chosen one of our girls.' She sympathizes with this chauvinism: 'I accept that I wasn't perhaps the most ideal choice.' She knows, too, that her Roman Catholic faith has been something of a stumbling block, with one member of the stoutly Anglican Royal Family refusing to speak to her 'until she had changed her religion'.

One member of the closed society in which Princess Michael now moves is Lord Dudley. In the early 1950s he was one of 'the Princess Margaret set'. In 1984 he wrote and taped a satirical ode to Her Royal Highness Princess Michael of Kent. Written and delivered in the spirit of the suggestive ode to *Eskimo Nell*, the turn drew attention to her foreign background, her social ambitions and royal aspirations. Written to amuse Princess Margaret and her 'set', it was first read out at a dinner party given by a leading publisher. Several of his guests found it so disgusting that they left the room. Prince Michael got his hands on a copy of the material which Lord Dudley had had printed and handed around to his friends, and which had gained circulation in London and in international circles. Prince Michael went to see one of Britain's leading libel lawyers who arranged a settlement under which Lord Dudley had to write what I have heard described as 'an extremely grovelling apology' for what the lawyer described as the worst libel he had read. One unfortunate result of this furore was that London 'society' was split down the middle with the supporters of Princess Margaret on one side and Princess Michael's on the other. Prince Michael refused to let his wife see a copy of the material because it was so ugly in tone and content. She may well wonder, when she now meets members of her 'society', which ones once laughed and still remember that hurtful attack.

15

The Princess and the Public

'She had the studio audience in the palm of her hand. You could feel a kind of mass adoration towards her. She was very frank and unpompous.' – Maria Aitken, who interviewed Princess Michael on her television show, *Private Lives*, 3 May 1984

In 1978 Lord Mountbatten told Prince and Princess Michael that it would take five years for the Princess to become accepted. Accepted by whom? By other members of the Royal Family? By the aristocracy? By the general public? We do not know how Lord Mountbatten would have answered these questions. We do know, however, that he was wise in the ways of royalty and of the problems that other newcomers had experienced.

We have seen that Princess Michael experienced a variety of receptions inside the 'domestic circle' of the Royal Family and in that upper-class society which surrounds the family. We have seen how even her friends talk of her 'German-like consideration for rank. She has to be acknowledged,' ignoring the fact that she is only one-quarter German. Did Lord Mountbatten expect that she would tone down this tendency? Or did he expect that she would learn from her 'mistakes' in this regard, that she would become less 'pushy' and so more acceptable?

Lord Mountbatten may have had a wider public in mind when talking of 'acceptance', for he could speak with experience of Britain's resentment of royal foreigners – in his own case, but also in that of his father, as far back as the First World War: Mountbatten had seen, in 1914, how the Press could make or break reputations. Perhaps, in 1978, he was warning Princess Michael that, if she wanted to gain acceptance from the British public, she would need to have an eye for what the Press said about her.

This leads to the question: 'How do we, the public, get our

knowledge about members of the Royal Family?' A minority may have gained an impression of Princess Michael from meeting her at some function or other. Others may have seen her on television or heard her on a radio programme such as *Desert Island Discs*. But the impressions gained during a fleeting visit or from television and radio will tend, usually, only to confirm already-held opinions; it is the daily and weekly Press which are the most important opinion-formers. The Press may also help to form opinion by *not* reporting certain things. Thus, for example, in 1935-6 the British Press did *not* tell the public about the relationship between the Prince of Wales (later Edward VIII) and the divorcée Mrs Simpson, persuaded into silence by Lord Beaverbrook.

Does the modern Press maintain a similar discreet silence about today's public figures? Would today's newspapers be as reticent as their predecessors were about, for example, Lloyd George's sexual proclivities? We might like to think that we have a 'free Press' which 'tells all, fully and frankly'. The truth, however, seems otherwise. Only after the enforced resignation of Cecil Parkinson did we learn that many reporters had long been aware of his affair with his secretary. There had been salacious hints at this relationship in *Private Eye* and in a news-sheet which circulates among MPs, but the *Eye* had named the wrong minister in its references to 'goings-on in the Cabinet' while the news-sheet's reports were not available to a wider public. So perhaps today's Press is still as reluctant to 'tell all' as was the Press of 1910 and 1936.

The newspapers can help form our opinion of a member of the Royal Family by the way in which they present their information. There are, for example, the adjectives used about the Princess of Wales: demure, shy, modest, glamorous and 'English'. The Princess enjoys 'a good Press', and the public responds by giving her its affection. Others who have this Press-inspired relationship with the public include the Queen Mother, the Duchess of Kent and Princess Alexandra. On the other hand, there are members of the family who get 'a bad Press': Princess Margaret and Prince Andrew.

The Press first brought Marie-Christine before the public at the time of her engagement to Prince Michael. Since then she has had a remarkably high public profile. In part, this is obviously due to the fact that she is now a member of the most written-about and most photographed family in the world. However, the wife of Prince Michael of Kent could easily have been a relatively unknown member of the 'royal firm'. If she is better known and more widely quoted than, say, the Duchess of Gloucester, the reason has to be found in her own character.

We have seen that Prince Michael receives nothing from the Civil List and that he has few regular royal duties. Princess Michael could, therefore, have lived much like the wives of his business associates – although, like other minor royals, she would have had the pleasure of Christmases at Windsor and summers at Balmoral and other family gatherings at Sandringham. But Princess Michael was unwilling, perhaps unable, to accept such an anonymous role.

Some people close to both Prince and Princess Michael point out that, at the time of their marriage, Lord Mountbatten was among their main supporters and advisers. It was Mountbatten who best understood that, since Prince Michael could not continue with his career in the Army, it was essential for him to develop a higher profile so that he might be better placed to be invited to join the various Boards which Mountbatten had in mind for him. Prince Michael would have to give up the relatively anonymous role that his position in the royal pecking order had almost forced on him. Mountbatten advised him to develop a public image of a hard-working member of the Family 'firm'. And the astute Mountbatten, say some of the Kents' friends, saw Princess Michael as a more than useful means of achieving just that high profile and better public image. Indeed, one such friend writes that 'as many see it, Mountbatten ... used Princess Michael to achieve what he wanted for Prince Michael.'

And, as we have seen, the Press welcomed the appearance of this newcomer on the royal scene. Physically imposing, the six-foot-tall and blonde foreign-born lady seemed more a princess than anyone else in the Royal Family – at least before the appearance of Lady Diana Spencer. Nor was she the sort of princess who might seek to shrink from view. She had married a royal prince and was clearly determined to enjoy her new status. But, as with Prince Michael, there seemed all too little for her to do: the Palace asked very little of her; there were very few invitations to undertake royal duties; there were no foreign tours, none of the 'walkabouts' that bring some members of the family before the public eye.

So/Princess Michael carved out her own special role. When she was interviewed for the World Service programme *Outlook*, she admitted that she was 'ambitious in a way that English people do not seem to be'. We may never know how much of this 'drive' was due to her mother's early teaching. ('No child of mine fails an exam'), how much to a Mountbatten-like determination to show the world that, she could succeed. So, she told listeners to *Outlook*, 'I like a challenge; it makes me try harder.'

In January 1985 the Princess gave an interview timed to appear on her fortieth birthday. In this she brought up the question of ambition and success. 'I think ambition is a very good thing. Without ambition, you don't get anywhere. If you don't want to succeed, you're not going to succeed. Should success fall into your lap like a ripe apple from a tree? I think you have got to climb the tree and shake that tree. I believe in work – I'm a worker bee and not a Queen bee who sits and waits for everyone else to bring the honey. The sweet smell of success doesn't exist unless you have worked for it.'

That fortieth birthday interview was merely the latest in a long line of interviews, for, as some of her critics noted, 'she talks a great deal to the Press ... too anxious to occupy the centre stage. Her quotes always appeared exaggerated, theatrical ...' There was, said her critics, something un-royal about the overt ambition, the seemingly constant references to money, along with her claims that she was anxious to earn more. If it were suggested to her that such detailing of income, expenditure and effort was not what the public expected of a princess, she replied, ' ... I don't terribly care any more about asking anyone's opinions.' On the contrary, she claimed on her fortieth birthday: 'I have understood what is required of me, I am prepared to play my role within its limitations and restrictions but I must be allowed, and I know I shall be allowed and encouraged, to develop that artistic side in me which is bursting to get out. It may not be good but it has got to be allowed to happen.' She then went on to explain how, to boost family income, she hoped to finish her first book in July. Originally, she explained, she had set out to write the story of Elizabeth of Bohemia (The Winter Queen). By January 1984 it had evolved into accounts of twelve princesses who left their own countries for marriage and to become Queens of other countries where they ruled. As Queens they had a great deal of influence in their new countries and the aims of the book is to examine the social and general changes they brought with them. 'I am not sure that it's going to be great but it's going to be the first effort. Probably as a first effort it will have far too much spotlight on it and not be allowed to sink as most people's first books are allowed to do. But I hope very much that my book will be a best-seller, that there will be a television series from the book and so on. I don't consider it pie in the sky. I don't see why, if I work hard at this book, I shouldn't have the reward. It may go wrong. But even if I get terrible reviews, I shall cry all the way to the bank,' she laughed.

In May 1984 there was a MORI poll which examined the public's perception of 'royal ladies'. People were asked to say which of them was, for example, the most glamorous, most liked, most understanding and so on. It came as no great surprise that the well-reported Princess of Wales was voted the most glamorous (in the opinion of fifty-seven per cent of those questioned). It is a reflection of the 'good Press' received by Princess Michael that she came second, with twenty-seven per cent of the vote. She was second, too, as 'the most attractive (thirteen per cent) to the Princess of Wales (sixty-four per cent). However, she received a 'nil' vote in response to the question: 'Which is the most understanding?' while she was nearly on a par with Princess Margaret in answers to the question: 'Which is the most unpopular?' (At first sight, then, it seems that Lord Mountbatten was over-optimistic in his expectation that 'it would take five years ...'.)

An examination of the MORI poll shows that Princess Michael was more popular with women (thirty-five per cent) than with men (eighteen per cent) and that she was more popular with older than with younger people. Are older people more perceptive than the young? How far are their opinions of the Princess influenced by their own memories of the hardship of war, by their appreciation of her struggle for recognition and by her 'pushiness' on behalf of Prince Michael? How far are the younger generation influenced by the sniping in *Private Eye*, or the Press judgement that Princess Michael is a 'fashion trail-blazer' if in a 'slightly outrageous style with a sense of adventure'?

'Every schoolboy knows' – or at least ought to know – that Princess Michael is a cat-lover. In January 1984 the reading public was told that she was 'heartbroken' by the death of her pedigree Burmese cat. Some of her critics saw in such Press comments yet another example of Princess Michael's publicity-seeking. The truth is that the cat disappeared on the day on which Princess Michael opened her garden at Nether Lypiatt to the Red Cross for the first time. As the cat liked travelling in cars, she put an advertisement in the local paper, just in case the cat had climbed into someone's car, been driven away, let out – and been unable to find its way home. Two weeks later it was found dead at the bottom of the road near the Manor House. It was the owner of the local paper shop who told the local press about this and a local journalist who drew the attention of the national Press. It was not, in fact, Princess Michael who told the newspapers. Nor, in February 1984, was it Princess Michael who informed the Press that she had two Burmese kittens. Her office had contacted a breeder to ask if he had any kittens for sale; it was the breeder who told the Press that she had picked up the kittens – and so helped to ensure that cameramen were waiting outside her door to photograph her arrival home with the kittens.

In January 1984, Princess Michael was a guest on Roy Plomley's programme, *Desert Island Discs*. When asked what object she would take if she were to be a castaway, she chose one of her cats. Plomley refused to allow the presence of anything animate: the Princess and he had a jokingly 'serious' discussion about the severity of the 'rules' and the wishes of the castaway. It was all done in a very bantering and jokey manner – as was evident to those who heard the programme or have listened to a recording. However, some critics insisted on pointing up the friendly exchange as 'a serious disagreement'. This tendency to seek any stick with which to metaphorically beat the Princess was also revealed by the 'otter story' which appeared in May 1984. The report was that she had obtained a trained otter to sing 'Happy Birthday' at her three-year-old daughter's birthday party. This was only part of the truth: a neighbour in Gloucestershire has a trained otter which is taken around the country to fêtes and other public gatherings to raise money for the World Wildlife Fund. This neighbour offered to bring her otter to Lady Ella's birthday party as a surprise treat. The owner had trained the animal to sing 'Happy Birthday' – which it did.

British newspapers have, in general, given Princess Michael a 'good Press'. There are reports of the three hundred or so engagements which she keeps each year, many for deserving charities – some, as in the case of the Refuge for Battered Wives, for relatively unglamorous ones. In reports and in photographs she is presented as 'smiling', 'glamorous', 'attractive' and 'outgoing'. This generally favourable impression was confirmed, for television-watchers, by her appearance on the show *Private Lives* in May 1984. She came over as a very honest person, admitting that she considered herself to have been very lucky to have been able to wear, as her first dresses, Audrey Hepburn's 'discards'. She described herself as 'a basket person' and told of the basket which she had had made while on honeymoon in Kashmir. In this favourite basket she regularly carried a camera, a tape-measure, a hairbrush and comb and a pair of dark glasses 'to avoid being bothered in the supermarket'. In this and other parts of the programme, she gave the impression of having a sense of humour, of being able to laugh at herself and of being very much a normal woman as distinct from some royal 'figurine'. Maria Aitken, who chaired the programme, spoke of her as being 'very frank and unpompous'. People who watched the programme described her as 'informal' and 'warm'.

The Princess was reported, in March 1984, as having 'nagging doubts about herself – particularly that she is not wanted by the British people'.[1] At the time of her fortieth birthday she seemed to have acquired a calmer, perhaps more mature attitude to her position: 'Even with hindsight I can't say what I wish I'd done or not done, at any one point, although I made a lot of mistakes. Now, I'm more tolerant ... and I get less fussed.' One of her eminent clerical friends and supporters commented at this time that she had been too forceful a character when she first entered the Royal Family and that, surely inadvertently, she had sometimes hurt the Queen. But, he went on, she is now much less assertive – perhaps, he added, because she is more assured and understands that she is accepted by the people: perhaps she does not have to try to 'push' as hard as she had once felt essential.

And there the book might have ended, with perhaps a reference to Lord Mountbatten's prophecy about her 'acceptance' in the process of being realized. However, as the world now knows, the Princess became the subject of unwelcome headlines and media attention with the launching of the stories about her father's wartime record. Headlines such as 'Princess's father was in SS and Gestapo' appeared above reports which, by their half-truths, innuendoes and allegations showed the Press indulging in the character-assassination of her father and linking the Princess with him in a 'guilt by association' tactic.

A researcher, Philip Hall, had got his hands on some material in Germany which could show that von Reibnitz had been part of the murderous clique which had conquered Europe and set out to exterminate the Jews and other opponents. He offered the story to the *News of the World*, part of the Murdoch group of newspapers. They decided not to use it: instead the story went to the *Daily Mirror*, part of the Maxwell group. The journalist who wrote the story telephoned Kensington Palace on Monday (15 April) to warn the Princess's Private Secretary that the story would be appearing in Tuesday's paper. He warned the Private Secretary that the editorial would be as much an attack on Princess Michael as on her father. And so it turned out.

We have already seen why the Princess did not know anything about her father's Nazi past. On the contrary, she had been brought up with the knowledge that her mother and father had been tried by the SS in 1944. The story of this trial had been repeatedly told to her by old family servants, who were still alive and living in Austria in retirement. She knew that her mother stood for two weeks (although eight months' pregnant with Marie-Christine) on public trial in the centre of the town where her family had been lords of the manor for hundreds of years. To these loyal people, it was this which they remembered of the war – because it was something which had touched them the most. As for Marie-Christine; because she was aware of the fact that her father had been tried by the SS, it had never occurred to her that he had in any way been a part of their activities, even in an honorary capacity.

The Berlin Documents' Centre, from which Hall had obtained his material, contacted Prince and Princess Michael's office to say how greatly they were embarrassed. The spokesman for the Centre explained that the material had been twisted so that it could be used against Princess Michael. They volunteered to send, immediately, copies of everything that Hall had received so that Princess Michael would know what had been made available to the researcher. This material took two days to arrive and a further three days to be correctly translated by lawyers and experts in the field of Nazi procedures. In all, a week or so elapsed before Princess Michael was in a position to produce the evidence which cleared her father's name.

Meanwhile, life went on; there was, for example, the State Visit to Britain of the President of Malawai, Dr Hastings Banda. On the evening of the day on which the *Mirror* headlined the SS-Gestapo story, there was a State Banquet at Windsor Castle in Dr Banda's honour. Princess Michael sent a message asking if she could be allowed to absent herself from this occasion; she was told 'No', and, greatly distressed, she went to the banquet. By then, as we now know, she had been interviewed for the TV-am programme, against the advice of Downing Street and the Palace.

She decided to 'go public' because shortly before she left for Windsor Castle she saw the BBC Six O'Clock News programme, in which eighteen minutes of the half hour's broadcast consisted of old film cuttings of Nazi atrocities, SS handling of Jews, appalling pictures of gold being extracted from teeth, mountains of corpses, what the Allies found when they opened Auschwitz and other camps, Jews being pushed into ovens and people being herded into cattle trucks. All the while, to Princess Michael's horror, her face was shown in the corner of the screen. It is this BBC News broadcast which has most upset her about the whole sorry episode of April 1985. The BBC was careful not to say that *she* had done any of these things: Princess Michael was only too conscious of what some people might infer from the implication of having her face on the screen while the horrors of the Nazi past were recalled.

Having seen this Six O'Clock News programme, she decided to give a television interview, in spite of the Palace statement that no interviews would be given. Timothy Aitken was one who urged her to do so, and she agreed with him that a statement from her was essential. Prince Michael is a board member of Aitken Hume which is connected indirectly to TV-am through Aitken Telecommunications and the Aitken family interests. He arrived at Kensington Palace as the interview was being recorded: he was not at all happy about it taking place, but after he had seen the BBC News, he told Aitken to go ahead with the entire interview. He and Princess Michael then quickly changed and went to Windsor where Michael Shea (the Queen's Press Secretary) asked if it was true that she had given the interview despite their instructions to the contrary. She said it was true, and that the interview would appear on the following morning (Wednesday, 17 April). She explained that the interview was pre-recorded because she would have found it impossible – after the State Banquet plus the shocks she had endured throughout Tuesday – to have gone to the study for a live programme on the Wednesday morning.

The Princess appeared pale and tired but very composed and she dealt with the questions put by Nick Owen. She explained that she had known nothing of her father's past: ' ... I don't consider myself a stupid person, to be quite frank with you, because things like that always come out. And for me to live trembling, fearing that such a knowledge would come out, would be very stupid ... if I had known, I would have made it known not only to my husband, not only to his family, but I would have been in a position to put the news out then and there so that it's not something that comes as a blow later on ...'

She explained that, after reading the *Mirror* story, she had rung her mother in Australia to say, 'Guess what they are trying to pin on me now?' Her mother's reply was, 'I am afraid that it is true.' Princess Michael told how she made a second telephone call – to her brother in Canberra, Australia. It was he who told her that he found out about their father's record only after von Reibnitz's death, when he had had to go through family papers. Among these, fortunately, he had discovered the documents concerning von Reibnitz's de-Nazification to which reference has already been made. He promised to send the document to London so that Princess Michael might publish it. Unfortunately, when it arrived, it was found to be only a certified copy. It was then that

Princess Michael started the frantic search in Germany, through lawyers and the kind assistance of the British Ambassador in Bonn and various British Consuls, to get the original.

Princess Michael then told Nick Owen that she had then 'phoned her stepmother and her half-sister (from her father's first marriage) and found that even 'people as close as that didn't know' about von Reibnitz's past. Admitting to being shell-shocked, she accepted that it was 'perfectly natural' for people to try to 'visit the sins of the father on his daughter'. When asked how she would feel about future public engagements, she admitted, 'I don't know what I shall feel ... I shall simply have to live with it. What the public's perception of me will be I simply don't know. I wasn't alive when it all happened. I hope they will judge me on my own performance, on what I am and what I stand for ...'

In fact, but only to a limited extent, she had already received some intimation of people's perception of her in the wake of the *Mirror* story and the BBC News broadcast. She recalls that, at Windsor Castle, and before anyone had seen her own interview, many people went out of their way to try to comfort her. In particular, she told a friend of Mrs Thatcher's great kindness and the warm sympathy of the Queen Mother.

I am grateful to the friend who told me how Lord Thorneycroft met the Labour MP, Eric Heffer, shortly after he had seen the TV-am interview. Heffer, he reported, was crying – perhaps in sympathy with the Princess. The MP was to issue a public statement during the day in which he complained that the tabloid Press had been guilty of the very crimes for which the world had once condemned the rulers of the Third Reich – character assassination and arguing that people were guilty by association with someone undesirable.

It is now clear that, because of the interview on the Wednesday morning, the heat was taken out of the situation: Princess Michael's decision to ignore the promptings of the Palace had saved the day, not only for her personally, but for the Royal Family collectively.

By Thursday of that fateful week, the pendulum had swung firmly in Princess Michael's favour. Serious researchers had already provided some of the evidence which would show that von Reibnitz was merely a 'minor' Nazi and had never been other than an honorary member of the SS, whose uniform he had never worn. From Australia came the news that the documentary evidence was on its way which would offer definitive proof that the *Mirror* had got it all wrong. In addition, and perhaps independently of such arguments, the public had decided that there was something radically wrong about trying to put her father's alleged crimes onto the shoulders of the Princess. A series of public opinion polls – one even commissioned by the *Mirror* – proved that some ninety-five per cent now held Princess Michael in as high esteem as they had ever done. As to the 'missing' five per cent? They held her in even higher esteem!

On Sunday 21 April Princess Michael went to Badminton to watch the Whitbread Horse Trials Championship. As she got out of her car, there was a burst of cheering and of applause that seemed, she later told a friend, to go on and on and to get warmer and warmer. This, she said, she found most encouraging.

Within a few days the Palace had received, translated and authenticated the findings of the Bavarian court. Von Reibnitz was seen to have been a 'minor' member of the Nazi Party; there had never been any truth in the *Mirror* story.

The tabloid Press lost interest in the Princess – at least for the time being. Perhaps, like Simon Freeman of the *Sunday Times*, the tabloids resented the fact that ' ... it was hard to find anyone with a truly nasty word to say about her. Strong-willed. Forceful. Charming. Interested in ordinary people ... It was equally hard to find anyone with grudges based on personal knowledge ...'[2] Perhaps we are meant to sympathize with the dirt-seeking investigative journalist who has sought in vain. However, readers (and Princess Michael) were warned that 'the pendulum could swing back ...' and it seems that some sections of the media will take a delight in helping to give it an anti-Princess Michael swing.

The preceding paragraph was written in June 1985. In July 1985 the 'anti-Princess Michael swing' was undertaken by Murdoch's *News of the World* which employed, it claimed, ten reporters and two cameramen to provide the material for its story concerning the alleged friendship between Princess Michael and a Texas businessman. The Queen's Press Secretary spoke of 'sewage journalism' and, not surprisingly, refused to comment at any length on the reports. Princess Michael herself, again not surprisingly, denied that there was any truth in the stories. Some of her supportive friends pointed out that, whatever the truth might be, the stories were typical by-products of the café society or *demi monde* where junior royalty, lesser aristocracy, millionaires and jet-setting entertainers mingle in a fun-seeking whirl. Her friends suggested that reporters were provided with the basis for their stories by some of the people involved in that moneyed and, seemingly, glittering world. And why, I asked, would any of them want to spread such stories – whether true or false? The answers given me in July 1985 tended to support some of the suggestions made earlier in this book. 'Some of the aristocracy are angrily jealous at the entry into their circle of the glamorous and, worst of all, Catholic, foreigner.' Her friends reminded me that, at one time, it had been Lord Dudley with his parodying song-poem, who had represented this section of 'society'. In July 1985, I was told, others were doing their worst by gossiping with the royal-watching reporters. Not that they needed much help. When Princess Michael appeared at a function, dressed and coiffeured in her most attractive way, she was described as 'flashy'. When, in the wake of the July rumours she went, with Prince Michael to Wimbledon, she was reported as looking dowdy and unroyal, with her hair loosely hanging to her shoulders. That anti-Princess Michael Catch-22 trap is easily exploitable by an eager Press.

In April 1985 the public showed – in a variety of polls – that it resented and rejected the attempt to attack the Princess through her father. At the time of writing, there has been no poll concerning public attitudes in the aftermath of the rumours concerning the Texas millionaire. Only the future will tell whether the Press or the Princess gains most public support.

And her own view of her future? In the interview which she gave for her fortieth birthday, Princess Michael spoke of being ambitious, of having the 'vigour' and 'willingness to be of service in public life. I am ready to be put to work.' She hoped to have a part to play in obtaining business sponsorship for the arts, the theatre, historic houses and museums. She intends to carry on with her writing and interior decorating. And, once the children are settled in their schools, she plans to take up full-time study. 'I never went to University,' she told Roy Plomley, explaining that she would very much like to take a degree in history when time permits. It is certain that, whatever her future, as 'royal worker' or student, Princess Michael will continue to be 'very Hungarian in the way that I enjoy everything. I like the big fences and I think life is a series of fences. Life is a cross-country course. Now you go through the gates but I am going to go for the shortest and quickest way and get a bit of fun going over the big fences.'

As those close to her said in May 1985, the Princess has acquired a new sense of maturity, a new toughness, from the 'very difficult ten days that I went through in April'. There could not have been much 'bit of fun' in meeting the 'fences' of misreporting and innuendoes. There was, however, a great deal of learning and of application of the philosophy which she inherited and which she has taught her children. 'Good things happen and bad things happen, there are good people and bad people and you must just keep your head above water and go on the way you were brought up believing in and doing what you know to be right even if everything goes against you.' She said that on her fortieth birthday. She could never have known how, in the coming months, she would demonstrate – to husband, children and the public at large – that she had the capacity to live up to her words.

Tables of Common Relationship between
Prince and Princess Michael of Kent

TABLE I

Prince Ferdinand August of Lobkowicz (1655–1715)

m. (1) 1677 Princess Claudia of Nassau (1660–80)

Prince Philip Hyacinth of Lobkowicz (1680–1737)
m. (2) 1721 Countess Anna Maria of Althann (1703–54)

Prince Ferdinand of Lobkowicz (1724–84)
m. 1769 Princess Gabriela of Savoy-Carignan (1748–1828)

Prince Franz Joseph of Lobkowicz (1772–1816)
m. 1792 Princess Caroline of Schwarzenberg (1775–1816)

Princess Maria Gabriela of Lobkowicz (1793–1863)
m. 1811 Prince Vincenz of Auersperg (1790–1812)

Prince Vincenz of Auersperg (1812–67)
m. 1845 Countess Wilhelmine of Colloredo-Mannsfeld (1826–98)

Princess Gabriela of Auersperg (1855–1933)
m. 1877 Prince Alfred of Windisch-Graetz (1851–1927)

Princess Maria Hedwig of Windisch-Graetz (1878–1918)
m. 1908 Count Friedrich Szapáry (1869–1935)

Countess Maria Anna Szapáry (b. 1911)
m. 1941 Baron Günther von Reibnitz (b. 1894)

Baroness Marie-Christine von Reibnitz (b. 1945)

m. (2) 1680 Margravine Maria Anna of Baden (1655–1701)

Princess Maria Louise of Lobkowicz (1683–1750)
m. 1703 Prince Anselm Franz of Thurn and Taxis (1681–1739)

Princess Maria Augusta of Thurn and Taxis (1706–56)
m. 1727 Duke Carl Alexander of Württemberg (1684–1737)

Duke Friedrich Eugen of Württemberg (1732–97)
m. 1753 Margravine Friederike of Brandenburg-Schwedt (1736–98)

Duke Ludwig of Württemberg (1756–1817)
m. (2) 1797 Princess Henrietta of Nassau-Weilburg (1780–1857)

Duke Alexander of Württemberg (1804–85)
m. 1835 Countess Claudine Rhédey de Kis-Rhéde (1812–41)

Duke Francis of Teck (1877–1900)
m. 1866 Princess Mary Adelaide of Great Britain (1833–97)

Princess Mary of Teck (1867–1953)
m. 1893 King George V of Great Britain (1865–1936)

Prince George, Duke of Kent (1902–42)
m. 1934 Princess Marina of Greece (1906–68)

Prince Michael of Kent (b. 1942)

TABLE II

Moritz, Landgrave of Hesse-Cassel m. (2) 1603 Countess Juliana of Nassau-Siegen
(1572–1632)   (1587–1643)

Friedrich, Landgrave of Hesse-Eschwege
(1617–55)
m. 1646 Countess Eleonore Katherine of the
Palatinate Zweibruken (1626–92)

Landgravine Christine of Hesse-Eschwege
(1648–1702)
m. 1667 Ferdinand Albrecht I, Duke of
Bruckswick-Bevern (1636–87)

Ferdinand Albrecht II, Duke of Brunswick-
Wolfenbuttel (1680–1735)
m. 1712 Princess Antonia Amalia of Brunswick-
Wolfenbuttel (1696–1762)

Princess Sophia Antonia of Brunswick-
Wolfenbuttel (1724–1802)
m. 1749 Ernst Friedrich, Duke of Saxe-Coburg-
Saalfeld (1724–1800)

Franz, Duke of Saxe-Coburg-Saalfeld
(1750–1806)
m. (2) 1777 Augusta, Princess Reuss zu Ebersdorf
(1757–1831)

Ernst, Duke of Saxe-Coburg-Gotha (1784–1844)
m. (1) 1817 Princess Luise of Saxe-Gotha
(1800–31)

Prince Albert of Saxe-Coburg-Gotha
(1819–61)
m. 1840 Queen Victoria of Great Britain
(1819–1901)

King Edward VII (1841–1910)
m. 1863 Princess Alexandra of Denmark
(1844–1925)

King George V (1863–1936)
m. 1893 Princess Mary of Teck (1867–1953)

Prince George, Duke of Kent (1902–42)
m. 1934 Princess Marina of Greece (1906–68)

Prince Michael of Kent (1942) m. 1978

Ernst Landgrave of Hesse-Rheinfels-Rotenburg
(1623–93)
m. (1) 1647 Countess Maria Eleonore of Solms
(1632–89)

Wilhelm, Landgrave of Hesse-Rheinfels-
Rotenburg (1648–1725)
m. 1669 Countess Maria Anna of Lowenstein-
Wertheim-Rochefort (1652–88)

Ernst Leopold, Landgrave of Hesse-Rheinfels-
Rotenburg (1684–1749)
m. 1704 Countess Eleonore of Lowenstein-
Wertheim-Rochefort (1686–1753)

Landgravine Christine Henriette of Hesse-
Rheinfels-Rotenburg (1717–78)
m. 1740 Prince Louis Victor of Savoy-Carignan
(1721–78)

Princess Gabriela of Savoy-Carignan
(1748–1828)
m. 1769 Prince Ferdinand of Lobkowicz
(1724–84)

Prince Joseph of Lobkowicz (1772–1816)
m. 1792 Princess Maria Caroline of Schwarzenberg
(1775–1816)

Princess Maria Gabriela of Lobkowicz
(1793–1863)
m. 1811 Prince Vincenz of Auersperg
(1790–1812)

Prince Vincenz of Auersperg (1812–67)
m. 1845 Countess Wilhelmine of Colloredo-
Mannsfeld (1826–98)

Princess Gabriela of Auersperg (1855–1933)
m. 1877 Prince Alfred of Windisch-Graetz
(1855–1927)

Princess Maria Hedwig of Windisch-Graetz
(1878–1918)
m. 1908 Count Friedrich Szapáry (1869–1935)

Countess Maria Anna Szapáry (1911)
m. 1941 Baron Günther von Reibnitz (1894)

Baroness Marie-Christine von Reibnitz (1945)

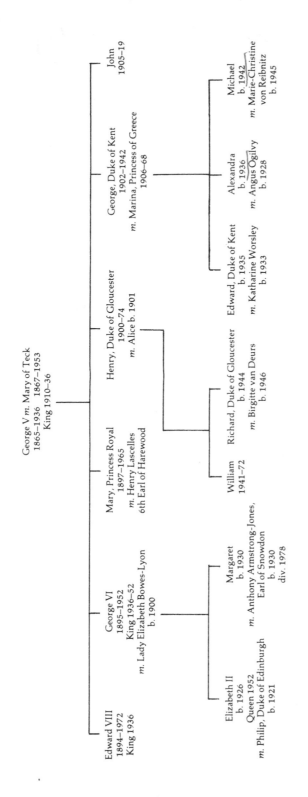

George V *m.* Mary of Teck
1865–1936 1867–1953
King 1910–36

Edward VIII
1894–1972
King 1936

George VI
1895–1952
King 1936–52
m. Lady Elizabeth Bowes-Lyon
b. 1900

Mary, Princess Royal
1897–1965
m. Henry Lascelles
6th Earl of Harewood

Henry, Duke of Gloucester
1900–74
m. Alice b. 1901

George, Duke of Kent
1902–1942
m. Marina, Princess of Greece
1906–68

John
1905–19

Elizabeth II
b. 1926
Queen 1952
m. Philip, Duke of Edinburgh
b. 1921

Margaret
b. 1930
m. Anthony Armstrong-Jones,
Earl of Snowdon
b. 1930
div. 1978

William
1941–72

Richard, Duke of Gloucester
b. 1944
m. Birgitte van Deurs
b. 1946

Edward, Duke of Kent
b. 1935
m. Katharine Worsley
b. 1933

Alexandra
b. 1936
m. Angus Ogilvy
b. 1928

Michael
b. 1942
m. Marie-Christine
von Reibnitz
b. 1945

Bibliography

Airlie, Mabell, Countess of, *Thatched with Gold* (Hutchinson, 1962)

Alexandra, Queen, *Prince Philip: A Family Portrait*, (Hodder & Stoughton, 1959)

Birmingham, S., *Duchess* (Macmillan, 1981)

Blum, Jerome, *The end of the Old Order in Rural Europe* (Princeton University Press, 1978)

Boothroyd, J.B., *Philip: An Informal Biography* (Longman, 1971)

Brown, Very Rev. Mgr. Ralph, *Marriage Annulment in the Catholic Church* (Kevin Mayhew, 1977)

Bryan III, J., and Murphy, C.J.V., *The Windsor Story* (Granada, 1979)

Cecil, Algernon, *Metternich* (Eyre & Spottiswoode, 3rd ed., 1947)

Channon, Sir Henry ('Chips'), *The Diaries of Sir Henry Channon, MP* ed. R.R. James (Weidenfeld & Nicolson, 1967, and Penguin, 1984)

Feiling, Keith, *A History of England* (Book Club Associates, 1974)

Field, Leslie, *Bendor: The Golden Duke of Westminster* (Weidenfeld & Nicolson, 1983)

Fisher, G. & H., *The Queen's Family* (W.H. Allen, 1982)

Fisher, H.A.L., *A History of Europe* (Eyre & Spottiswoode, 1952)

Hamilton, W., *My Queen and I* (Quartet Books, 1975)

Hibbert, C., *George, Prince of Wales* (Longman, 1972)

Hough, R., *Edwina, Countess Mountbatten of Burma* (Weidenfeld & Nicolson, 1983)

Jones, Thomas, *A Diary With Letters, 1931-50* (Oxford University Press, 1969)

Judd, D., *King George VI* (Michael Joseph, 1982)

Knight, Stephen, *The Brotherhood* (Granada, 1984)

Lacey, Robert, *Majesty* (Hutchinson, 1977)

Lacey, Robert, *Aristocrats* (Hutchinson, 1983)

Lane, Peter, *The Queen Mother* (Robert Hale, 1979)

Lane, Peter, *Prince Philip* (Robert Hale, 1980)

Lane, Peter, *Europe since 1945* (Batsford, 1985)

McNair-Wilson, D., *Hungary* (Batsford, 1976)

Mansergh, N., *The Coming of the First World War* (Longmans, Green & Co., 1949)

Montagu of Beaulieu, Lord, *More Equal Than Others* (Michael Joseph, 1970)

Morrow, A., *The Queen* (Granada, 1983)

Morton, F., *A Nervous Splendour, 1888-9* (Widenfeld & Nicolson, 1980)

Musulin, S., *Austria: People and Landscape* (Faber & Faber, 1971)

Musulin, S., *Vienna in the Age of Metternich* (Faber & Faber, 1975)

Nicolson, H., *Diaries and Letters, 1930-39*, ed. N. Nicolson (Fontana, 1969)

Nicolson, H., *Diaries and Letters, 1945-62*, ed. N. Nicolson (Collins, 1968)

Ormrod, R., *Una Troubridge: The Friend of Radclyff Hall* (Cape, 1984)

Reibnitz, Baron Paul von, *History of the Lords and Barons von Reibnitz, 1241-1901* (Berlin, 1901)

Rose, K., *King George V* (Weidenfeld & Nicolson, 1983)

Scott, George, *The RCs* (Hutchinson, 1967)

Seaman, L.C.B., *A New History of England, 410-1975)* (Harvester Press, 1981)

Shakespeare, N., *The Men Who Would Be King* (Sidgwick & Jackson, 1984)

Talbot, G., *The Country Life Book of the Royal Family* (1980)

Taylor, A.J.P., *Bismarck* (Hamish Hamilton, 1960)

Trevelyan, G.M., *An Illustrated History of England* (Longmans, Green & Co., 1956)

Waterlow, C., and Evans, A., *Europe, 1945-70* (Methuen, 1973)

Westminster, Loelia, Duchess of, *Cocktails and Laughter* (Hamish Hamilton, 1983)

Wheeler-Bennett, Sir John, *King George VI* (Macmillan, 1958)

References

1. A Background of Families

1. *Royalty, Peerages and Nobility of the World*, 91st volume, p.532
2. *Debrett* (1980), p.20
3. Jerome Blum, *The End of the Old Order in Rural Europe* (Princeton University Press, 1978)
4. Stella Musulin, *Austria: People and Landscape* (Faber & Faber, 1971), pp.112-14
5. Ibid., p.224

2. The Family and the War, 1939–45

1. Quoted in *The Times*, 17 April 1985
2. Ibid.
3. B. Stransky, *East Wind over Prague* (Hollis & Carter, 1950), pp.22-3
4. Geoffrey Levy, *Daily Express*, 12 March 1984

3. Growing Up in Australia, 1951–68

1. Geoffrey Levy, London, and Catherine Olsen, Sydney, in *Daily Express*, 12 March 1984
2. Sydney *Daily Telegraph*, 4 April 1981
3. Levy and Olsen, *op. cit.*

4. Mrs Thomas Troubridge, 1971–7

1. Quotes in *Daily Express*, 13 March 1984
2. Quoted in *Majesty*, August 1984, p.24
3. Quoted in *Daily Express*, 13 March 1984

5. The Annulment of the Troubridge Marriage

1. *Majesty*, August 1984
2. *The Times*, 14 July 1978

3. Ibid., 30 June 1978
4. R. Brown, *Marriage Annulment in the Catholic Church* (Kevin Mayhew, 1977), p.10, quoting *The Church in the Modern World*, para.48
5. *The Diaries of Evelyn Waugh*, ed. M. Davies (Weidenfeld & Nicolson, 1976), p.305
6. Brown, *op. cit.*, p.5
7. Ibid., pp.5-6

6. The Queen and the Engagement

1. *The Times*, 3 March 1978
2. Ibid.
3. Ibid., 1 June 1978
4. Ibid.

7. The Churches and the Marriage, 1978

1. Press Association report, 31 May 1978
2. *The Times*, 3 March 1978
3. Ibid., 1 June 1978
4. Archbishop Heim to the author, 14 December 1984
5. *The Times*, 19 June 1978
6. Ibid., 30 June 1978
7. *The Tablet*, 23 June 1978
8. *The Times*, 3 July 1978
9. Ibid.
10. *The Times*, 4 July 1978

8. The Royal Wedding, 30 June 1978

1. *Sunday Telegraph*, 2 July 1978
2. *The Tablet*, 23 June, 1978
3. *The Times*, 4 July 1978
4. Private conversation
5. *Sunday Telegraph*, 2 July 1978
6. Quoted in *The Times*, 17 April 1985

9. A Catholic Marriage – At Last, 1983

1. Private conversation
2. *Catholic Herald*, 5 August 1983
3. *The Times*, 30 June 1983
4. *Catholic Herald*, 5 August 1983

5. R. Brown *op. cit.*, pp. 15–16
6. *Western Mail*, 6 April 1983
7. Letter dated 11 February 1980
8. Letter dated 11 March 1981
9. Letter dated 13 April 1981
10. Letter dated 7 August 1981
11. *The Universe*, 28 July 1983
12. Ibid.
13. *Western Mail*, 27 July 1983
14. *Catholic Herald*, 5 August 1983

10. The House of Kent

1. E. Longford, *Victoria RI* (Weidenfeld & Nicolson, 1964), p.20
2. Ibid.
3. *Sunday Telegraph*, 22 December 1968
4. J. Bryan and C.J.V. Murphy, *The Windsor Story* (Granada, 1979), pp.56–7
5. *Chips: The Diaries of Sir Henry Channon*, ed. R. Rhodes James (Penguin, 1984), p.268
6. Bryan and Murphy, *op. cit.*, p.57
7. R. Hough, *Edwina, Countess Mountbatten of Burma* (Weidenfeld & Nicolson, 1983), p.119
8. Bryan and Murphy, *op. cit.*, pp.100-101
9. The Duchess of Windsor, *The Heart has its Reasons* (David McKay Inc., 1956), p.188
10. Bryan and Murphy, *op. cit.*, pp.101–2
11. K. Rose, *King George V* (Weidenfeld & Nicolson, 1983), p.390
12. D. Judd, *King George VI* (Michael Joseph, 1982), p.133
13. D. Morrah, *Princess Elizabeth, Duchess of Edinburgh* (Odhams, 1950), p.52
14. D. Morrah, *The Work of the Queen* (William Kimber, 1958), p.10
15. D. Judd, *op. cit.*, p.135
16. Hough, *op. cit.*, p.134
17. From an interview given on Princess Michael's birthday

11. Princess Michael and Other 'Ladies of Kent'

1. *Majesty, op. cit.*, p.27
2. Channon, *op. cit.*, pp.27, 72, 172, 438
3. A. Morrow, *The Queen* (Granada, 1983), p.52
4. R. Crossman, *The Diaries of a Cabinet Minister, volume 2*, Jonathan Cape, 1976, p.544
5. G. Talbot, *The Country Life Book of the Royal Family* (1980), p.170
6. Channon, *op. cit.*, pp.220, 338–9, 402
7. Bryan and Murphy, *op. cit.*, p.568

8. P. Lane, *The Queen Mother* (Robert Hale, 1979), pp.54–5
9. P. Lane, *Prince Philip* (Robert Hale, 1980) chapters 16–20 and 25–8
10. Bryan and Murphy, *op. cit.*, p.354
11. Channon, *op. cit.*, p.518
12. *Daily Mirror*, 9 May 1984
13. Quoted in N. Shakespeare, *Men Who Would be Kings* (Sidgwick and Jackson, 1984), pp.134–5
14. *Daily Star*, 1 May 1984
15. *Ibid.*

12. The Princess and her Homes

1. J. Dean, *HRH Prince Philip: A portrait by his valet* (Robert Hale, 1954), p.45
2. Letter to author, 27 July 1985
3. Letter to author, 4 March 1985
4. *The Times*, 13 April 1985

13. The Problem of the Civil List

1. Channon, *op. cit.*, p.512
2. Lacey, *op. cit.*, p.309
3. Quoted in Hamilton, W. *My Queen and I*, p.45
4. *Financial Times*, 3 December 1971
5. *Guardian*, 11 December 1971
6. *Hansard*, quoted in Lacey, *op. cit.*, p.313
7. *Daily Express*, 15 March 1984
8. *Sydney Morning Herald*, 24 November 1981
9. *Ibid.*
10. *Daily Express*, 15 March 1984

14. The Princess and the Royal Family

1. *Majesty*, August 1984, p.27
2. *Daily Express*, 3 March 1984
3. *Ibid.*
4. *Daily Star*, 1 May 1984
5. *Daily Express*, 12 July 1984
6. *Daily Express*, 5 May 1984

15. The Princess and the Public

1. *Daily Express*, 15 March 1984
2. *Sunday Times*, 21 April 1985

Index